BY HAND:

Low-Cost, No-Cost
Decorating

Robert Kangas

Reston Publishing Company, Inc.
A Prentice-Hall Company
Reston, Virginia

Library of Congress Cataloging in Publication Data

Kangas, Robert.
  By hand.

  1. Handicraft. 2. Waste products. 3. Recycling
(Waste, etc.) I. Title.
TT157.K35 1983   684   82-19563
ISBN 0-8359-0603-2
ISBN 0-8359-0602-7 (pbk.)

Also by the same author:
The Old-House Rescue Book

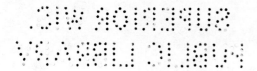

Copyright 1983 by
Robert Kangas

10 9 8 7 6 5 4 3 2 1

Printed in the United States of America.

Contents

10 MISCELLANEOUS PROJECTS 201

ACKNOWLEDGMENTS

The drawings at the beginning of each chapter are from the Dover Pictorial Archive Series. Chapters 1, 4, 6, 9, and 10 are from *Original Art Deco Designs*, by William Rowe. Chapters 2, 3, 5, 7, and 8 are from *Art Deco Designs and Motifs*, by Marcia Loeb.

The restoration and preservation of neon signs project was prepared under the guidance of Leonard Davidson of Davidson Neon Design Studio, Philadelphia, Pennsylvania.

1

INDEPENDENT DESIGN

People who are interested in furnishing and outfitting their homes have a problem. It seems that all the good stuff, the elegant/useful/striking/intriguing things (shown in magazines and decorator's showrooms and in some people's homes), is out of reach. It's too expensive and/or you need a professional decorator or architect to order it for you because it's just not generally available. It seems to be reserved for rich individuals and corporations.

People who live in older apartments or houses have another problem. It's difficult to find new furnishings and objects that fit into the mood created by the classic architecture they inhabit. High ceilings, wide moldings, hardwood floors, solid doors, and deep-set windows seem to call for furnishings of similar quality. The furniture available today (except for high-priced originals and reproductions)

is often of poor construction, with veneers and printed vinyl material on top of composition wood products. The cost of good-quality solid woods and natural fabrics is simply too high for them to be included in reasonably priced furniture.

Still other people can't abide the popular taste in household objects, from lighting fixtures and lamps to basic household appliances. They avoid trends, ignore advertising, and don't want to be caught up in this year's color or model or style. They are sure of their own taste in these matters but frustrated by the fact that it's difficult to find simple, classic, enduring design in many popular objects.

Another group of people are strapped for money. Perhaps they have sacrificed much of their income to buy a house or rent a desirable apartment, or are dealing with the financial demands of a growing family, or—like most of us—find that no matter how much money they have, it's never enough. These people need to furnish and equip their homes too, and for them it's a constant battle to set priorities. Buy a high-quality piece of furniture and eat at home for the next two months, or buy something cheaper and be able to afford an occasional restaurant meal?

NEED FOR A COMPATIBLE LIVING ENVIRONMENT

We all need certain basics in our homes—seating, tables for eating and working, a place to sleep, storage for clothes and household goods, and display for entertainment products. We also need and want useful items that help us work at projects, prepare and serve food, entertain friends and family, and enjoy leisure time. Home is, after all, the place we go every day to relax, eat, be with friends and family, sleep, work, entertain, study, play, read, watch television, and listen to music. Home has always been a place to do lots of different things, and with the availability of new entertainment and communications systems it is sure to be the center for ever more activity, work, and recreation.

The objects we furnish our homes with are not only utilitarian but are also filled with symbols, status, and self-image. They are often the only things we have direct control over. Not many people can build their own houses or supervise the design and construction of their living spaces. However, we all can directly participate in the selection and placement of furniture, fixtures, art, and other household objects. People inevitably want to infuse their homes with ideas and feelings that reflect their image of themselves and how they want to be seen by others. Self-expression runs through every human activity. Banks build and furnish their offices to reinforce the idea of security (for your money), and business establishments are furnished and

FIGURE 1-1. A knife rack made of white pine.

FIGURE 1-2.   Utilitarian kitchen fixtures of white pine.

FIGURE 1-3.   A recycled cast iron gas stove.

decorated to put forward the idea of efficiency (for your patronage). If such images work for corporations, they can work for individuals and families, too.

We all need to design and create our living environment, and whether it's for reasons of taste, money, utility, or image, there is no one more qualified or interested in doing it than ourselves. Only we can decide what it is that we want to live with. If we take the trouble to work with what's available, we can shape our own useful and decorative objects from old pieces, raw material, and unusual materials to fit our unique situation.

UNDERSTANDING IMAGE, STATUS, AND VALUE

This book is about things that can be recycled, adapted, and created by the individual. It's a practical book on a practical subject, but it must also of necessity get into areas such as status, self-image, and history. One of the things that will guide us as we work along is a consciousness of how these things can affect how we look at and feel about common objects.

For example, what is it that produces value in certain objects? In some goods it is age (antiques), character (a very comfortable chair, perhaps), quality of work and material (fine glassware and silver), and often uniqueness or scarcity (a one-of-a-kind art object or limited edition print or photo). In the projects and suggestions throughout this book you will be working with all of these factors, and they will all contribute to the effect you achieve.

Often the images and status values of one time will have to be removed to reveal the value that you see in the piece now. For example, many pieces of solid wood furniture have a veneer of another kind of wood applied over the original wood. The image popular at the time of manufacture called for this trickery. Today you might value the basic lines of the solid wood, so you would remove the veneer and finish the solid wood to arrive at a piece that pleases you. This kind of detective and recycling work could save you money because if the original piece had a damaged or peeling veneer it would probably be passed up by other people who were only seeing the piece for its original image.

The objects you will be working with will possess some mix of age, character, quality, and uniqueness. Sometimes it will be age and quality that you feature when you restore and refinish an object, as with an old table, chair, chest, or frame that you come across. More often it will be character and uniqueness that you will bring out when you adapt and create objects. Anything hand-wrought has a touch of the one-of-a-kind to it; when you build and adapt you create something new and unexpected out of common materials, and that imparts uniqueness. Character speaks for itself in any object— it's the useful, well-made, and comfortable quality that we all admire, regardless of status and image considerations.

DEVELOPING A FLAIR FOR RECYCLING AND ADAPTING

Many new movements and ideas have emerged in this century about architecture, interior design, and the way we should live in our buildings and with our

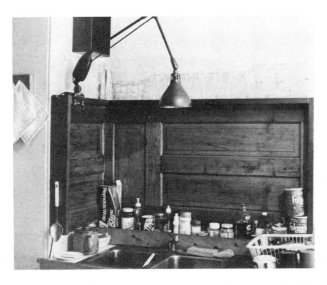

FIGURE 1-4.   A solid wood door used as a backsplash.

objects. If you read design magazines and books and attend lectures and museum exhibits, you will become familiar with them. This book freely borrows from and uses these ideas for the good things that each has to offer.

Use Common Objects in an Uncommon Way

Part of developing an eye for recycling/adapting/creating objects is to realize that there is nothing entirely bad about an ob-

FIGURE 1-5.   Industrial light fixtures.

FIGURE 1-6.   A 1930s camera and a 1940s telephone.

ject—at worst, a small part of it can be used. So it goes with design ideas and schools of thought; they exist to teach us and guide us, and sometimes to lead us, but not to rule us. One idea can be turned upside down and combined with another, just as you can take a pipe that was designed to carry water and make it carry illumination instead.

This use of the common in an uncommon way is the basis for inexpensive, independent, distinctive design. You want to bring the unexpected into your home, things that belong to industry, commercial concerns, the farm. For the most part these things haven't been discovered for their domestic uses and effects. They are available at the cost of their raw materials and manufacture. You can transform them into useful and decorative objects without paying for status and symbol.

Look for Old Objects

You can also search for out-of-time objects—furniture and fixtures that belong to another age, possibly the near-antique (20 to 90 years old). Many of these things

have great design and construction value and they might have been filled with status and symbol when they were first made. Now because of the current fashion they are available at low cost, and their status value in the general market is nil. You may be attracted to these pieces for their intrinsic quality and usefulness, or you might want to restore or adapt their looks. Often the image value of these dated pieces returns when they are installed in the proper setting along with similar objects.

FIGURE 1-7.   A 1950s wall clock.

Adapt Designs from Nature, Art, and Books ————

Another avenue is finding and adapting designs and objects that occur in nature or in other media such as photography, books, and art. It is possible to transfer images and textures from one thing to another using simple art and craft techniques. These methods offer great flexibility to a person who is interested in unique design and who can see possibilities in different physical forms.

FIGURE 1-8. Designs from an art deco stencil book.

Make Use of Broken Objects ————

Part of being an independent thinker/designer/creator is to be aware of and make use of outmoded and broken material. There are many useful and decorative things to be found as surplus, junk, and salvage. Whether you live in a city, small town, or the country, there are plenty of nearby people and organizations who throw out useful material. Recycling these objects is a big part of learning and enjoying design. These no-cost and low-cost items can be experimented on, used recklessly, and changed radically, and can teach you a great deal about your own capabilities and the adaptibility of the material you work with.

SATISFACTION OF "DOING-IT-YOURSELF" ————

A last component to consider is the satisfaction of working with your hands as well as your mind to furnish and outfit your home. Going over each piece to restore it or adapt it to create it out of raw material provides another kind of knowledge of it that adds to its value. Starting with simple projects, you will find your confidence and skill building with each procedure you try. This confidence and hand-wisdom will guide you as you work on more complex and ambitious projects.

Knowing how something works, how it is built, how to repair and adapt it provides you with a special kind of perspective. Common things will never again be terribly baffling or loaded with undue symbol and status simply because you

FIGURE 1-9. An unrestored veneered radio.

FIGURE 1-10. The reverse side of the radio. Line cord and one tube need to be replaced to return the unit to working condition.

don't know what lies underneath. Sales-people or professionals in the field won't be able to bamboozle you with their jargon or pressure techniques, which often rely on surface appearances.

Your new knowledge will also be an aid to striking out on your own and decid-ing what things (perhaps currently un-fashionable or unorthodox) please you. Times, locations, and your needs and tastes change, so you should be armed with knowledge and a flexible attitude to be able to live comfortably and with style, whatever your situation may be.

FIGURE 1-11. Two vintage appliances. The carbon-arc sunlamp is displayed as a curiosity. The oscillating fan is still used.

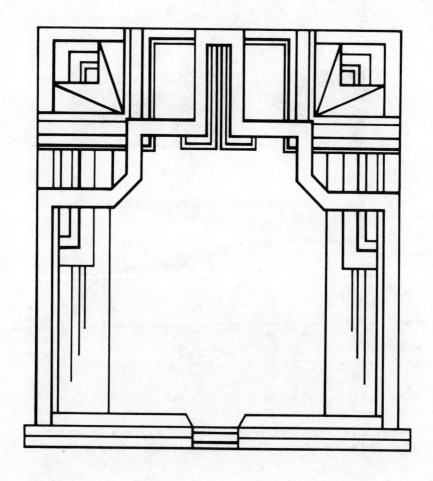

2

SOURCES

Regardless of your location, there are plenty of sources for materials, furniture, appliances, equipment, and the hundred other things that can be recycled into useful household goods. The city dweller will find newspaper listings of surplus and used goods, numerous shops that offer specialized items, and rich pickings on the streets just before trash pick-ups. The suburban recycler might rely on local yard sales and flea markets, plus classified advertising publications and even visits to the township dump. People who live in the country can find many useful items at auctions, in farm-supply catalogs and stores, and even from their natural surroundings.

Your objective is to gather low-cost and no-cost materials from a variety of sources so that you can experiment freely with them. By using bits and pieces of material—castoffs, broken items, bargains at sales and junk heaps—you can combine items or cut them down to come up with something new. Because you haven't invested much money you can make mistakes, and it's no great tragedy if the piece doesn't turn out exactly as you envisioned it. This frees you to do your best work as you play with these items.

You have to keep in mind things that could *become* useful. Often you buy or acquire something and then keep it until it suggests a combination or use that finally shows it off, investing in an inventory of small parts and items so that when you see something in life that you'd like to imitate, you have the materials available.

WHERE TO LOOK

What you need to get started is a guide to where suitable material can be found and an idea of the range of items available. The following list will get you started in your search for inexpensive materials and items.

Abandoned and Condemned Buildings. Buildings that are slated for demolition or are abandoned can often provide interesting material. Some useful items include doors, ornamental and architectural woodwork, hardware, glass panes, tile and masonry products, flooring and framing wood, iron and steel products, plumbing fixtures, and kitchen equipment.

If a building is scheduled for demolition you can approach the demolition contractor and ask for permission to salvage items from the building. The demolition contractor usually will have the right to deny or grant your request. Often the contractor will allow you to buy the right to remove certain items for a fee. These salvage fees are negotiable and are often quite low for small residential buildings. The fees rise and competition for salvage rights increases when the building is large and of commercial or historical significance.

In the case of an abandoned building that is not being demolished, you must approach the owner. If you have the address of the building, you can find the owner by going to the records department of your city hall or county seat. This is public information, and someone will assist you in searching the records for the owner of the building. Approach the owner by letter or phone and express your interest in salvaging material from the building. If the property is damaged or vandalized, the owner might let you take what you want in exchange for cleaning and sealing the building.

Antiques Exhibits. Often you will see a notice for an antiques exhibit and show. These events often take place at a local mall or in conjunction with a charity function or local celebration. These exhibits are *not* good places to buy inexpensive items. In general, exhibits are run by dealers who offer high-quality mer-

FIGURE 2-1. Heating registers taken from a demolished building.

chandise at top prices. However, antiques exhibits are excellent places to learn about old furniture and other objects. You can find out a lot about prices and quality, and you get the chance to examine good pieces at first hand. Expand your knowledge by talking to dealers and browsing through the entire show.

Antiques Shops. Like antiques shows, shops are generally not good places to find inexpensive items, but they are good for browsing and learning about quality and price ranges. If you do see something that you like in a store you can often get it for less than the asking price (10 to 20 percent markdowns are possible); store owners expect to haggle a bit. It is also possible to get a genuine bargain on rare occasions. Sometimes in a store that specializes in certain items, the owner will be careless in pricing an item that is out of that store's genre. You might get a good price on a floor lamp in a store that specializes in small china and glassware. One of the reasons to go into antiques stores is to get enough general knowledge so that you can recognize and take advantage of the occasional bargain when it shows up.

Antiques stores are not prime sources for our purposes because by definition antiques are 100 years old or older. Most items that we will be working with are 30 to 90 years old—semi-antiques (or just old stuff)—and will be found in places other than antiques stores.

Attics, Cellars, Garages, Barns, Warehouses, Abandoned Businesses. By offering to clean attics, cellars, and other places for what you might find, you can often get some interesting material for an afternoon's work. Approach the people who control these resources. Perhaps they don't share your interest in older things and will be glad to let you have whatever you come across. You can also buy pieces from neighbors, friends, and family. After all, quality and aesthetics are relative—many people just don't find these things exciting or valuable. You can approach the owners of buildings that have vacant storefronts left by defunct business concerns. Often many old and interesting fixtures, signs, and equipment will have been left behind.

Auctions. Attend established auction houses where merchandise is brought to the house to be displayed and sold) or on-site affairs (where the auction occurs at the home, farm, or business being sold). When it comes to finding inexpensive goods, auctions are extremely variable. You can find good values or you can be frustrated by the high prices for common goods.

The key to finding good values usually lies in determining the auction overhead cost. If the auction occurs on-site at a remote location and with simple tables used to display goods, it could produce some good values. A low-overhead auction can still make a profit with goods from $1 to $50. If the auction occurs at an auction house with a fancy address and lush accommodations for the customers, it's likely to be a high-priced affair. An auction with high overhead costs is likely to have goods priced at $100 and more.

Auctions are good hunting grounds for people who have the time to select the ones they are interested in. Newspapers carry in their leisure sections or classified pages notices of auctions that sell everything from industrial goods to art objects

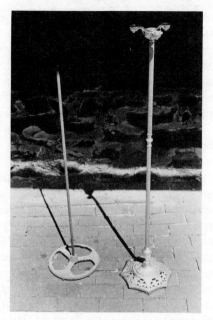

FIGURE 2-2.   An assortment of lamps from an attic. If you don't like the style of a lamp, you can strip it down to its stalk and base and use that as a fixture.

to household goods and furniture. Auctions are also announced in special magazines about collectibles and antiques. Ask your newsdealer for copies of the ones in your area. Some auction houses are also listed in the Yellow Pages of the phone book, and you can call for information on their regular exhibition and sales days.

Beaches, Fields, Forests, Natural Areas. These areas provide excellent hunting for shells, bones, rocks, woods, plants, leaves, and other natural products to use in your projects. A seashell can be glued to a nightlight to make an unusual shade. A nicely shaped piece of driftwood can form the basis for a chandelier. Shapes of natural things can be transferred to stencils for decorating walls, table tops, and other flat surfaces.

FIGURE 2-3.   A seashell night light.

Country Fairs and Farmers' Markets. Usually better prices can be found here than in antiques shops, but the prices will be higher than those typically found at flea markets and swap meets. The prices usually relate to the overhead costs. If an operator can rent a stall or table cheaply at one of these markets, the cost of his or her merchandise will be less. The operators tend to be weekenders who have other jobs and who store their stock in their homes and at the market. Their goods will cost less than a conventional storeowner's but more than those of the amateurs who display and sell at other kinds of markets.

Dumps and Landfills. In general you can only find dumps and landfills in rural areas. Most city and suburban trash services incinerate or compact their refuse. The price is right for whatever you find, and you can find some surprisingly good things at a dump. File cabinets, furniture, cardboard tubes, steel and iron scrap, and appliances are just a few of the items that turn up at dumps. People who use dumps will often place useable material that they discard in a special place at the dump, and you are welcome to take it. Trash picking has a long and honorable history, and more people do it than you might expect.

If you live within convenient driving distance of a dump or landfill, it is worth checking from time to time for useable materials and items. Some times of the year are better than others for dumps, and the spring cleaning season—when everyone is on a clean-out-and-throw-out regime—can produce some truly outstanding items.

Flea Markets. Very good prices on all kinds of items can be found at flea markets. These markets are usually weekend affairs, held in large parking lots where amateurs can pull up their cars and display and sell whatever they bring. Because it only costs a few dollars to become a seller, the overhead cost is low and the merchandise is sold at near-giveaway prices. Along with amateurs selling all manner of household goods will be a few semi-professional dealers who may

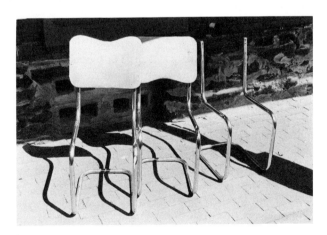

FIGURE 2-4. Chrome chair frames. Found at a dump, these frames could be recycled with wood or canvas seats and backs.

FIGURE 2-5. A typical flea market find. With the top sawed off and the copper and brass polished, this old soda-acid extinguisher would make a handsome umbrella stand.

specialize in one kind of item (oak furniture, rattan objects, etc.). Often these dealers will have good-quality items at fair prices.

Bargaining is the rule at flea markets, and if you press you can usually get substantial reductions on asking prices (20 to 40 percent is common). Some amateurs sell objects at ridiculously low prices (they have just cleaned their attics and garages and are on the way to the dump with them), and you can often get broken but repairable items for less than $1.

Furniture Warehouses. In urban areas there are plenty of used-furniture dealers who handle large lots of used fur-

niture from bankrupt and out-of-business hotels, schools, institutions, and businesses. Often real estate brokers and lawyers use these dealers to take stock from large apartment buildings, dormitories, and resorts that are being remodeled or demolished.

The selection and prices at these warehouses are great. Usually the warehouse is located in a low-rent district in a converted factory, supermarket, or other recycled building. Because the overhead is low and the stock is obtained from distressed sources, the values are good. You can expect to find all kinds of furniture (often well-made heavy items intended for commercial use), lamps, and office equipment, plus assorted objects and accessories such as rugs, water coolers, shelving units, and kitchen appliances. The merchandise is generally 20 years old or older, and its style is out of fashion. (This may suit your plans for adapting or restoring.) Dealers expect you to bargain, especially if you buy a number of pieces at once. Reductions of 10, 20, or 30 percent are common.

Garage Sales, Yard Sales. These sales are run by homeowners who are cleaning out their houses or selling excess goods before a move. Prices can be very good because the primary purpose is not to make a huge profit but to get rid of obsolete or unused merchandise. Check the classified sections of your newspaper for notices of private sales. Also look for notices on community bulletin boards, suburban telephone poles, and in church and neighborhood newsletters.

The most important strategy with yard and garage sales is to be there early. These sales generally offer only a few desirable items. You should be there before others to pick up the ones you want. You can bargain if you want, but generally prices are fair at these sales.

Museums. Museums often sell interesting and inexpensive merchandise. Museum shops are a good source for small products, design books, posters, prints, and photographs. In addition to art items, some museums even sell antiques and furniture. These pieces are often donated items that don't fit into the museum's collections. Prices for furniture and antiques are generally high, but this is a source that many people aren't aware of.

Museums are also an excellent source for ideas. By experience and contact with the fine pieces and design shown in museums, you can train yourself to recognize quality. When you develop this eye for quality and good design it will serve as a guide to hunting for objects at your other sources.

Museums don't always concern themselves with fine art and hand-wrought objects. There are museums and exhibits devoted to science and technology and commercial and popular design. These museums celebrate the best in these areas and can contribute to your appreciation of quality and design in machine-made goods.

Rummage Sales. Sponsored by social, civic, religious, charitable, and fraternal organizations, rummage sales rely on donated goods and are extremely low-overhead operations. Prices are generally excellent, but clothes and other nondurable items dominate. It is worth checking bulletin boards and local and neighborhood newspapers for notices, especially before Christmas and Easter or during the organization's annual fund drive.

Swap Meets. These are usually held in large parking lots, drive-in theaters, racetracks, or fairgrounds. People pull in and deal from their cars or trucks. There are wide variations in price and quality of goods, but because of low overhead, values are generally good. Swap meets are very informal (even more so than flea markets), and the sellers are apt to spend just as much time browsing and buying as the customers (the original idea being that people could trade their items). Some swap meets are organized around specific items such as collectibles, furniture, and housewares, but it's likely that you will find just about everything offered at any swap meet you attend—and of course cash is acceptable if you don't have anything to swap.

Thrift Stores. Located in cities and towns, thrift stores are an excellent source for all kinds of goods, especially furniture and appliances. The biggest charity operators are the Salvation Army, Goodwill Industries, and St. Vincent DePaul Society. There are plenty of private operators in business as well. Prices are good because the merchandise is donated or surplus and the overhead is low (these stores are often located in low-rent converted buildings).

A lot of people use thrift shops because they don't have very much money to furnish and outfit their homes and because they don't favor modern goods anyway. Thrift shops are a kind of time machine back to 20 years ago and more. The goods and furniture here can be better quality than those offered in regular stores.

Trash Day. In cities you have to get to the discarded items before the trucks and compactors come. The best way is to

FIGURE 2-6. Useful decorative items that were found on the street.

cruise the streets the night before refuse is scheduled to be picked up. Look on city streets, in dumpsters, and near trash containers behind businesses and apartment complexes. There is no formal etiquette for city trash picking—if you see it and it's what you want, pick it up. You can call the local city government to find out what days trash is picked up in various districts of the city. Some of the better picking is to be found in wealthy neighborhoods, older inner-city areas, and in business and commercial districts. You can find furniture, appliances, household goods, building materials, cabinets, lamps, and practically everything else on the street.

WHAT TO LOOK FOR ⸻

When you are out looking for materials in flea markets, thrift stores, warehouses, and other less-conventional places, you never know what you might find. Following are some of the items you should be aware of:

Broken or Dirty Items. Mirror and picture frames, cupboard and cabinet fancy hardware, architectural wood and plaster moldings, furniture legs, stair newels and balusters, cast iron and steel parts (brackets, stove and vent grates, fencing) masonry details and tiles, radio/TV/record player/sewing machine cabinets and bases.

Printed Material. Picture postcards, sheet music, menus, playing cards, train and bus timetables, calendars, letterheads, tickets, posters, trade and consumer catalogs, comic books, magazines, newspapers, illustrated books, stock certificates, deeds, cancelled checks.

Automotive Objects. Radiator and hood ornaments, horns, mirrors, clocks, gearshifts, cigarette lighters, license plates, radios, bumpers, grilles, auto body parts, seating, mechanical parts, novelty accessories.

Glassware and Ceramics. Stained glass, colored glass, pressed/cut/etched glass, bottles (in classic or odd shapes), jars and jugs, commercial containers (milk, soda, beer, etc.), plates, bowls, saucers, cups, tiles, pots, and crocks.

Lighting Fixtures and Lamps. Floor lamps, table lamps, wall and ceiling fixtures, theatrical lighting instruments, lighted wall plaques, illuminated clocks/mirrors/pictures, novelty lamps (often featuring shapes of airplanes, zeppelins, nudes, scene-in-action tableaus, etc.), glass/metal/fabric shades.

Small Decorative Objects. Door stops, cigarette and make-up boxes, compacts, decorative hardware items (glass/brass/porcelain knobs, hinges, pulls, etc.), ash trays, small statues, trophies, desk sets.

Popular Culture Items. Sports/TV/radio/automobile-related items, advertising memorabilia (promotional items, catalogs, premiums), tobacco and cigarette containers, tin boxes and cans, lunch boxes, army/navy items and surplus, metal/plastic/wood/neon signs, movie and photographic prints and related material, life-size figures in tin and cardboard.

Old Equipment. Radio and TV tubes, 78- and 45-rpm records, cameras, safes/banks/safe deposit boxes, obsolete electrical equipment (health machines, mechanical equipment), thermometers, bottle openers, soda fountain equipment, novelty devices (cigarette dispensing and lighting machines, concealed home bars, etc.), vintage electronic equipment (radios, TVs, phonographs, tape machines, intercoms, telephones, etc.).

FIGURE 2-7. A bench seat from a van. Automotive seating can be used as household furniture.

FIGURE 2-8. A flowerpot and a tail-pipe. Both objects can be wired as lamps with little effort.

Uses

Such items might be things that most people overlook when they are among used merchandise. These objects (and others like them) could form the basis for an exciting project. A table top without legs could be bought cheaply and teamed with some legs (that you picked up somewhere else or cut from new material) to make a useful piece. Old printed material can often be purchased cheaply by the bundle or box. You might cover the walls of a small room with sheet music, old catalog pages, or the sections of a foreign newspaper. Such improvised wallpaper could transform an undistinguished space into an intriguing one.

Other objects from automotive, household, and commercial sources can be adapted to decorative or functional uses. A ceramic flower pot could be made into a hanging lamp with the addition of a lamp socket, cord, and line switch. An old enamel and stainless steel soda fountain milkshake machine could be a practical and attractive piece for a large kitchen. An interesting looking camera, gearshift, or tin box can simply be an inexpensive item to brighten a shelf or table.

CLASSIFIED AD PUBLICATIONS

One of the richest sources of goods and materials deserves a complete discussion. These are the classified publications that allow private parties to list merchandise for sale and pay for the advertising only if and when they sell (usually the fee is ten percent of the listed price of the item). Because there is no risk to the seller in listing merchandise, people are encouraged to offer all sorts of interesting things, and many will be good values. A great advantage to the buyer is that you can browse through these publications at your leisure and make your selection as if you were at a flea market. The publication also requires each seller to list the price for the item, so you know exactly what value the seller places on the item.

There are drawbacks. Often sellers will provide misleading information or incomplete descriptions of their merchandise. You must call the seller and interview him or her to determine whether or not the item closely fits your idea of it. And of course you have to go to the seller's house to see and finally buy the item.

Sometimes sellers over-price their merchandise out of ignorance or greed. When you sense this you can bargain. Often price reductions can be obtained, especially if the seller hasn't been getting many inquiries about the item. The seller is still required to pay a percentage of the listed price to the publication regardless of whether the item is sold at a discount or even given away, so bear this in mind when you ask for reductions from the asking price.

Buying from the classified ad publications is not for everybody. It takes courage to interview a seller over the phone to determine the quality of the item and then to go to the seller's home (perhaps in an unfamiliar neighborhood) to bargain and make your purchase. You really have little cause for worry. The people who buy and sell through this medium are usually quite friendly and used to the process. The stakes are generally low, and no one is going to be humiliated or insulted if you don't buy an item or if you ask for a price reduction based on some legitimate problem. The bargains are numerous and the action is enjoyable once you get used to it, so you shouldn't ignore this very productive and democratic marketplace.

Ask your newsdealer for copies of the publications in your area. Nearly every part of the country is covered by one, and some urban areas have two or more competing publications. Your newsdealer can also tell you when the new issues are dropped off at the stand. You might want to pick up the paper as soon as it is distributed so that you get the jump on other buyers who want desirable items as they are listed.

Advertisement Categories

Following is a list of typical categories of merchandise with some of the items you might want for recycling, repair, or adaption. As you can see from the variety, these publications are truly print versions of flea markets and thrift stores.

Air conditioners and fans

Portable air conditioners
Window fans
Portable and desk fans
Dehumidifiers
Humidifiers

Antiques and collectibles

Glassware and ceramics
Furniture
Old electronic equipment
Stoves and appliances
Books and printed material
Mechanical equipment
Popular culture objects

Appliances

Mixers
Toasters
Food scales
Coffee makers
Ice cream makers
Irons and ironers
Blenders
Juicers

Auto accessories

Car and truck wheels
Bumpers and body parts

Mechanical parts
Curved glass and mirrors
Seating units

Building supplies

Woods (rare and common)
Salvaged glass and windows, thick glass
Wire and cable, rope
Nails and fasteners
Metals of all kinds
Cast iron sinks and tubs
Paints and finishes
Doors (solid, hollow, carved)
Hardware, locks, brackets
Electrical fixtures
Masonry units, tiles, slate
Cabinets of all kinds
Decorative iron and steel units
Industrial shelving
Metal scaffolding
Plastics and foams
Shutters, salvaged building parts
Cork
Metal guttering
Wood molding of all kinds

Business equipment

Barber chairs
Cabinets, tables, chairs, desks
Weight scales
Storage racks, display racks
Mannequins
Display gondolas
Display cases
Clothing racks
Neon signs
Grills, hot plates, warmers
Soft-drink coolers, vending machines

Background music systems
Jars, containers, bins
Pinball and electronic games
Wine barrels
Ice machines
Copying machines
Counters, bars
Telephones, answering machines
Safes, cash registers
Butcher blocks
Commercial refrigerators, freezers
Water coolers

Decorative articles

Plant stands
Throw pillows, floor pillows
Gas logs
Door knockers, door hardware
School desks
Mirrors
Posters
Animal hides
Café doors
Candle holders

Educational and hobby items

Old microscopes, telescopes, mechanical
equipment
Books, encyclopedias, maps, postcards,
photos
Old trains, toys, dolls, collectibles
Kilns and pottery equipment
Weaving equipment
Leather-working equipment
Stained glass supplies

Electronic equipment

Test equipment
Intercoms

Telephones
Communications and data processing devices
Video equipment and games
Radios/TVs
Stereo equipment
Vintage electronic gear

Furniture

Tables, lamps, chairs of all kinds
Sofas, ottomans
Sofa beds
Bookcases
Cabinets, hutches, étagères
China closets, wardrobes, chests
Bars and stools
Coat racks, clothes trees
Mattresses, box springs
Water beds, adjustable beds, folding beds
Headboards, frames, bunk beds
Vanity tables

Health and medical

Sun lamps
Whirlpool units, hot tubs
Exercise equipment
Air cleaners

Household furnishings

Rugs, weavings, wall hangings
Clothes hampers
Medicine cabinets
Chests and trunks
Roll-up shades
Folding chairs
Lecterns, book stands
Benches

Kitchen equipment

Cabinets of all kinds
Work tables
Dining tables
Sinks
Chairs, stools
Range hoods
Backsplashes
Shelving
Storage containers
Refrigerators, freezers
Dishwashers
Stoves
Ovens
Cooktops
Vintage refrigerators and stoves

Lamps and lights

Floor lamps
Table lamps
Clamp-on lamps
Chandeliers
Wall and ceiling fixtures
Pole lamps
Lampshades
Fluorescent lights
Indoor/outdoor floodlights

Office equipment and supplies

Typewriters of all kinds
Desks, chairs
Drafting tables
Copying machines, duplicators
Telephones, answering machines
Desk lamps
File cabinets

Plumbing and heating

Wood-burning stoves
Cast iron tubs and sinks
Antique faucets and fittings
Water coolers
Porcelain bathroom fixtures
Medicine cabinets
Shower stalls and fittings

Tools and machinery

Grinders, sanders, polishers
Saws
Drills
Work benches
Vises and clamps
Tool boxes
Bending and forming tools
Scaffolding
Routers
Jig saws
Welding equipment
Paint sprayers
Soldering equipment

SPECIALIZED SUPPLY STORES

Something to remember when you are looking for special items or want to jog your imagination with the unexpected is the wealth of specialized stores and sources that exist. Shopping at specialized supply stores can put you in contact with items that you don't normally think of as decorative or useful in the home environment.

One of the best specialized supply stores is the auto supply store. Just about every community has one of these, and as you can see from the partial list that follows, there are plenty of useful items to be found. Shopping at a discount auto supply store can give you supplies at a very low price, and since most stores have everything on display you can inspect, compare, and handle the items.

Auto supply store

Flexible plastic and metal moldings
Pinstripe tapes
Colored plastic and cloth tapes
Tail pipe extensions
Small mirrors of several shapes
Mylar, foil, and mirror sheets
Small plastic baskets, pails, cubes
Plastic and cloth tarps
Chain and cable of all kinds
S-hooks and hardware fittings
Rope and cord
Simple electrical supplies
Fiberglass kits
Epoxy and polyester body putty
Glues and adhesives of all kinds
Spray paint of all kinds
Power and hand tools, socket sets, torch kits
Rubber and metal hose and duct
Clamps of all kinds
Work gloves and safety equipment

Related to auto supply stores are auto supply and accessory catalogs. These catalogs are put out by national retailers who supply people with discount parts and supplies for cars, trucks, vans, RVs, and motorcycles. The partial list of interesting supplies from a typical auto supply store catalog shows the rich pickings to be found here.

Auto catalog

Metal trunks suitable for use as tables, chests

Metal and plastic caddies and trays

Small two- and three-burner gas stoves (for RVs—adaptable for home use)

Small kitchen exhaust hoods

Small stainless steel sinks (possible home bar use)

Aluminum van ladders (could be used for lofts, bunk beds, or access to tall shelves)

Various shape bubble windows (could be made into lighting fixtures)

Canvas and nylon tarps (for sunshades, hangings, outdoor furniture)

Seat covers of all kinds (for covering recycled auto seats into couches)

Leather and vinyl repair kits

Glass etching kits

Glass tinting spray

Paint stripping tools

Paint sprayers

Airbrushing tools

Aircraft and boat style lights

Various design auto lights and colored lenses

Gooseneck inspection and map lights

Over 40 different chrome and illuminated hood ornaments

Auto body tools (shapers, rasps, flexible sanders)

Hardware kits (metric and standard screws, washers, nuts, bolts, pins, etc.)

Clamps and pipe-hanging hardware

Stainless steel and galvanized tubing

If you want to get deeper into specialized sources you can try going to professional and industrial supply houses. These are the places where electricians, plumbers, and tradesmen in masonry, metal, and construction go for their supplies. These sources are often located in industrial districts, in nondescript warehouses and sheds, and in unfamiliar neighborhoods. They are worth seeking out, however, (using the Yellow Pages) because the selection of materials will be greater and prices will generally be lower than at consumer-oriented outlets.

Many people don't take advantage of these supply sources because they feel that they are out of place in the environment, and they are put off by the fact that very little merchandise is on display. You generally must ask for what you want (or ask to see a catalog of merchandise) when you walk in. If you need additional help in ordering supplies, you can come into the supply house in the late afternoon (usually a slow time at the counter) and get a clerk to help you select what you need. Times to avoid these places are the early morning (when the pros are ordering what they need for the day's work) and around lunch (when the counter is usually understaffed and pros may be back for additional materials for the afternoon).

Additional sources include retail stores that specialize in certain items. Many of these stores put out catalogs that can be valuable tools for study and inspiration. Certain retail stores (notably variety and discount department stores) have sections that feature plenty of well-designed items at inexpensive prices. These are mass-produced goods that have stood the test of time and are in constant demand. They include small hardware items (mirror hangers, anchors, and shelf brackets), housewares (towel bars, plastic bins, metal buckets and tubs), and general merchandise (lampshades and parts, mirrors, and picture frames). A partial list of these and other sources follows.

Other sources

Appliance parts and supplies stores
Army/navy and surplus stores
Art supply stores
Auto wrecking yards
Building wrecking yards
Crafts shops
Demolition sites
Discount department stores
Electrical supply stores
Electronics catalogs
Electronics supply stores
General merchandise catalogs
Hardware stores (general and industrial)
Home improvement stores
Institutional equipment and supply stores
Lumber stores and yards
Masonry supply stores
Office furniture and supply stores
Pawnshops
Plumbing supply stores
Restaurant and bar supply stores
Roadwork sites, excavations
Roofing supply stores
Steel and metal supply houses
Tile and decor stores
Used appliance stores
Variety stores

FOR SALE: MISCELLANEOUS ————————

In cities there is constant change. Offices, theaters, shops, and stores are constantly remodeling, moving, or going out of business. Fixtures, furniture, and stock from these business are offered for sale at bargain prices. Many items can be used as is. Others may need to be refinished or adapted. Still others have no obvious use until you come up with one. Many of these items come up in newspaper classified columns. A sampling from one Sunday newspaper:

"American black walnut discs ¾ inch thick, 3 and 5 inches in diameter over 30,000 available at 5 cents each." These are probably industrial scrap, left over from a manufacturing operation. Possible uses include making bases for small projects like lamps, or for displaying small art objects, or perhaps as wall covering (attached with mastic directly to walls or to backing pieces of plywood or chipboard).

"Antique building parts, pine flooring, Greek revival doors and frames, mantels, shutters." Surplus from a building demolition. Good for quality wood and for adaptation of objects to wall pieces.

"Blueprint files, drafting stools and tables, office chairs and desks." These are often out-of-style pieces handled by a jobber who deals in office surplus. The items can often be used as is or painted and adapted to home hobby use (photography, woodworking, crafts).

"Candy showcase 6 feet long, excellent condition, best offer." These showcases are often of fine wood with nice, thick glass panels. It might make a good display bookcase or a place for treasured art or collectible objects.

"Church benches (10) solid oak, $25 each or best offer." These pews are a bargain for their craftsmanship and quality wood. Pews can be used as guest seating (with the addition of foam and fabric cushions) and can even be cut and bent around corners to take full advantage of their length if you use wood or steel underbracing to support the two pieces.

"Fluorescent fixtures, good used 2 lite, 8 feet long with lamps, $8 each." These fixtures probably come from a commercial or public building renovation. At this bargain price you can afford to use them as hidden light sources in a hall or large room, perhaps covering the lamps with a colored gelatin filter to soften and change the light.

"Hardwood showroom; ash, bubinga, cherry to teak, walnut to zebra, dimensionals, flitches, burls." In this category are often found ads by businesses that supply unusual materials. This company deals in quality woods and would be a good source for a craftsperson seeking a few odd pieces for a project.

"Hub caps—300 to 400, selling as lot only." Plenty of unexpected merchandise is available. Perhaps you could use the caps as wall covering in a large room, hanging them on finishing nails driven partway into the wall surface.

"Industrial and residential shelving from 1–59 feet, 1000 units available, used metal lockers also." You could organize your storage by purchasing these metal storage systems. The units would probably need painting, but their honest and strong looks could be an asset to your home if you like expressed structure as a design element.

"Movie seats from closed up movie theater, best offer." Theater seats often come in units of two, four, or six seats. You might mount one or more units to your floor (or a portable base) with lag or machine bolts. Theater seats with their steel or iron frames, wood and upholstery seats, have an appealing combination of textures that remind us of pleasant hours spent watching entertainment. If you have a large-screen TV and VCR you can create your own movie theater with these seats.

"Restaurant equipment, ovens, boxes, assorted equipment, booths, refrigerators, tables, chairs, etc." Big city restaurant supply outfits handle plenty of used fixtures and furniture. These objects can often be used or adapted for home use. If you have a large kitchen you can use a professional stove or refrigerator. Used booths and banquettes can be adapted to living room and dining room use.

"Type cases, wood (50) make offer." These compartmented cases are left over from the days when metal type was used in printing shops. They are often of good-quality wood but are stained and scarred from years of use. These cases make excellent organizers for hobby parts or can be mounted on the wall as display and storage for small art objects or collectibles.

THE YELLOW PAGES ————

One of the most useful tools for hunting supplies, materials, and services is the local Yellow Pages. This source will put you in touch with the people and places that can provide you with what you need. Not only can you find what you are looking for, but you can call to check prices. In some major metropolitan areas there can be as much as a 25 percent difference in prices for the same item from different suppliers. It pays to call around and get the best deal.

In some areas, the Yellow Pages are published in two editions, one for consumers and one for businesses. You need both editions to shop intelligently. Go to the local telephone business office to pick up the latest editions of both directories.

Often the best values can be found with firms that do most of their business in industrial goods. That doesn't mean that they won't sell to you; often they will. That's why you should call to check on availability, whether catalogs and price lists are available, and what minimum quantities (if any) need to be purchased.

What follows is a master list of categories from the Yellow Pages that you can use as a guide for your own research. Each category is classified as primarily consumer-oriented, business-oriented, or both. This will give you an idea of which directory to check first and what kind of supplier to expect when you do call.

Categories from the Yellow Pages

Abrasives#
Adhesives, glues, and equipment#
Air conditioning, supplies, and parts#
Aluminum products#
Amusement devices
Anchors, expansion#
Animation mechanisms#
Antiques dealers*
Appliances, household—supplies and parts
Architects' supplies#
Army and navy goods*
Art galleries—dealers*

Artists' materials*
Auctioneers*
Auto bumpers and grilles#
Auto parts and supplies—new, used, rebuilt
Auto seat covers, tops, and upholstery*
Awnings and canopies
Bags—burlap, canvas, cotton*
Bakers' equipment#
Barbers' equipment and supplies#
Bar fixtures#
Barrels and drums
Bathroom accessories*
Baths—equipment and supplies*
Beauty salon equipment and supplies#
Beds
Bed springs#
Benches and worktables#
Bicycles and parts*
Bins#
Blankets#
Boat covers, tops, and upholstery*
Bolts and nuts#
Bookcases#
Bookdealers—used and new
Boxes—metal, wooden, paper#
Brass and brass products#
Brick—new and used
Bronze tablets and plaques#
Brushes*
Building materials—new and used*
Building restoration and preservation*
Bulletin and directory boards#
Butchers' equipment and supplies#
Cabinets—equipment and supplies#
Camping equipment and supplies*
Caning equipment and supplies*
Canvas goods#

Cardboard#

Carnival supplies*

Carpet and rug dealers and cleaners

Carts*

Caterers' equipment and supplies#

Caulking materials and equipment#

Cellophane and cellulose materials and products#

Cement products*

Ceramic products#

Ceramics equipment and supplies*

Chains#

Chairs#

Chimes and bells#

Chimney lining materials#

Chinaware and glassware*

Christmas lights and decorations

Church furnishings*

Clamps#

Cleaning compounds#

Clay products#

Closets and accessories*

Collectibles*

Concrete blocks and shapes#

Conduit and fittings#

Cooking utensils*

Copper products#

Cork and cork products#

Countertops*

Craft dealers and galleries*

Craft supplies*

Decals#

Demolition contractors#

Discount stores*

Document preservation and restoration*

Doors*

Dowels#

Drafting room supplies#

Draperies, curtains, and fixtures*

Drawing materials*

Drills#

Dry goods*

Dumps—rubbish#

Electric equipment and supplies

Electric motors—repairing and supplies*

Etched products#

Expanded metals#

Fabric shops*

Farmers' markets*

Farm supplies*

Fasteners#

Fences—posts, fittings*

Fiberglass materials and products#

Fireplace equipment*

Flags and banners*

Flea markets*

Floor materials*

Floors, industrial#

Foam and sponge rubber*

Foil and foil products#

Furniture frames#

Furniture—new, used, unfinished, outdoor, leasing, etc.*

Games and supplies#

Garden centers*

Garment racks#

General merchandise

Gift shops*

Glass—auto, plate, window

Glass block

Glass rods and tubing#

Glass—stained and leaded*

Glassware decorators*

Gourmet shops*

Gratings#

Grilles, registers, diffusers#

Guards—window and door*

Gutters and downspouts*

Handles#

Hardware

Heating equipment—supplies and parts*

Hobby and model construction supplies

Home centers*

Hose and tubing—rubber and plastic#

Housewares

Industrial equipment and supplies#

Inks—printing and lithographing#

Interior decorators' and designers' supplies#

Iron#

Ironwork*

Job lot merchandise#

Junk dealers*

Kitchen cabinets and equipment

Laboratory equipment and supplies#

Ladders and scaffolds*

Lamination services*

Lamps and lampshades

Lath#

Laundry supplies#

Lawn and garden equipment and supplies*

Leather goods#

Letters, signs#

Library equipment and supplies#

Lighting fixtures—supplies and repairs

Lockers#

Locks and locksmiths*

Lumber—new and used

Magazines—used*

Magnets and magnetic devices#

Manhole covers#

Maps*

Marble*

Marine equipment and supplies*

Mats and matting#

Mattresses and bedding*

Metals—base#

Metal specialties#

Metal trim—moldings#

Millwork#

Mirrors and resilvering

Mosaics*

Motel and hotel equipment and supplies#

Museums*

Needlework materials*

Notions*

Novelties#

Office furniture and equipment

Office supplies, stationery#

Optical goods#

Packing and crating*

Paint*

Painters' equipment and supplies#

Pallets and skids#

Paper boxboard#

Paper products#

Paper tubes and cores#

Partitions#

Party supplies*

Perforated metals#

Photographic equipment, supplies, and services

Picture frames

Picture hangers#

Pictures*

Pillows*

Pipe and fittings—new and used#

Pipe bending and fabrication#

Pipe hangers#

Plaster—ornamental*

Plastics products

Plastics, raw materials#

Plastics—rods, tubes, sheets, etc.#

Platforms, portable#

Plating, replating*

Plumbing fixtures and supplies—new and used

Plywood and veneers*

Porcelain enamel repairing and refinishing*

Porcelain products#

Posters#

Quilting materials and supplies#

Quilts*

Racks#

Railings

Railroad ties#

Ranges and ovens—supplies and parts*

Rattan, reeds, willows#

Razors and blades#

Recycling centers#

Reels, cable#

Resins#

Restaurant equipment and supplies#

Rock shops*

Rods—threaded#

Rollers—wood, metal, rubber#

Roofing supplies and materials

Rope#

Rubber products#

Safes and vaults

Sail fabrics#

Sail makers*

Sandblasting#

Scaffolding#

School furniture and equipment#

School supplies*

Scrap metals, plastics, rubber#

Screen printing equipment and supplies#

Screws#

Seating#

Second-hand stores*

Service station equipment#

Sewer pipe#

Shelving#

Showcases#

Shutters

Signals#

Signs—equipment and supplies

Slate*

Slings—cargo nets#

Slipcovers*

Soaps and detergents#

Solvents#

Spools#

Stair treads#

Stationers*

Statuary*

Steel distributors and warehouses#

Steel—used#

Stencils and supplies#

Stools#

Store fixtures—new and used

Surplus and salvage merchandise#

Tabletops*

Tanks—concrete, fiberglass, plastic, wood, etc.#

Tarpaulins#

Telephone equipment and systems

Television and radio—repairs, supplies, and parts*

Terra cotta#

Theatrical equipment and supplies*

Thrift shops*
Tile—ceramic and nonceramic
Tin#
Tools—industrial and commercial#
Toys*
Traffic signs, signals, and equipment#
Trophies*
Truck equipment and parts#
Trunks#
Tubing, metal#
Twines and cordage#
Upholsterers' supplies#
Upholstery fabrics
Variety store merchandise
Vending machines#
Venetian blinds*
Ventilating equipment#

Vertical blinds#
Wallpapers and wallcoverings
Waste containers#
Waste—cotton, wool, etc.#
Welding equipment and supplies#
Welding repairs*
Wheels#
Window blinds
Windows*
Wine storage equipment#
Wire and cable#
Wire cloth#
Woolen goods#

#Business
*Consumer
No symbol means check both business and consumer editions.

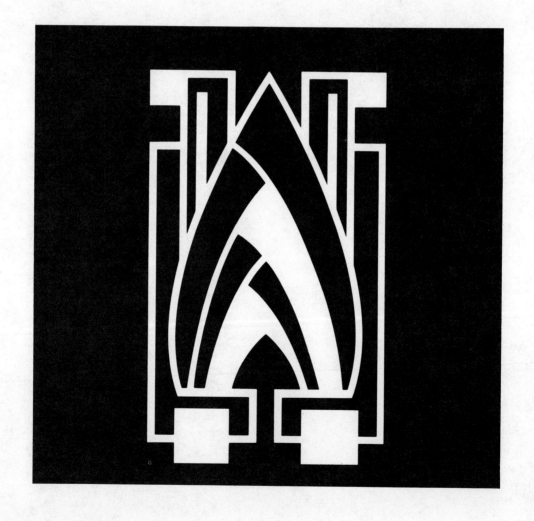

3

TOOLS

Part of doing things for yourself is having and knowing about hand and power tools that can help you in your repair and recycling work. You don't have to own every tool in the hardware store (or even all the ones listed in this chapter) to get a job done. Some tools simply make the work go faster, more accurately, or more easily. Some specialized tools can be borrowed or rented instead of bought outright. No tool, no matter how fancy or expensive, is going to substitute for your effort and desire to do the job correctly.

The tools described here are some of the classics that you will use over and over for the projects in this book and for other repair and construction work. Because you will be using these tools for work and not for show, you needn't be concerned about buying very expensive premium tools with fine finishes and rare

materials. Look for tools that are intelligently designed to do their job well. Just as you should avoid ultra-expensive tools, you should beware of cheap tools that may break or wear quickly, produce inaccurate results, or perhaps injure you. The descriptions provided will mention quality points to look for and can help you steer a middle course when you go shopping for the proper tool.

In general, the tools described in each classification are listed in descending order of their usefulness to our work. The most important tools are listed first. Most of the tools are inexpensive, and some of them you can construct yourself from common objects. The few power tools listed are among the least expensive and most popular ones available. You should have no trouble finding them at competitive prices.

ORGANIZING YOUR TOOLS

One thought before we move on to the tools themselves: You can waste up to a third of your working time if you don't have your tools assembled and organized properly before you work. It is very frustrating to have to search for a half hour each time you start a project and then conduct 15-minute mini-searches periodically during the project. Careful and experienced craftspersons keep their tools organized. Some people use a large steel toolbox. Others wear leather belts with loops for tools, and still others wear aprons with pockets and loops. The important thing about any of these systems is that the tools are organized before, after, and during the project so time and energy aren't wasted looking for them.

One simple and inexpensive approach to organization is to buy six to eight plastic or metal pails. You can place your tools in the pails according to function. You might adopt the classifications used in this chapter to organize your collection. With pails, you can see in an instant whether the tool is there or not, and you can put large and bulky tools in a pail that you can't place in a conventional box or on a belt.

Another system is to organize your tools according to size. You might use a fishing tackle box for small tools and instruments, several pails for bulky tools, and a wooden crate for power tools and their extension cords. Whatever system you devise is fine as long as it frees you to work quickly, accurately, and safely. Any system that makes working more efficient contributes to the pride and pleasure you will feel in your accomplished projects. Look to professional carpenters, linemen,

repair and service people for inspiration—they are organized because this kind of work is their livelihood. They can reach instinctively to the place where their tool should be, on a belt, in an apron, or in a box or pail.

FASTENING TOOLS

Claw Hammer

This is your basic fastening tool. Buy one with a 16-ounce head (forged, not cast) and a wood, steel, or fiberglass handle. The rubber-cushioned fiberglass hammers transmit the least shock to your hands and are worth the extra cost. Professionals favor hammers with a slightly convex-shaped driving face. This shape lets you drive a nail flush to the surface of the wood without marring the surface of the surrounding wood.

Screwdrivers

Your repair and recycling work will involve a number of different sizes and types of screws. Because of this you should have a complete set of screwdrivers for maximum flexibility. A good set will include three slotted drivers (small, medium, and large), two Phillips head drivers (large and medium), and three additional slotted drivers (mini, stubby, and offset) for working in tight places. Look for quality features such as fully ground blades; sturdy, square shafts; and large, padded handles. Screwdrivers that have long shafts let you get better torque and pressure on the screw than short-shaft tools.

In addition to the basic set above, you may need a set of precision screwdrivers (also known as jewelers' or hobby screwdrivers) for very small screws found in models, jewelry, and fine objects. These drivers are usually sold in sets of five or six sizes and have rotating handles that allow you to hold the driver on the screw and twist at the same time.

Adjustable Wrench

This is one of the most useful tools you will own. The full name is *adjustable open-end wrench*. The most useful size to own is 12 inches (other sizes are 4, 6, 8, 10, and 16 inches). This tool will accommodate any size metric or standard nut, bolt, or flat fitting. Use the wrench on construction projects, plumbing fixtures, auto and home equipment, fixtures and furnishings—almost anything that can be loosened and tightened.

Socket and Ratchet Wrench Sets

These are very useful and efficient tools to have. Originally designed for automobile and machine repair and maintenance, socket sets are a must for many repair and construction projects around the home. Sockets allow you to work in tight areas and apply solid pressure on tough fittings. Auto supply and discount department stores carry inexpensive socket sets that are fine for nonprofessional use.

Because of their automobile orientation, sockets come in metric or standard sizes. For greatest flexibility buy a ¼- and ⅜-inch square drive combination (metric and standard) set. This will include sockets for most bolts and fittings you will encounter, a nut driver handle, and a ratchet handle (you can drive fittings

with as little as 10 degrees of arc to work with). Accessories that you can add to your basic set include screwdriver bit sockets, universal joints, and broken bolt and stud removers. If you can't find an inexpensive combination set and must purchase either a standard or a metric set, buy the standard set—it will get you through more situations around the house than a metric set.

Hot Glue Gun

This inexpensive device (about the same cost as a good adjustable wrench) uses an electric heating element to melt solid glue sticks and dispense a thin bead of glue into joints. The tool is shaped like a small pistol and can be handled easily in tight situations. The great virtue of the system is that you can glue something without the use of clamps. The glue reaches its full strength 60 seconds after it's applied. This means that you can glue fragile and oddly shaped things and use your hands to hold the pieces together until the glue takes. The system works for larger construction projects too. The cost of the glue sticks is about what you would have to spend on screws, bolts, or other fasteners. The advantage is that you can repair, fasten, and assemble without the use of holes, threads, washers, or other time-consuming procedures. Solid glue sticks are available that will bond wood, tile, leather, cloth, certain plastics, metals, and so on.

Propane Torch Kit

A hand-held propane gas torch is ideal for soldering copper and brass pipe and fittings. Not only can you repair and adapt plumbing fixtures, but you can

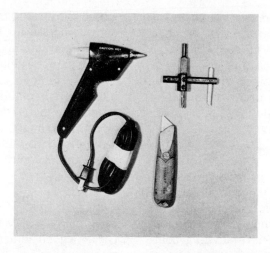

FIGURE 3-1. Specialized tools. A hot-glue gun bonds materials almost instantly. An adjustable hole drill cuts circles in wood and plastic. A utility knife cuts cardboard, carpet, tile, and other thin materials.

create interesting and functional objects with copper, brass, and solder. Most jobs can be handled with a medium flame fitting (often called a pencil-burner). If you purchase a torch kit you will often get a flame spreader fitting (good for paint removing) and a soldering iron fitting (for electrical soldering and fine metal soldering) along with the basic torch.

Soldering Iron or Gun

This is used for making permanent precision electrical connections in wiring and for repairing and adapting electrical and electronic equipment. A pencil-tip soldering iron is fine for occasional work if you select one with at least a 45-watt rating and replaceable tips. The iron will take from 1 to 3 minutes to reach operating temperature but will be quite serviceable for the occasional job. A more expensive soldering gun with a rating between 150 and 250 watts is needed for constant

duty and for near-instant heating. The better guns have a work illumination light and replaceable tips for general duty, plastic cutting, and fine work.

Hand Staple Gun

This is useful for installation of carpet, wallcoverings, upholstery, fabrics, screens, and other sheet materials. A hand-operated stapler is fine for domestic use (more expensive electric and air-powered staplers are available). Be sure to carefully check the stapler and its operation before buying—some staplers can pinch your skin no matter how you hold them. Most staplers take two or three sizes of staples suitable to different tasks.

Caulking Gun

A very inexpensive tool, this metal skeleton accepts cardboard tube cartridges of caulk, industrial mastic, roof cement, butyl rubber, panel adhesives, and so on. The gun make it very easy to dispense and control applications of these and other adhesives and sealers.

Nail Set

This is an inexpensive tool that lets you set the head of a finishing nail or brad below the surface of the wood so that the hole can be covered over with putty. This procedure is necessary in fine cabinetry or other carpentry work where you want an unbroken wood surface. Buy a nail set with a square head so that it won't roll away from you when you put it down.

Adhesive Trowel

Available at a tile store, roofing supply house, or general building supplies dealer, an adhesive trowel is necessary for laying and setting tiles and surface materials of all kinds. A versatile trowel will be made of an oblong of flexible steel with notches of various sizes cut on all sides. A handle of wood or plastic is attached to the center of the trowel. You use the side of the trowel that has the size notches called for by the manufacturer's instructions on the adhesive package. In general, you use large notches to spread adhesive for thick material and smaller notches to spread adhesive for thinner materials. The notches provide the proper bonding characteristics for the material you are using.

Allen Head Wrenches

Also known as *hex key wrenches*, these special L-shaped wrenches operate set screws, inspection plates, and other devices that you may occasionally work on.

Available in sets for metric or standard sizes, the best buys are the sets that are attached to a ring or handle so that you don't misplace them.

Rubber Mallet

These are used for working with delicate woods, metals, and plastics. Use a rubber-headed mallet to knock apart furniture that is to be reglued or to tap delicate assemblies together. Mallets can be found at auto supply stores and larger hardware stores.

Rivet Gun

Often called a *blind rivet tool*, these guns let you bind sheet materials, fiber, metal, leather, and other materials. The tool uses a special rivet that expands internally when set by hand pressure. The advantage to the tool is that it lets you rivet from only one side of the material—great for irregularly shaped objects, tubes, and in-place repairs.

CUTTING TOOLS

Circular Saw

This is one of the most important power tools you can own. A saw with a 7¼-inch blade will make cuts in lumber up to 2¼ inches thick and should be able to handle all of your projects. The least expensive saws have plastic housings and very basic depth-of-cut and bevel adjusting devices. These saws are generally fine for home use. The more rugged metal-housed (and heavier) saws are for constant professional use, and that is reflected in their price. The important things to check are the feel of the saw (does it handle easily, are controls logically placed?) and the design and function of the safety features (the trigger switch, retractable blade guard, and sawdust chute).

Part of the circular saw's usefulness and versatility is in the blade you select for each job. There is a great variety of blades available. The common ones are: *combination* for general sawing with and against the grain, *rip* for fast sawing with the grain, *crosscut* for accurate cutting across the grain, and *plywood/veneer/paneling* for accurate, clean cuts with these thin materials. Still other blades are available to cut sheet metals, fiberglass, masonry products, and very dense woods.

FIGURE 3-2. A storage closet. A circular saw and 3/8-inch drill are the only power tools required for this project.

Electric Drill

This tool is just about indispensable for construction, repair, and recycling work. Happily, good drills are not terribly expensive. You want a ⅜-inch variable speed reversible drill. Like circular saws, the least expensive models will be plastic-housed and built for occasional duty. With the variable speed option you can drill successfully in a number of materials and use such accessories as screwdriver bit and socket sets, hole drills and saws, and grinding and shaping bits. The reversing feature will come in handy with accessories and for the times when your bit becomes stuck in the material.

A ⅜-inch drill will accept bits with a shank diameter of up to ⅜ inch. Select "high-speed" drill bits (not "carbon") for durability, and use carbide-tipped bits for drilling in masonry and ceramics. For drilling ½-inch and larger diameter holes in wood you can use an auger bit that you modify to fit your ⅜-inch drill. An auger bit will have a pyramid-shaped tang on the end of the shank (for fitting a hand-operated tool called a *brace*). This tang will not allow you to fit the bit into your power drill, so you simply cut the tang off with a hack saw. The plain shank will now fit your drill, and you can use the auger to cut large holes in wood. Be sure to use low speed and pressure to imitate the action of the hand-operated brace.

You may also want to use a set of countersinking and counterboring bits. These special bits are used to drill pilot holes and countersink the surface of the wood to accept flat-head wood screws. Each bit makes the pilot hole and the countersink in one operation. These bits are sold in sets to accommodate the nine or ten most common screw sizes.

Hack Saw

An inexpensive tool for sawing metals, pipes, hard rubber, certain plastics, even hard wood, a hack saw is actually just a frame with a handle that accepts 8-, 10-, or 12-inch disposable blades. The frame adjusts to take any length blade.

Hack saw blades vary from 14 to 32 teeth per inch. Select a blade that will keep at least three consecutive teeth in contact with the work at all times. In general, use a fine-toothed blade on thin stock and a coarse-toothed blade on thick stock. Install the blade on the frame with the teeth facing away from the handle, and tighten the wing nut until the blade is under strong tension.

Crosscut Hand Saw

Most of your sawing will be done with a power circular saw, but a hand saw can be useful for small jobs or for when you don't have electric power available. A 26-inch crosscut saw with nine teeth per inch will be the most versatile for making smooth cuts in seasoned wood.

Razor Blade Utility Knife

Available at art supply, auto supply, and hardware stores, this tool is very useful for cutting and scoring different materials. Select a knife that has a sturdy metal handle that's comfortable in your palm and offers a place to store extra blades. This knife offers the security and stiffness of a hand tool with the sharpness and accuracy of a razor. Use it to cut materials such as tile, fabric, canvas, thin wood, plastic, cardboard, and mat board.

Pocket Knife

These can range from a simple penknife to a multi-purpose and very expensive camper's and wilderness knife. Perhaps the best compromise is a basic electrician's knife, which has a single heavy-gauge blade for cutting and stripping insulation and a combination screwdriver/wire stripper tool. Since wire stripping and preparation is likely to be the primary use for the knife, you can't go wrong with a sturdy electrician's knife.

Tin Snips

These are used for cutting sheet metals, gutters, ducts, and some plastics. Buy a sturdy pair of compound-leverage aviation snips (the most versatile kind) about 12 inches in length. Be sure to check for quality in the handles, the most likely failure point in this tool. You don't want the handles to flex or bend at a critical moment. Snips can be found at a roofing supply house or industrial hardware store.

Tubing Cutter/Reamer

This tool is used for cutting copper, brass, and thinwall plastic pipe. Most of your cutting jobs can be handled with a wheeled pipe cutter that accommodates pipe up to 1-inch diameter. Larger pipes can be cut with a hack saw. Get a cutter that has a built-in reamer to remove burrs from the cut ends of the pipe.

Glass Cutter

This is used for cutting sheets of glass to the size and shape required. Buy one with a tungsten steel cutter wheel. (The tungsten carbide wheels are more expensive and are for prolonged professional use.)

Hole Drill and Saws

For cutting large-diameter holes (up to 4 inches) in wood, metal, and plastics, there are two ways to go. An adjustable hole drill is fairly inexpensive and will cut wood and most plastics. This single tool chucks into your ⅜-inch drill and can be used at low speed to drill holes from ½ to 3 inches. A high-speed hole saw is a more expensive proposition, but it will cut holes up to 4 inches in steel, brass, aluminum, copper, or iron. You must buy a separate saw for each size hole that you wish to make. In addition, you must buy a mandrel piece that chucks into your ⅜-inch drill to hold and position the saw blade.

Single-Edge Razor Blades

These are very useful for precise scoring and cutting operations, as well as for scraping and refinishing. Buy your blades from a paint store or industrial hardware store in boxes of 5, 25, 50, or 100. Blades are disposable and will quickly dull and break, but they are important tools for certain jobs.

Hobby Knives

These tools are found at artists' and drafting supply houses and hobby and model shops. A typical knife consists of a finely balanced aluminum handle with a holder for a very sharp blade. Blades are interchangeable and replaceable for different tasks. They are useful for cutting paper, fabric, cardboard, matboard, thin woods, plastics, or stencils.

Back Saw and Miter Box

A back saw is a 14- or 16-inch hand saw with about 12 teeth per inch, which has a steel brace running at the top of the blade to stiffen the entire saw. The saw is used with a wood, plastic, or steel miter box to make precise angled cuts in wood. The saw and miter box combination is useful for picture frame and furniture construction. Plastic pipe can also be cut accurately in a miter box. For general use an inexpensive plastic or hardwood miter box is adequate. The more expensive and versatile steel frame adjustable miter boxes are only justified for someone who is serious about making a lot of furniture and frames.

Sabre Saw

Along with a power circular saw and a drill, an electric sabre saw is one of the most popular and common power tools around a home. The sabre saw cuts a great variety of materials with different blades and can cut straight lines, circles, and irregular shapes. There are some very inexpensive saws available with single-speed motors and stripped-down features. A good mid-priced model would have variable-speed or two-speed operation, a bevel device, a straight line guide, and a circle cutting guide.

Blades are available to cut a wide variety of materials such as woods, metals, masonry products, plaster, plastics, leather, rubber, tile, and cardboard. In general, sabre saws are at their best cutting thin materials—the more blade teeth per inch, the smoother the finished cut.

FORMING AND SMOOTHING TOOLS

Putty Knife/Taping Knife

These two tools are indispensable. The putty knife should have a blade about 2 inches wide and be made of fairly stiff steel. You will use it for patching, scraping, forming, smoothing, digging, and a host of other jobs. A taping knife should have a 6-inch-wide blade of flexible steel. Its primary use is to spread plaster, adhesives, joint compound, and other soft materials.

Scrapers

For stripping old paint, wallpaper, rust, dirt, and other films or finishes from fur-niture, fixtures, and household goods, there are many different kinds of scrapers available. A good selection will be found in a large paint store or industrial hardware outlet. The most useful kind of general purpose scraper is a 4-inch razor scraper with replaceable blades. Buy one with a sturdy metal shaft about 1 foot long and a large padded handle. A scraper of this kind will give you plenty of leverage and strength to remove finishes, and you can keep putting new 4-inch razor blades into the head as you require.

Some other scrapers worth considering are triangular and tear-drop shaped scrapers (nonreplaceable heads), flat metal hand scrapers in rectangular and curved shapes, and wood-handled, pulling-motion floor scrapers. All of these fixed-blade scrapers can be sharpened with a burnishing tool or a fine file.

FIGURE 3-3. A wire brush, a razor scraper, and a taping knife—three important tools for cleaning, refinishing, and forming operations.

Files

Very useful for repair and maintenance work, files sharpen tools; clean up joints to be fitted and attached; and make guide cuts in metal, glass, and ceramics. There are many different types and grades of files. For general work a 10-inch mill bastard file is good for removing metal quickly. For finer work and sharpening, an 8-inch mill smooth file will serve. For sharpening saw teeth, scoring glass tubing, and working in tight places, a tapered triangular file about 6 to 8 inches long is ideal. There are also round, half-round, square, and needle shapes available in various sizes and grades to handle specialized jobs such as model making, sheet metal working, or wood and plastic.

Most people don't bother to purchase and use a wood handle with their files. They should. Handles are inexpensive, and they protect your hands from possible injury if the file slips or hangs up while you are working.

Power Sanders

Most of your finishing work can be accomplished with hand sanding, steel wool, and other manual procedures, but for large projects and some materials it is advisable to have a power sander of some sort. The most versatile of the finish sanders is known as a *dual action machine*. It offers both reciprocating (back and forth) and orbital (small circle) actions in a single machine. Orbital action cuts through material quickly, while reciprocating action produces a finer surface and with special pads can even buff and polish a finished product.

For more money you can buy a belt sander, which is suited to refinishing large, flat areas quickly and smoothly. With a 3-inch belt machine rated at one horsepower or better and with a dust bag attachment, you can quickly refinish wood, plaster, stone, marble, glass and metal.

Power sanders are optional for most small projects, but they can be very helpful for big jobs on flat surfaces. Use silicon or aluminum oxide sandpaper in power models; it lasts longer and clogs less frequently than cheaper flint papers.

Wood-Forming Tools

To remove wood from irregular shapes and to form shapes from raw wood, you need several tools. A *wood rasp* is a fast-cutting tool in a flat, half-round, or round shape. A flat and a round rasp, each 12 to 14 inches long, will handle many jobs.

For working on irregular shapes in recycling and design work, a *surform* tool is very handy. It will work on sharply curved and tight places. Auto supply houses carry some interesting forming tools for working on auto bodies. Some of these can be useful in your work, particularly flexible rasps that cut fiberglass, filler putty, and plastics.

Whetstone

This is an inexpensive tool for sharpening and burnishing your tools so that they will work smoothly and efficiently. A good whetstone will be made of hard natural or man-made stone, one side coarse, one side fine. As you sharpen your tools on first the coarse and then the fine side, put light oil on the stone to keep the surface clean and unclogged with dirt and grease.

Tube Bending Kit

Used for thinwall conduit, copper flexible tubing, and other flexible tubing up to ½-inch diameter, a kit consists of five or six tempered spring coils that allow you to bend tubes into shapes smoothly and without kinking. It is useful for lamp construction, design work, and artistic projects.

MEASURING AND MARKING TOOLS

Steel Tape Measure

This is your most important measuring tool. Buy one with a 1-inch-wide blade, a sturdy metal or plastic case, a locking device for the blade, and a clip for your belt.

The length of the blade is not too important; most good measures will be from 16 to 25 feet in length. The important thing is to get a wide blade with highly visible markings. This single feature will make more difference in your accuracy than any other attribute.

Yardstick and Straightedge

An aluminum or steel yardstick with engraved and painted markings is a valuable marking and measuring device for small projects. If you are going to be cutting glass sheets, you should have a wooden yardstick or an absolutely straight piece of flat wooden molding (¼ × 2 inches will do nicely). Wood won't slip on glass as easily as metal will.

Carpenter's Square

Also known as a *try square*, this wood and steel square is used for testing and marking lumber for perfect cutting. Generally the wood handle is 5 inches long and the steel blade is 8 inches. When the wood handle rests on a straight edge, the steel blade describes a perfect 90-degree angle for checking and marking.

Levels

These are used for leveling furniture, mounting fixtures in square, and similar jobs. For general use buy a 24-inch model with an aluminum frame (for lightness, easy handling, and resistance to warping). You can also purchase a plastic frame level about 3 to 5 inches long for leveling small projects such as shelves.

HOLDING TOOLS ──────────

Combination Pliers

These are also called *slip joint pliers* or *hose clamp pliers*. Get a pair 6 or 8 inches long with insulated handles (for comfort and safety when working near electricity). Use these for general holding and forming projects.

Needlenose Pliers

These are used in electrical work for forming wires into loops for attachment to terminals and screws. Get a pair with insulated handles about 6 or 8 inches long. The best kind has side cutting blades to cut wire and cable.

C Clamps

Made of iron or steel, two of these clamps will handle many of your projects. Clamps that will open to 3 or 4 inches with a 2-inch throat depth (distance from the edge of the work) are a good choice for starters. Typically C clamps are available that will open from 1 to 8 inches in 1-inch steps. The larger clamps are expensive and should only be bought if called for by a big project or a series of smaller ones. There are other ways of clamping and holding large objects that involve less expense.

Spring Clamps

These inexpensive spring-loaded clamps are made of stamped steel and are great for brief or light-duty clamping. Buy three or four 2-inch capacity spring clamps at a discount department store, auto supply store, or home center.

Multi-Pliers

Also called *adjustable joint pliers*, these are excellent for handling and holding pipe and fittings. They combine the actions of an adjustable wrench and a pair of common pliers. They are available in 10- and 12-inch lengths, with five to seven grooved positions. A pair of these tools makes good sense for general work.

Lock-Grip Pliers

This tool combines the functions of pliers, wrench, vise, and clamp. It doesn't perform any one of these functions well enough to replace the original tool, but it is a useful extra set of hands in many situations. A 10-inch model with straight jaws will be most useful for repair and fabrication work.

Sawhorses

For working in comfort and security on large pieces (doors, lumber, certain pieces of furniture, etc.), a pair of sawhorses is needed. You can make your own by purchasing four metal or plastic sawhorse brackets and cutting 2 × 4 lumber into legs and cross pieces. The suggested height for the horses is 24 to 30 inches; the suggested width for the crosspieces is 36 to 44 inches. In addition to the brackets you will need four 6-foot 2 × 4s and one 8-foot 2 × 4.

If you are going to be doing a lot of fine work and cabinetry, you might consider buying a *vise bench*. This specialized tool acts like a small workbench, a big vise, and several clamps. It can hold just about any shape securely for construction and repair.

Pipe Wrench

Also known as a *Stillson wrench*, it is necessary for removing and fitting steel pipe. Two wrenches are needed for pipe fitting (one to hold the pipe and one to turn the fitting). For most work two 14-inch wrenches will serve—they will accommodate pipe up to 2 inches in diameter. These wrenches are only for steel pipe; do not use them on plastic, copper, or soft brass.

Vise

There are many different vises including woodworking, picture framing, drill press, and machinist types. Good vises are not cheap, so they are definitely for the serious worker. The most versatile would be a machinist's vise with a 4-inch capacity. Look for such features as a locking swivel base (so that when the vise is bolted to the work surface it can be used in any position), well-aligned jaw faces, and built-in anvil surfaces. Some vises are clamp-on models, which can be set up on a sawhorse, countertop, or wherever needed.

Homemade Holding Devices

You can create your own inexpensive holding devices for working on items. One of the easiest devices is a series of rubber bands cut from bicycle, motorcycle, and auto tire inner tubes. These bands can do an admirable job of holding and clamping material. Cut the bands narrow or wide according to the tension needed for the job at hand.

Another easy device is a cord or rope tourniquet. Simply wrap your object sev-

FIGURE 3-4. A Deco table. A clothesline tourniquet was used to clamp this table when it was reglued.

eral times, tie off the cord or rope, and tighten the bands by putting a stick or dowel in between the lines and twisting.

A very useful homemade device is an alligator-clip work stand. Take a scrap piece of 2 × 4 lumber and drill two ⅛-inch holes in the wood. Place the holes 8 inches from each other. Take two 8-inch lengths of coat hanger wire and dip an end of each into epoxy glue. Place the coated ends of the wire into the drilled holes. After the epoxy has cured, take two 2-inch-long alligator clips (available at electronics supply stores) and attach one to each free end of the coat hangers. Bend each of the coat hangers into a loop with a pair of needlenose pliers, and place the loop under the screw on the body of the alligator clip.

You now have a work stand for holding very delicate and small objects. The coat hangers can be bent into any angle necessary, and the clips will hold objects securely. A variation on this is to use plastic or wood spring-clamp clothes pins instead of the alligator clips.

Pipe Clamps

These are used for holding and clamping very long objects. You buy a two-piece set consisting of a fixed screw mechansim and a sliding backstop that adjusts along the length of a pipe to fit the piece being worked on. You must buy a length of threaded steel pipe in addition to the clamp pieces. In general a set for ½-inch pipe is adequate, along with a 5-foot section of ½-inch threaded steel pipe. For more demanding projects a ¾-inch set-up is required.

REFINISHING TOOLS

Paint Brushes

When applying paints, finishes, varnishes, paint removers, strippers, and cleaners, a good selection of brushes is essential for efficient work. Many people won't take the time to properly clean and store brushes between jobs. To get around this problem, you can purchase disposable nylon and synthetic bristle brushes. These brushes are inexpensive, and you can let them freeze up with paint after you are done with them. Disposable brushes are a good bet for certain critical jobs where you want an absolutely clean brush to avoid contaminating sensitive liquid finishes or chemicals. Most fine cabinetmakers and furniture refinishers use disposable brushes to apply varnishes and other clear finishes.

Most of your work can be handled with 1-, 2-, and 3-inch-wide flat brushes. If you are doing a lot of finishing work it would be handy to have a selection of these on hand, perhaps four or five of each size. You can find these inexpensive brushes at paint stores, hardware stores, and home centers. You can also invest in a few good quality wood-handled natural bristle brushes for special situations. You must be prepared to clean and store these brushes for future projects. For painting and finishing carvings, moldings, frames, and other ornate objects, a 1-inch diameter round sash brush is ideal. The stubby fat bristles of this brush are good for getting paint into small details. For stencil work and detail painting of large objects, a 1½-inch round sash brush is a good investment.

Wire Brushes

These are invaluable for cleaning rust, corrosion, grime, and other debris from objects in preparation for refinishing and recycling and are particularly good for getting softened paint out of turnings and carvings. A good general-purpose brush will have a 1-foot-long curved wooden handle with flexible bristles about 1½ inches long. Another useful model is somewhat shorter, with a straight wood handle and stiff 1-inch bristles. For cleaning large flat objects, a 4 × 8-inch flat brush with 2-inch bristles is efficient.

There are also circular wire brush attachments that you can chuck into your ⅜-inch drill for power cleaning of objects. These round brushes come from 1 inch to 4 inches in diameter depending on the size of the object you are working on.

Steel Wools

Steel wool is essential for certain refinishing and recycling jobs. Extra fine (#000) is for rubbing down furniture and fine objects, both before and after applying a finish. It is also useful for removing and reconstituting thin finishes in combination with a liquid solvent. Fine grade (#00) is for buffing woods with paint stripper and solvents and for plain buffing of copper, brass, aluminum, or steel. Medium grade (#0) is for cleaning copper and brass tubing and fittings prior to soldering, and for general cleaning and buffing of hard materials in preparation for finishes and adhesives. Coarse grade (#2) is for deep cleaning and buffing of pitted and corroded materials and for removal of thick paint and varnish in combination with strippers and solvents.

Sandpapers

Used for hand sanding as well as in pad machines and belt machines, most papers now are made from a synthetic abrasive product that is more durable than any natural product such as flint or garnet. Most of your smoothing and forming jobs can be handled with the standard coarse, medium, and fine grades. In general you use sandpaper for working with raw materials and when you radically adapt old materials. Use steel wool for working with existing furniture and objects.

Cleaning Brushes

An assortment of cleaning brushes can be useful for cleaning and preparing small and ornate objects. A selection of soft, medium, and hard toothbrushes is handy for very small objects. A plastic-handled dishwashing brush with nylon bristles can be used for cleaning fancy and detailed objects. Auto supply stores offer an interesting selection of special purpose brushes including brass bristle brushes, long-handled tire cleaning brushes, metal cleaning brushes, and auto parts cleaning brushes.

SAFETY AND TESTING TOOLS

Goggles

These should be your first safety investment. Purchase impact-resistant plastic goggles that will protect your eyes. Get the kind that protect your entire eye area, and are not just glasses with side shields. Look for goggles at an auto supply store, industrial hardware outlet, or home center. Wear your goggles whenever material is in the air—during stripping, refinishing, drilling, sawing, sanding, hammering, and so forth.

Respirator

These are used to protect you against harmful dusts and other materials that you may encounter when you are working. There are permanent models with washable or replaceable filters, but you may prefer to buy the inexpensive disposable kind that come in packs of six or twelve. Auto stores, large hardware stores, and industrial hardware outlets carry a good selection of respirators. Wear a respirator during sanding, spray painting, cleaning, and other operations when dust and fine particles are thrown into the air.

Gloves

To protect your hands from unexpected sharp edges and slivers, you should have a sturdy pair of leather gloves with 4-inch canvas cuffs. These gloves should be worn when you are selecting and handling lumber, going through raw and salvaged material, and during cutting and forming operations. For less demanding jobs, an inexpensive pair of cotton work gloves will protect your hands and still give you plenty of dexterity for smaller objects and more delicate operations.

Neon Circuit Tester

Available at most electrical supply houses and home centers, this inexpensive tester will tell you whether or not current is flowing in a line or circuit. This test for hot wires should be the first thing you do before you handle or work on any electrical installation. The tester is useful in repair and testing of electrical appliances and equipment and is absolutely essential if you are going to be doing any modification to your home's electrical system (for example, wiring in a fixture that you have recycled).

Multitester

Often called *volt/ohm/milliameters* (or *VOMs*), these are available at electronics supply stores, hobby shops, and electrical supply houses. These meters and testers perform a number of useful functions in the testing and repair of electrical and electronic equipment. They range from simple, inexpensive models up to complex instruments costing hundreds of dollars. Your needs will probably best be served by an economy or pocket-sized

Cap. 2
EAST END

FIGURE 3-5. An iron fence pot rack. A magnetic stud finder is needed to locate the hidden wood joists for installing this fixture.

VOM. (Just about every manufacturer makes an instrument for the home market.) A guide included with your instrument will instruct you in its use. Typically you will be able to test for voltage leaks, short circuits, electrical resistance, electrical polarity, and AC and DC voltages. These and other tests and readings will help you to pinpoint problems and failure points in appliances and equipment that you are recycling.

MISCELLANEOUS TOOLS

Stud Finder

This is a very inexpensive but handy tool for locating the position of studs under plaster or other finished surfaces in your house. You will need to know the position of studs and joists to attach shelves, fixtures, and other objects securely to walls and ceilings. The stud finder consists of a plastic holder enclosing a magnet on a pivot. As you move the finder over the wall surface, the magnet will move perpendicular to the wall when it finds a stud. (The nails in the stud cause this to happen.) Using a stud finder is more accurate and cleaner than using your hammer to tap the wall or searching for studs by trial and error.

Cat's Paw Pulling Bar

This is useful for removing woodwork, carvings, moldings, and architectural details. A cat's paw is different from a common crowbar—it has a head that can be driven behind delicate pieces without undue damage. A cat's paw bar will also remove nails from wood with less damage than a crowbar or claw hammer. It is available in two sizes, 6 and 16 inches. You should have both sizes if you do a lot of salvage work.

Center Punch/Cold Chisel

Center punches are used for making holes in soft sheet metals and for making starter indentations in metal for precise drilling.

You can buy a set of punches or individual punches as required. Look for alloy steel construction with square shanks. Related to punches are cold chisels, useful for cutting sheet metals and removing rivets and frozen bolts. A ½-inch by 6-inch cold chisel is a good starter tool for general work.

SOURCES FOR TOOLS ———

One of the best sources for general hand and power tools is a discount department store with a large hardware department. These discount operations often feature name brand merchandise at substantial savings. The only drawback is that you can't get advice and counsel from the store personnel. If you know what you want and can judge features and quality, these outlets can be a great resource.

General consumer hardware stores and home centers are places where you will pay retail or close to retail prices for tools but can find some of the more uncommon or specialized tools. You can also get advice from the employees of the store about different models, styles, and qualities.

Industrial hardware stores almost always charge full retail prices to the walk-in customer. However, the store employees here are very knowledgeable about tools, and you should be able to find just about every tool and accessory currently available.

Shopping at specialized supply houses can be rewarding. Prices will range from full retail to a slight discount (5 to 10 percent). Some of the more interesting tools will be found here. Electrical supply stores offer long-reach drill

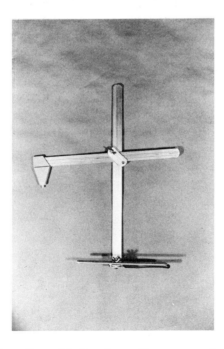

FIGURE 3-6. An adjustable bottle and jug cutter. Available through hobby stores or catalogs, this device makes bottle cutting easy. The plastic cone positions the cutter as it circles the bottle.

bits, testers, knives, and strippers. Roofing supply houses have trowels of all kinds, tin snips, bending devices, and metal-working tools. Plumbing supply stores feature tubing cutters and reamers, pipe benders, propane torch kits, and unusual wrenches. Auto supply stores carry socket sets, brushes of all kinds, safety equipment, and power tools. Electronic supply stores have soldering guns and irons, test equipment, and wrenches and screwdrivers for delicate work. Art supply stores offer precision knives, measuring tools, and clamps.

Power tools are often heavily discounted in loss leader advertisements for discount stores and home centers. The drill, circular saw, sabre saw, and power sander you want will probably be on sale somewhere in your area during the month. If you can wait, watch the newspapers for these tool advertisements. You should check carefully to make sure that the tool has the features and quality you want, however, since some stores offer a stripped-down model for the sale.

Shopping from a mail order catalog is another way to get tools, especially the very specialized and uncommon items. Just about every interest and hobby is represented by a catalog of supplies and tools, and you can find some truly intriguing tools this way. The only drawback to this method is that you can't judge a tool by hefting it and examining it closely until it has been delivered, and then it may delay your work should it not prove to be satisfactory.

In general, it is not likely that you will find good values in used hand tools. In the first place, used hand tools rarely come on the market—everyone, it seems, holds on to or passes on tools. In the second place, the few hand tools that do come on the market may be of obsolete design or poorly maintained. The cost of sharpening and repairing saws, drills, and other tools can be equal to or greater than the price of new tools.

However, the second hand market can be excellent for large power tools such as table saws, radial arm saws, drill presses, large furniture clamps, or vises. Of course you would have to be doing a lot of work at home to justify the investment in these large items.

4

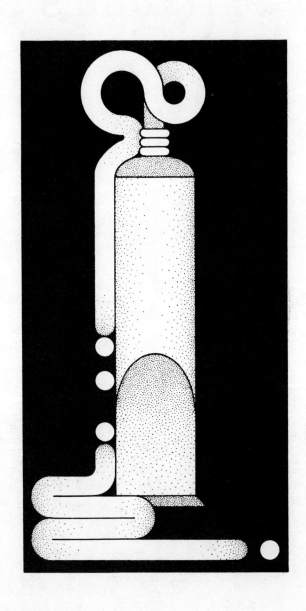

MATERIALS

In your recycling and construction work you're going to come across many different materials. This chapter covers the most common ones. The descriptions that follow will help you to know what you are working with and what you might need to have on hand to take care of projects that come up beyond the ones in this book.

A flexible stock of materials can liberate you to go in new directions with your projects, for just having certain items handy can suggest new uses. You are almost a small manufacturing firm when you have raw materials that can be used in a number of different ways. For example, you can cut white pine to serve as shelving or cabinetry, as backing for a wall plaque, or as a base for a unique floor lamp. A couple of lengths of galvanized steel duct and some fittings might turn into a lamp, a storage unit for rolled up towels or sheets, a cover for exposed pipes and wires, or a slim trash can for the bathroom.

Not all of the materials described here have to be bought new. Salvaged steel and cast-iron pipes can be found, hardware can be recycled from old houses and furniture (especially ornate cast hinges and latches), and used glass abounds from a number of different sources.

You don't have to buy all of the fasteners mentioned here individually. There are kits of fasteners available that provide a good assortment for repair use. Some items will prove so useful that you will want to keep them in good supply. You can buy screws and nails in bulk; bolts, nuts, and washers by the bag; and glue sticks by the box.

Wood is about the only material that you must closely inspect as you purchase it. Because of warpage, splits, knots, and other imperfections, you should shop at a lumber yard that will allow you to do your own selecting. You may pay a premium for the privilege, but it's worth it.

Most yards will allow you to reject pieces as they are pulled from the pile. If you are extra choosy and reject a good bit of material before you are satisfied, you should offer to assist the yard person in restacking the pile before you leave. You can also give the yard person a few dollars in appreciation of the extra time spent with you.

You should expect to have to waste about 10 percent of the wood you buy because of bad ends, inconvenient knots, splits, and slight warps. However, you should save small pieces for minor projects such as mounting plates or paper holders.

It's almost impossible to get permission to wander around steel warehouses, masonry supply yards, and electrical supply storerooms. You will have to rely on illustrated catalogs to give you an idea of what's available. Browsing through these catalogs can be very inspiring—there are lots of unusual shapes and devices that we don't often see revealed in daily life, and these may have excellent design possibilities. Do some detective work and get these catalogs; they will teach you and lead you in interesting directions.

WOODS

White Pine

In 1 × 12- and 1 × 6-inch sizes, this is going to be a versatile stock lumber for many of the projects in this book. Having boards of white pine around will allow you to work on nearly any project without having to go out and hunt down a special size. With your circular saw and other tools you can cut white pine down into sizes as small as 1 × 1 inch. It can be sanded, buffed, painted, urethaned, oiled, stained, waxed, or left natural. Scraps of white pine left over from larger projects can be fashioned into towel and

FIGURE 4-1.   A towel rack. White pine is a very economical lumber since even small scraps can be made into useful items.

paper holders, knife racks, and other small objects.

Buy white pine in the utility grade (#2) for most projects. The boards will have occasional knots, but you should select stock that is free of warps and splits. More expensive clear grade (#1) boards will be free of knots and should be perfectly straight. Use clear white pine for critical smaller jobs such as cabinets and formal shelving. Commonly found lengths of 1 × 12 and 1 × 6 pine are 6, 8, and 10 feet. Buy the length most practical for the project—6 and 8 feet for cutting down, 10 feet for long continuous shelving and floor-to-ceiling storage unit construction.

Two-by-Fours

Perhaps the most universal lumber, 2 × 4s are used extensively in construction, framing projects, and renovation and remodeling jobs. You will have some use for 2 × 4s in larger projects, perhaps as a brace or underframe for furniture or platforms. They are usually cut from spruce, pine, or fir varieties. You can buy the standard or utility grade (#2) for most projects. When selecting 2 × 4s, look for lumber that is straight and free of splits and patches of softness and check to make sure that each piece weighs about the same as the others. Weight is one measure of the wood's density and moisture content. You want all of your 2 × 4s to be as uniform as possible so that they act alike when you build with them.

Furring Strips

These are 1 × 2- and 1 × 3-inch pieces of wood (typically 6, 8, and 10 feet long) sold for use behind gypsum board, panel-ing, and other wall materials. Furring strips are rough lumber, but they can be useful for small structures, hidden frames (for fabrics, hangings, or wall pieces), and even some exposed applications. Rough-surfaced furring strips are often sold by the bundle at a low price. Smooth furring strips are sold individually, and you can find strips that are straight and true. These are the ones you can use in precision applications.

Four-by-Four Lumber

These square posts (generally 6, 8, and 10 feet long) are heavy and sturdy timber. You might use them for table legs, pedestals, lamp bases, or for heavy duty framing or structural use. Look for posts that are straight and square on all sides. Most posts will have some small splits (wood this thick tends to split as it dries), but that will not materially affect its strength.

Stair Tread

Made of yellow pine, this lumber is specially cut and milled for use as step stock. Available in 8- and 10-foot lengths, stair tread comes in widths from 8 to 12 inches. One long edge of stair tread has a rounded nosing already milled into it. The other long edge is flush and can be trimmed to fit.

Because of its special design, stair tread resists flexing and warping. This makes it a perfect material for bench seating, shelving, and other demanding uses. A length of stair tread laid over a low, flat-topped radiator makes an instant bench. A length of stair tread attached to a wall with braces or dowels into the studs makes a quick and strong shelf for heavy objects.

**FIGURE 4-2. A particleboard desk. A 3 × 5-foot slab of particle-
board over terra cotta flue liners makes a quick and inexpensive
piece of furniture.**

Particle Board

Available in 4 × 8-foot sheets in thicknesses of ¼, ⅜, ⅝, ¾, and 1 inch, particle
board is a very dense and hard material
made of wood chips, sawdust, and adhesive. It is smooth surfaced and takes a
good finish when primed and painted
with oil- or epoxy-based paints. Because
of its easy workability and inexpensive
price, particle board is a good choice for
certain furniture and cabinetry projects.

Hardboard

Along with wood and composition product paneling, hardboard is available in
4 × 8-foot sheets in thicknesses of ⅛, ¼,
and ½ inch. Hardboards are made from
wood fibers and adhesives bonded by
heat and pressure in a process very much
like paper making. The resulting product
is a smooth-surfaced sheet that has a

number of uses in craft and construction
work. The best stock hardboard to have
around is a tempered product (treated to
resist moisture) in the ⅛- or ¼-inch
thickness.

Plywood

For use in construction and craft projects
where great strength is called for,
plywood is a manufactured wood made
up of cross layers of wood veneer over a
central core. It is a very strong product in
nearly every direction because of the
overlapping plies. Like other manufactured materials, it comes in 4 × 8-foot
sheets. Thicknesses are ¼, ⅜, ½, ⅝, ¾,
and 1 inch.

For general use in furniture and crafts
a ½- or ⅝-inch interior (non-waterproof
adhesive) grade panel is fine. Choose either both sides rough, one side smooth, or
both sides smooth according to the de-

gree of exposure your project will give the plywood. You pay extra for each smooth side.

PLASTICS

Polyester and Epoxy Fillers

For repair, design, and craft work there are a great many fillers, putty products, and pastes available. Perhaps the best selection can be found at a large auto supply store. Fillers stick well to metal, wire, wood, and certain plastics. (Always read the label of your brand for authoritative information on application.) They are extremely useful for repairing and forming projects. Fillers can be smoothed and formed while soft and then filed, sanded, and cut when hard. Most fillers can be painted when hard.

Many fillers are supplied in two units, a paste in one can and a hardener in a separate tube or bottle. Still others are ready to use in a single can or tube. In general, the mix-method fillers are more durable and allow for more manipulation on the part of the worker. Some of the more common materials in fillers and pastes include wood fibers, ceramic powders, metal fibers and powders, chopped fiberglass strands, and plastic powders. For repair projects you are usually best off selecting the filler ingredient closest in character to the base material.

Fiberglass and Resins

This material offers some exciting possibilities for repair and design work. It is available from auto supply stores, craft shops, and commercial supply houses. Fiberglass cloth, matting, resins, hardeners, and coloring materials are the supplies needed. Perhaps the best introduction is to experiment with an inexpensive kit designed for auto repair. Projects are made by laminating layers of cloth and mat with resins, using freehand techniques or forms such as balloons, tubing, and wire structures. Possible projects include custom-designed lampshades (with printed material laminated between fiberglass cloth), freeform lighting fixtures, and repairs of irregular surfaces such as old advertising signs, life-size figures, or curved items.

Plastic Laminates

These are very hard, semi-rigid panels used as countertop or furniture facing material. Laminates are available in 4 × 6- or 4 × 8-foot sheets in $\frac{1}{16}$- or $\frac{1}{32}$-inch thicknesses. The range of colors, textures, and patterns available is large—you need to look at a catalog to see them all. Laminates are made up of resin-soaked kraft paper sheets with surface layers of melamine resin paper (for color and pattern effects).

Laminates must be glued with contact cement to a solid subsurface such as chipboard, lumber, or plywood to give them strength and rigidity. Laminates are cut with a crosscut handsaw or power saw, with the laminate firmly clamped between two pieces of lumber to prevent splitting and chipping. After the laminate is glued and set firmly in place with a rolling pin, the edges are finished with a smooth file. Cutting openings for fittings and the finishing of laminates is tricky work, but it can be very rewarding to a patient and careful craftsperson.

Acrylic Panels and Forms

Also known as Plexiglass, these are used in light diffusers, skylights, and windows. They are break resistant, and they don't tend to yellow in the sun or under strong light. They are also available in various forms such as bubbles and domes, and can be purchased at plastics supply houses, auto supply and RV stores, and building products dealers. Buying scrap panels from sign shops and plastics stores is less expensive than buying uncut full sheets.

Plastic Foams

Polyurethane shake foams are available for a wide variety of uses. Instant-setting shake foams that will fill any cavity from a small hole are available from hobby and plastics supply stores. These can be useful for protecting sensitive equipment from vibration and moisture or for adding rigidity to a fragile structure. High-, medium-, and low-density precast foams are available for use as padding in upholstery, furniture making, and other special projects.

Acetate Film

This is used for tracing shapes and experimenting with design. Buy a clear acetate sheet from an art supply store or crafts shop. With it you can trace designs from books, posters, and other flat material by simply placing the sheet over the material and following the lines with a grease pencil. If you are displeased with the work or are done with it, you can erase the pencil markings with a soft cloth and use the acetate sheet over and over.

Casting Resins

Most often polyester resins are employed, and they allow the amateur to embed small objects, flowers, and other ornamental items into a block or other shape. Perhaps the best way to get started is to purchase a complete kit with resin, hardener, molds, pigments, and mixing tools. Later you can purchase supplies separately as you need them. Castings are typically built up in layers, the blocks sanded and smoothed and finally polished with a special cutting and smoothing paste.

Related to casting resins are epoxy resins that can be used to provide an enamel effect on wood, glass, tile, and other objects. These resins can also be used to embed small objects such as pebbles or dried leaves in a flat surface in order to make an entirely new surface above the original one.

METALS

Steel

The most common and useful metal in modern products, steel is an alloy of iron and carbon. As the carbon content of steel increases so does its hardness and strength. *Mild steel* (also called *common steel*) is a low-carbon, soft steel. It is easy to bend, file, cut, and drill. You will find it in pipe and tubing, appliance and machine parts, wire and sheet products, and in hardware and fittings.

Tinplate is a mild sheet steel covered with a thin coating of tin. Tinplate is easily bent and can be soldered with a propane hand torch. You will find it in older household goods, utensils, gutters, ducts, pipes and tubes, and other common objects.

Galvanized steel is a mild steel coated with zinc to prevent rust and is found in gutters, fittings, pipes, buckets and tanks, ducts, and a host of other products. The zinc coating is applied by hot dipping (the best quality) or by electroplating.

Stainless steel has a high chromium content. Expensive and difficult to work with, you will mostly adapt or use fixtures or utensils that have already been fabricated from stainless steel. It is a very useful material because of its strength and rust resistance.

Cast Iron

Found in older objects made before mass steel production existed, it is also used in certain modern objects such as gratings, plumbing parts, manhole covers, and other heavy objects. Cast iron is very brittle and cannot be easily bent or hammered. It can be sawn, drilled, and filed.

Wrought iron is a softer iron and can be hammered and bent with relative ease. It can also be cut, drilled, chiseled, filed, and soldered. It's ideal for decorative and design work.

Copper

A soft, easily worked, reddish metal, it can be drilled, cut, chiseled, stamped, and soldered. It comes in sheets, tubes, blanks (precut shapes and sizes suitable for craft and manufacturing work), and wire.

Aluminum

This is a soft, light metal that can be formed into a great variety of shapes. Building supply dealers and home centers often have a whole section of aluminum products on display including tubes, fittings, sheets (solid and perforated), moldings, wire, bars, and rods.

Brass

An alloy of copper and zinc, brass can often be found in castings, fine hardware and fittings, and plumbing goods. It can be soldered with a hand propane torch.

GLASS

Window

This type of glass is also called *common sheet glass*. For most uses grade A will serve nicely. Grade AA has the fewest imperfections. The major choices are for single strength (for most applications), double strength (for situations where $\frac{1}{8}$-inch thickness is desirable), and heavy (for shelving and other structural uses calling for $\frac{3}{16}$- or $\frac{7}{32}$-inch thickness). Common window glass can be found at hardware stores, home centers, and lumber yards.

Plate

This is sheet glass specially ground and polished to give an undistorted image in mirrors. Heavy plate glass is used in large shelves, table tops, and furniture and fixture construction. It is very expensive and comes in thicknesses of $\frac{3}{8}$ to 1 inch.

FIGURE 4-3. Beveled glass and poster sandwich. The silvering was removed from an old mirror and the glass mounted over a poster. The broken top of the glass seems to fit the style of the art.

Mirror

In older mirrors the glass is quite often thick (⅛ to ¼ inch is common), and the edges may be beveled. This glass, even with its distortions and imperfections, is highly prized. Should you come across old mirror glass you can leave it as it is (if the silvering is good or only slightly deteriorated), have the silvering restored by a resilvering shop, or scrape off the deteriorated silvering and use the glass itself for framing and displaying some art.

In modern mirrors of moderate quality the glass is known as *float glass* (or *float plate*). It gives the look of plate glass but at less cost. Float glass mirrors typically use glass of ¼ inch or less.

Auto

Automobile glass, also called *safety glass*, is a laminated glass with sheets of glass between transparent or slightly tinted plastic layers. This strengthens the glass and makes it break into dull-edged pieces when it does shatter. Auto glass has limited use in home design and decoration projects, but because it's widely available in interesting shapes at junk yards, it has possibilities for the ingenious craftsperson. (A windshield hung on the wall with photos, art, or graphics mounted on the reverse perhaps?) Auto glass is not easy to cut or form at home, so you are limited to using the existing shapes.

PLUMBING SUPPLIES

Copper Tubing and Pipe

The basic material for domestic water supply systems can also be an exciting design material. Copper tubing comes in rigid forms in ½- and ¾-inch diameters and 10- and 20-foot lengths. Flexible copper tubing comes in ⅜-, ½-, and ¾-inch diameters and in lengths from 5 to 50 feet. Rigid copper pipe is available in 1- and 1½-inch diameters and 5- to 20-foot lengths.

Copper and Brass Fittings

To connect copper pipe and tubing there are many different copper and brass fittings, all of which are soldered (also called *sweated*) on. The most useful fittings are: sleeves (to connect runs of pipe); 90- and 45-degree elbows (to make turns and angles); tees (to form branches); reducing tees (to form a branch of smaller size from the main one); threaded adaptors (to join a threaded fitting to a soldered joint); reducing adaptors (to join smaller to larger pipe); and caps (to shut off a run of pipe).

All of these fittings are available in either copper or brass. You might prefer to have all copper fittings to match the copper of the pipe or tubing in your design, or you might want the contrast and different texture of brass in your project. Fittings, tubing, and pipe are available at plumbing supply houses, hardware stores, and home centers.

PVC Pipe and Fittings

Polyvinyl chloride pipe and fittings designed to carry water and wastes can be an intriguing design and construction material. It is available from professional plumbing supply houses and some larger home centers and catalog houses. The basic colors are white, gray, and tan or cream. The pipe is put together by sawing straight pieces, wiping the ends of the pipe with a solvent cement, and fitting them together. Within a minute the joint will be firm, and in 2 or 4 hours the joint will be permanent. Joints can also be made in a number of other ways including friction fit and screws and bolts.

Useful sizes of PVC pipe and fittings include ¾-, 1-, and 1½-inch (for light-duty projects) and 4-inch (for heavy-duty projects). Because you don't want to paint your pipe after you have constructed something (paint easily scratches and flakes off hard plastic), you must ask for the specific color you want and make sure that the color of the pipe and fittings match. Obviously if you were buying the material for concealed plumbing, it wouldn't matter.

There are other nonmetallic and non-ceramic pipes available that are worth investigating. DVW (drain, vent, waste) pipe is a thinner-walled, less expensive pipe than PVC, available in 1-inch or greater sizes. Fiber pipe might also give some interesting uses.

Steel Pipe

Available in galvanized and black finishes, steel pipe is a material that has several design and construction uses. Short steel pipe legs screwed to a sheet of plywood (using threaded steel flanges) makes a quick and adaptable platform. The height of the platform can be changed quickly by screwing different length pipes to the flanges on the underside of the plywood. Steel pipe can form a hanging frame for kitchen utensils or for movable lighting fixtures.

The most useful sizes for our work will be ½-, ¾-, and 1-inch diameters. Steel pipe comes precut and prethreaded in lengths from 1 to 12 inches and from 1 to 10 feet. Galvanized pipe will resist moisture and has a bright silver finish. Black pipe can be painted and is fine for interior work. Fittings for steel pipe include sleeves, elbows, tees, reducing and enlarging adaptors, and caps. In addition, steel pipe can use threaded flanges with countersunk screw holes for attaching to walls, floors, and other materials. Steel pipe hangers are also available to suspend pipe from the ceiling. Pipe and fittings can be found at plumbing supply stores. Flanges and hangers can be found at industrial hardware stores.

Ducts and Smoke Pipe

Generally made of galvanized sheet steel, ducts are interesting and adaptable shapes that you can use to create some unusual designs. Select round pieces that have plain and crimped ends so that an assembly goes together with simple hand manipulation. In addition to plain, straight sections, there are flexible elbows that turn and adjust, outlet pieces with plain collars and register grilles, and reducing adaptors for joining different size ducts.

Rectangular ducts are more bulky than round varieties, but they have possibilities for creating architectural shapes (false columns or movable dividers) and can also be a cheap and fast cover for some mechanical equipment or utility object that happens to be in your living space.

Related to ducts are smoke pipes of galvanized and stainless steel. These pipes generally have the same plain and crimped joints and fittings as round ducts and can be used in the same way. A complete set of pipes and fittings wired with some low-wattage bulbs could form an unusual floor lamp, or you could hang short sections of 4- or 6-inch-diameter pipe from the ceiling and wire them with lights as a ceiling fixture. Pipes and ducts with their plain and honest structure and materials can be an interesting element in certain interiors.

Round ducts and pipes come in 3-, 4-, 5-, 6-, 7-, and 8-inch diameters. Rectangular duct generally is available in 12 × 8-, 16 × 8-, 20 × 8-, 24 × 8-, and 28 × 8-inch sizes. Ducts and pipes are commonly hung by stout wire or a perforated steel strapping. The steel strapping offers the most secure hold on all shapes and can be secured with small-gauge bolts and nuts. Ducts and accessories can be found at plumbing and heating supply houses, air conditioning supply houses, and some large home centers.

Clay and Cast Iron Pipe

Available in 4-inch diameters, clay and cast iron pipe are heavy-duty materials. The design of both types of pipe is such that each piece has a plain end and a belled end. This design feature makes these pipes ideal for use as table pedestals. Simply order the pipe in the length that will suit the table being built. Thirty inches is appropriate for a dining table; 24 inches is about right for a side table. The belled end should provide enough stability for a small side table; the pipe might need to be attached to a circular base for stability if you used it for a large dining table. Epoxy cement would provide the proper bond between the pipe and a wood table top. Since these materials are difficult for the amateur to cut accurately, you will have to rely on stock lengths or have the supplier cut the pipe for you. The best source for these pipes is a professional plumbing supply house.

ELECTRICAL SUPPLIES

Switches, Plugs, Cords, and Wire

These are the basics of electrical repair. Your best selection will be found at an electrical supply house. They may not have very many items on display, but they are sure to have nearly anything you ask for in stock. See if your supplier offers a catalog, and study that before you go shopping. The second best bet is a large home center. These stores often have a decent selection of parts and supplies on display. The prices are generally higher than at electrical supply houses, but you can at least browse at your leisure.

The switches you are likely to need are canopy toggles, turn screws, and push on/off. These are small switches with wire leads coming out of their bodies that you can use to repair appliances and equipment. Each of the switches mounts with its own hardware in a small drilled hole.

One other switch can be useful in wiring jobs. A line switch is installed directly on the power supply cord at a convenient position to control the fixture or lamp. Line switches come in various sizes and styles for lamp cords and heavy-duty cords. Select a wheel or toggle switch for easy operation.

Plugs are used in wiring power supply cords (line cords). The easiest plug to use with a new power cord is a self-tapping style. There are various brands and designs available, but the working principle is the same. You simply insert the flush-cut end of a power cord into a slot on the plug body. Press a lever on the plug flush with its body. The lever locks the line cord into place and pierces the cord's insulation with two conductors that make the electrical connection. Common colors for self-tapping plugs are white, cream, brown, and black.

Power cords are used with plugs and switches in rewiring jobs. Worn, cracked, and frayed cords are the number one safety and performance problem with most old lamps, appliances, and electrical equipment. Most of your jobs can be handled with lamp cord, which is adequate to take care of lighting fixtures, electronic equipment, some small appliances, and other low-wattage items. Buy 18-gauge, 2-conductor lamp cord (called *18/2 cord*) in the standard colors of white, cream, brown, or black.

Lamp cord is sold by the foot, and you can buy any quantity. If you have a lot of work to do it will pay you to go to a professional electrical supply store and get a reel of 18/2 (250 feet). Your price per foot will be about half what you pay for lesser quantities.

Hook-up wire is related to lamp cord and is available at electronic or electrical supply stores. Use single conductor wire to repair and modify electronic equipment or create special circuits for items you design. Most of your jobs can be handled with plastic insulated 18-gauge stranded wire. A roll of 100 feet should get you started. If you are going to be doing a lot of complicated rewiring, a package of assorted colors of hook-up wire can be helpful (the colors help code the various circuits). In an emergency you can always pull apart 18-gauge lamp cord and use each single conductor as a length of hook-up wire.

Lamp Parts

For repair, design, and recycling of lamps, most of your work can be handled with inexpensive sockets that screw or clamp onto the core pipe of the lamp. Sockets provide a means of mounting a threaded base light blub and also have threads and mounting surfaces for shades and other hardware. Order a keyed socket for most applications. (*Keyed* means that there is a turn switch or push switch mounted in the socket.) A keyless socket is for lamps with a switch mounted on the lamp cord or elsewhere on the fixture.

FIGURE 4-4. A floor lamp. Common lamp parts were used to restore this vintage fixture to safe and efficient operation.

FIGURE 4-5. A porcelain table lamp. A streamlined fixture that is still being manufactured is teamed with a wood base and a 25-watt torpedo bulb.

For design and recycling work you can purchase threaded tubes and sockets that allow you to extend or modify the central pipe of the lamp. These parts are available in steel or brass. The tubes (also called *nipples*) come in lengths ranging from 2 to 12 inches.

For mounting a large shade to the lamp and socket, there are harp kits that screw onto the core pipe of the lamp and extend around the socket and bulb to pro-- vide support for a shade. A kit consists of a threaded piece of stamped metal that accepts the harp frame. The frame of the harp has a threaded stud on top that se- cures the mounting piece of the shade.

For mounting a small shade directly to the socket, a threaded holder piece (often called a *shade fitter*) is used, which screws to the male threads on the end of the socket and then secures the rim of a pressed or blown glass shade with thumb screws.

Simple Sockets and Fixtures

For utility lighting, hidden applications, and design work you might want to take advantage of the many inexpensive sockets and fixtures available. A classic socket that is very inexpensive is a porcelain or plastic cleat-type socket. These small circular pieces allow you to mount a light bulb, attach wires, and secure the whole assembly to a flush surface. We will be using cleat sockets for many lighting projects in this book. They offer the best and most secure light bulb mounting for hidden applications. In general, use porcelain cleat sockets in preference to plastic models. The porcelain resists heat-related stress better than plastic.

Another inexpensive classic socket is a porcelain circular socket (about $4\frac{1}{2}$ inches in diameter) with or without a pull chain switch. These sockets can be mounted with screws and fitted with low-wattage bulbs for durable and reliable hidden lighting, or you can expose them and rely on their honest, simple looks to carry the day. Related to these workhorse sockets are some more design-conscious porcelain fixtures. Some of these fixtures are still being produced in streamlined 1930s and 40s designs and are a very easy and inexpensive way to give your home an unusual touch. Outfit one with a longish, low-wattage bulb and a paper or colored gelatin shade, and you have a sophisticated small lamp.

Vintage and reproduction ceiling fixtures can be mounted on wood bases and used as table lamps. Some of these fixtures are very inexpensive and incorporate interesting pressed or blown glass domes or shades. These ceiling fixtures can also be mounted at eye level on the wall as lighted wall plaques. Their close proximity to the viewer changes their effect and makes them seem to be something other than what they are. Once again low-wattage bulbs and/or dimmers are used to soften their effect as they are adapted from their original use to a more decorative level.

Along with simple sockets and fixtures are inexpensive but nicely designed glass shades. These shades are designed as replacements for existing fixtures. You might not see them on display in a home center, and they may be tucked away in an obscure corner of an electrical supply store. You must seek them out. Some of these pressed, blown, cut, and frosted glass pieces can be adapted to make interesting small lamps or can be used in combination with an old fixture that you have come across. In general the shades have mounting rims that accept only the fixture for which they were designed. You must either attach the shade yourself by gluing or cementing or seek out a suitable adaptor (ask for help from the store personnel on this).

Light Bulbs

Of all the changes you can work on lighting fixtures and lamp parts, perhaps the greatest change will be in the selection of light bulbs for them. Especially for exposed or nearly exposed applications, the size, shape, and wattage of a light bulb will tremendously affect the look of the piece. Shop at a large electrical supply house for the best selection of bulbs. Pay particular attention to the low-wattage bulbs (7½-, 10-, 15-, and 25-watt models) in clear and frosted glass. Many bulbs are available in interesting shapes such as torpedo, globe, stubby, candelabra, bullet, flame, and elongated. Don't overlook colored bulbs as well as floodlights, black lights, and other special-purpose bulbs.

Solderless Terminals

Soldering electrical connections is an excellent way to make reliable and permanent repairs. There are, however, some interesting alternatives. Wire nuts are inexpensive devices that can be used to connect and insulate electrical connections. Buy a package of plastic wire nuts for 18- to 14-gauge wire. These will handle most of your projects. Simply twist the wires together and then twist the wire nut over the bare wires. Always twist wires and nuts clockwise. The wire nut will tighten the connection and will cover and insulate the connection from other wires.

A solderless wiring terminal kit is a good investment for anyone planning to

do a lot of appliance repair work. Solderless connectors are used extensively in appliances, and it is very convenient to be able to use the same type connectors in repair and modification work. Perhaps the best way to get started is to buy a complete kit from an auto supply store, electrical supply house, or electronics supply shop. A kit will include a hand tool that crimps terminals (essential for these kinds of fasteners) and probably cuts and strips wire as well. The rest of the kit will include ring and spade terminals (for posts and screws), butt splices (for connecting two wires), taps (for taking branches off a circuit), and male and female disconnect devices (for quick assembly or breakdown). You can buy refills for any individual items if you run low.

Thinwall and Rigid Conduit

Designed for use in rough situations to protect electrical wire, steel conduit is an interesting design material. It can be used in lamp and lighting fixture construction, or it can be used to carry electrical wiring between switches or dimmers and lighting installations in exposed applications. Conduit applied directly to a wall or ceiling and used with utility steel switch and outlet boxes becomes a design element. The bright steel finish of the conduit and the honest look of the steel and conduit fittings contribute to a "high tech" architectural look.

It is recommended that you use thinwall conduit for cost saving and bendability. Conduit and fittings are available in ½-, ¾-, 1¼-, 1½-, and 2-inch diameters. For general interior design work ¾-inch is best. Fittings include metal straps for fastening conduit to walls or ceilings (use one about every 4 feet), threaded couplings for attaching two pieces of conduit, and threaded connectors for attaching conduit to switch and outlet boxes. An inexpensive bender is available to make up to 90-degree bends in thinwall. To complete your installation you simply run power supply wires or cables through the conduit to connect your fixtures to house current.

Outlet Strips

These were originally designed for kitchen and workshop use, where you want to keep a number of appliances plugged in for instant availability, but they can be adapted for other applications. One would be to mount the strip on the ceiling in the center of a pipe lighting grid. Clip-on lighting instruments with coiled cords could then be positioned anywhere on the grid and plugged into one of the sockets on the strip. This would eliminate costly and tricky individual wiring of each instrument and allow for maximum flexibility.

High-quality strips are made of sturdy metal with secure mounting slots for screws or anchors. Lengths range from 8 to 72 inches, with from 4 to 10 outlets. The strip should be wired with heavy-duty cable (14-gauge or better) and permanently connected to the house wiring system. Strips can be found at electrical supply stores, home centers, and large hardware stores.

Transformers

In order to adapt and take advantage of automobile and boating lighting equipment (small lamps, running lights, etc.) you need to convert standard house current (115 volts) to a lower voltage (10 to 12 volts). Happily, an inexpensive solution is available. A common doorbell transformer from a discount store, hardware store, or electrical supply house is perfect. A 10- to 16-volt transformer will power most of the low-wattage, 12-volt lighting devices that you take from auto and boating sources. Simply wire the primary side of the transformer to the house current (with lamp cord and a plug) and wire the secondary side (low-voltage terminals) directly to the lighting device.

Don't try to use a doorbell transformer to run several auto or boat lighting devices at once or to power 12-volt DC electronic equipment (radios, CBs, etc.). For this kind of adaptation, you will have to go to an electronic supply store and buy a house current adaptor. These adaptors provide the proper capacity of regulated direct current needed to run these items efficiently. Adaptors are relatively inexpensive and are perfect for recycling an old auto radio into a unique and functional household object.

FIGURE 4-6. A hood ornament lamp. This automobile fixture is powered by a common doorbell transformer hidden in the pine box.

Transformers are needed to power vintage neon signs that you may want to install in your home. Neon transformers take house current and step the voltage up to 3,000 to 15,000 volts while reducing the current to 20 to 30 milliamps (thousandths of an ampere). When working with old neon set-ups, get the advice of a sign shop on the proper size transformer, or take the rating plate from the old transformer in with you.

MASONRY SUPPLIES

Tile

For covering table and counter tops and for facing other furniture and construction projects, tile is a good choice. Ceramic tile is really the only choice for durability and good looks. Shop at a retail store that specializes in tile or go to a commercial tile supply house. You might select imported hand-painted tiles for design effects or go with plain domestic tiles for simplicity. One of the most rugged and handsome choices will be quarry tile—a hard red earthenware product supplied in 6 × 6-inch squares. Quarry tile is impervious to stains, liquids, and most scratches.

Along with tile you will have to purchase adhesive and grout for filling the gaps between tiles. Follow the dealer's and manufacturer's recommendations for adhesives and grouts. Colored grouts are available that can contribute to the effect you achieve.

Concrete Blocks and Shapes

Masonry supply yards stock decorative concrete blocks (often called screening

blocks) in a number of interesting designs. You can also find cast concrete shapes such as L, Y, T, and others. These blocks and shapes lend themselves to building outdoor furniture. For your own safety, most masonry yards won't let you browse around the yard looking at the stock, but they will show you a catalog so that you can get an idea of what's available.

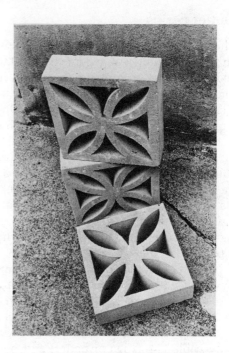

FIGURE 4-7. Decorative concrete blocks.

Terra Cotta Flue Liners

Found at masonry supply yards, these hard red or yellow clay shapes are inexpensive and adaptable. The standard length of flue liners is 2 feet. Some of the dimensions available include 8 × 8, 8 × 12, 8 × 16, 16 × 16, 16 × 20, 20 × 24, and 24 × 24 inches.

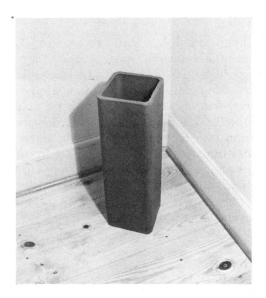

FIGURE 4-8. A terra cotta flue liner.

The liners can be stacked on their sides to make pedestals for table or desk tops. A single 8 × 8-inch liner standing on end makes an umbrella stand. A 16 × 16-inch liner filled with dirt is a generous size plant holder. Single liners can be fitted with circular tops to make side tables or breakfast tables. The possibilities are endless, and the liners are inexpensive and have a naturally good looking finish. This is a very good field for experimentation.

Glass Block

Glass block is useful for translucent partition construction, lamps and lighting devices, and design work. Glass blocks are 4 inches thick and are available from masonry supply yards in 6-, 8-, and 12-inch squares. Glass blocks are normally cemented together with mortar and reinforcing wires and straps. For small, noncritical jobs, you can try bonding with industrial mastic, silicone caulk, aquar-

ium cement, and epoxy and polyester body fillers.

FASTENERS

Nails

The most common fastening device, nails are suited for rough work and framing jobs, certain wall and ceiling fastening situations, and (with some of the finer grades of nails) certain precision applications. Common nails have sturdy heads and pyramid-shaped points. A good selection to have on hand would be from 1 to 4 inches long in 1-inch steps.

Finishing nails are thinner versions of common nails, with small heads designed to be put below the surface of the wood with a nail set. A versatile selection would run from 1 to 2½ inches long in ½-inch steps.

Masonry nails are extremely hard nails that resemble common nails except for spiral grooves cut in the shank. They can be driven into mortar joints, soft brick and block, and other masonry surfaces. Some masonry nails come in cut style as well as the more common round shank style.

Cut nails are available in roughly the same sizes as common nails. Cut nails are flat shank nails with tapered bodies and oblong heads. Often used in rough carpentry and flooring, cut nails provide a distinctive look whenever they are used. The oblong nail head becomes part of the design.

Roofing nails are very sharp, large-headed nails that have been dipped in zinc for rust protection. They are useful for outdoor construction projects and anywhere moisture is present. Their heads cannot be hidden, so you must plan on incorporating their looks in the design of any exposed application.

Tacks are useful for securing fabrics, hangings, carpet, and other light materials. A good selection would be ½-, ¾-, and 1-inch lengths. In addition to standard blued steel tacks, there are decorative tacks for upholstery work in exposed places. These decorative tacks all have shanks approximately ½ inch long.

Screws

Screws are very useful for furniture making and repair work. The two major types of wood screws are the *slotted head* (common wood screw) and the *Phillips head* (cross head screw). Both types come in flat-head and round-head style. Use flat heads for most of your work and round heads for fastening thin materials (plastic and metal sheets) to wood. Both flat heads and round heads are sized by the length of the screw and the gauge of the screw body. A good general selection to have on hand would be: flat heads—¾-inch #6, 1½-inch #10, 2-inch #14, and 2 ½-inch #18; round heads—½-inch #4 and 1-inch #6.

Sheetmetal screws are for fastening sheet metals, ducts, gutter parts, certain plastics, and even chipboard and hardboard. A round-head slotted style is the most versatile to have around. You want *type A* self-tapping screws (these have coarse threads that make their own way through a drilled or punched hole). A good selection would be ½-, 1-, and 1½-inch lengths with #8 or #10 diameters.

Lag Screws

Often called *lag bolts*, these coarsely threaded fasteners are used when a screw would be too short and a nail or spike wouldn't hold. They are often used in loft, ladder, and utility furniture construction, and are available in lengths from 2 inches to 16 inches and in diameters from ¼ to 1 inch. General-purpose lag screws should be approximately 3 to 6 inches long and ⅜-inch in diameter. Drive the screw head with an adjustable wrench or a socket wrench.

Bolts

Bolts are used for fastening large pieces of lumber or metal, when great strength is needed, or for making furniture that can be disassembled easily. *Carriage bolts* are usually for wood-to-wood joints. They have a round head with a square underside that grips the wood to keep the bolt from turning when tightened. The other end of the bolt uses a nut and washer (the washer keeps the nut from chewing into the wood). Bolts are available from 4 to 16 inches in length with diameters of ⅜, ½, ⅝, and ¾ inches.

Machine bolts are generally made for metal-to-metal joints, but they can be used in wood-to-wood or wood-to-metal. The head and nut will be either hexagon or square shaped. They are available in lengths from 1 to 20 inches and in diameters of ¼ to 1 inch. Use flat or lock (split ring) washers to secure the joint from vibration and damage.

Stove bolts were originally designed for holding the cast iron plates of wood and coal burning stoves together. They tend to be thinner than machine or carriage bolts (shanks from ⅛ to ¼ inch are typical), and they have slotted heads (round or flat). Lengths range from ½ to 20 inches and longer. Stove bolts have square or hex nuts and are not as precisely made as carriage or machine bolts. Use them for less demanding joints in all materials.

Washers and Cotter Pins

Flat steel washers are used to provide reinforcement to nuts and bolt heads and to give additional strength to the whole assembly. An assortment is needed to handle the different size bolt diameters and nut sizes. Lock washers are made of spring steel and are split and bent so that they place constant pressure on the object and the nut. This prevents slippage due to vibration or unusual loads.

Cotter pins are used in repair work on appliances and mechanical equipment. They secure nuts, bolts, pins, shafts, rods, and other items that could work loose during operation. Every time you remove a cotter pin from an assembly you should replace it with a new one for security and safety.

Perhaps the best way to keep a good supply of washers and cotter pins handy is to buy an assortment in a plastic case at the auto store, hardware store, or discount department store. These assortments provide a good selection of types and sizes for home use.

Plastic and Masonry Anchors

These are used for hanging pictures, mirrors, wall hung fixtures, and the like. A plastic anchor and wood screw is an inexpensive system for securely holding fairly heavy objects. Drill a hole the exact diameter of the plastic anchor. Insert the anchor in the hole; then insert a matching wood screw into the anchor. As the screw drives into the anchor it expands the plastic to wedge it tightly in the hole. Anchors and wood screws are sold together in packages. A 1- or 1½-inch-long anchor should be sufficient for most jobs. Anchors will work in solid plaster walls, hollow gypsum board walls, and masonry walls (using a carbide-tipped drill to make the hole).

For very secure anchoring in masonry walls, both interior and exterior, a lead masonry anchor (or cincher) is used. Select a ½-inch-diameter anchor for general use. Drill a ½-inch hole in the masonry with a carbide-tipped drill. Place the anchor in the hole and drive it with the setting tool (usually supplied with the anchors). The setting tool and hammer cause the lead to expand and tightly set the anchor in the masonry. Remove the setting tool and attach the fixture or hanging with the machine screw that came with the anchor.

Plastic anchors are available in variety stores, hardware stores, and discount stores. Masonry anchors are available at electrical supply stores, industrial hardware stores, and large home centers.

Toggle Bolts, Molly Bolts

These are used for more demanding installations in hollow walls of plaster, gypsum board, and paneling. *Toggle bolts* are flat- and round-headed bolts with special spring-loaded expandable wings instead of nuts. They hold well in softer, more crumbly material because they expand behind the material, not in it. Toggle bolts come in ⅛- and ¼-inch diameters and 3- to 6-inch lengths. You must drill a larger hole than the bolt's diameter to accommodate the folded wings. First the item to be fastened must be attached to the bolt, and then the assembly must be inserted into the wall. This procedure can be clumsy with a large fixture, so you might want to first mount a hook or bracket to the toggle, fasten it, and then mount the fixture to the hook or bracket.

Molly bolts are expandable anchors that work with hollow walls. You must buy the bolt that will fit your wall thickness. Molly bolts are available to accommodate wall thicknesses of ¼ to ½, ½ to ¾, ¾ to 1¼, and 1¼ to 1¾ inches. To install, you drill a hole large enough to accommodate the assembly, tap the unit into place, turn the slotted screw head until a firm resistance is felt, remove the screw, position the fixture, replace the screw, and tighten the fixture into place. One of the advantages of a molly bolt is that you can remove and replace the screw without disturbing the bolt's grip on the wall.

Solders and Fluxes ————————

These are used for making permanent and strong joints in metals, plumbing materials, and electrical and electronic equipment. Solder is composed of tin and lead in various proportions according to the work to be done. Ordinary plumber's solder is a thick wire solder sold in rolls. It is composed of half tin and half lead and is fine for plumbing and general work.

When using plumber's solder to make joints in metals, plumbing, and other structural projects, use an acid-based flux to clean and prepare the sur-

faces for a good bond. Flux cleans the metal before soldering and keeps it clean during the heating and soldering process. Apply the flux to all surfaces with a ¼-inch brush (often supplied with the flux). After the joint has been made and the metal is cool, the flux residue should be cleaned off with a stiff brush, warm water, and detergent to prevent the residual acids of the flux from corroding the metal.

There are also acid-core solders that have flux contained in the solder wire. These can be fine for noncritical work, but you will want to use a brush-on paste flux for big and demanding jobs.

Electrical soldering calls for different solder and flux. Most often a thin, rosin-core solder is used (available from electronic and electrical supply shops). The standard wire size is .062, which allows the worker to get the solder into delicate joints and tight places. A rosin-based, brush-on flux generally is not needed because the joints in electrical soldering are usually very clean to begin with, and the heat source (an electric gun or iron) is a clean one. Acid flux or acid-core solders are never used on electrical connections because they would inevitably corrode the work.

GLUES AND ADHESIVES ————————

White Glue —————————————

Often called *carpenter's glue* or *polyvinyl acetate (PVA) glue*, this is a general-purpose woodworking glue for joints that don't have to be waterproof. The pieces have to be clamped or otherwise held while the glue sets (full strength comes in

24 hours). The glue can be cleaned up with a damp cloth while wet. When dry it is nearly transparent. White glue is a good general glue to have around; it is cheap, nontoxic, and can be used for paper, leather, and cloth as well as wood.

Related to common white glue is *aliphatic resin glue*—a wood glue for more demanding work. Often tan-colored, this adhesive acts like white glue but gives a better bond and resists water. It's worth the extra cost for certain furniture and heavy-duty projects.

Epoxy Cements and Putties

These are very useful for a host of repair and construction projects. Epoxy adhesives come in two containers (resin and hardener) and are mixed together before application. (Be sure to follow package directions carefully.) Clear, colored, and filled epoxy products are used for nonporous materials such as ceramics, metals, glass, some plastics, chinaware, stone, and tile. Epoxy is a good choice for a hard, waterproof, heat-resistant repair or bond. Filled epoxy putties (using resin filled with ceramic, metal, and plastic powders) can be very useful for large patching jobs or where a deep joint or crack must be filled. A wide selection of epoxy cements and putties can be found at a good auto supply store.

Hot Melt Glue

Sold in the form of sticks to be used with a hot melt gun, this glue can be used to bond porous and nonporous materials. Hot melt glue sets up in 20 to 30 seconds and reaches nearly full strength in 60 sec-

onds. It is ideal for clamp-free repairs and for constructing small objects (using glue instead of screws or nails). There are two basic kinds of glue sticks, one for wood and general bonding and another for plastics, vinyl, and other nonporous surfaces. Buy your sticks in 1-pound or larger boxes for economy.

Cellulose Cement

Often called *plastic cement*, this common household adhesive is sold in tubes. It is good for minor repairs on ceramics, paper, glass, leather, wood, metal, and some plastics and is primarily for small decorative objects. The bond is fairly weak and won't stand up to much water. The cement will bond most objects without clamping. Simply coat both sides of the repair, let the cement get tacky, place the two surfaces together, and then hold for 60 seconds. It is available at hardware stores, hobby shops, and variety stores.

Panel Adhesives/Mastics

Packaged in cardboard tubes with plastic nozzles that fit caulking guns, these adhesives are sold to bond lightweight wallcoverings such as paneling, cork boards, and decorative foam and plastic panels. Related to adhesives are heavier duty products known as *mastics*. Both mastics and tube adhesives are heavy, paste-like products. You might use them to mount and secure wallpieces and thin wood, plastic, or metal sheets. Related to tube mastics are adhesives for floor and countertop tiles and coverings. These tile adhesives come in cans and are spread with a brush (paintable-style adhesive for thin products) or a trowel (heavy-duty adhesive for thicker products).

Silicone Caulks and Adhesives

Sold in tubes with adjustable plastic nozzles, these products are excellent for sealing joints from wind, weather, and water. The product is actually a treated rubber that cures in about 24 hours into a permanently flexible seal that can adhere to most nonporous surfaces. The product is not paintable, so you must select a color that you can live with (common ones are white, clear, and gray). You can buy the product in a caulking gun cartridge or a small squeeze tube.

Rubber Cement

This is useful for bonding cork, felt, leather, paper, rubber, and cloth. For greatest strength, don't buy common paper-bonding rubber cement at a stationery store, get heavy-duty rubber cement at an auto supply store. (It's used for tire and tube repairs.)

Cyanoacrylate Glue

This can be a handy adhesive for certain jobs. It will bond most nonporous materials almost instantly, so you don't need a clamp. Use it for metal, china, glass, most plastics, small parts, and jewelry. Cyanoacrylate will not fill even small gaps, so the parts must fit tightly. The glue can get a tremendous grip on surfaces, but you must avoid exposing the glue or the surfaces to high humidity or high temperatures before they are joined.

Resorcinol Glue

A high-strength, waterproof glue for quality woodworking, the glue comes packaged in two cans. One is a red-colored resin, and the other is a white or tan hardener. Mixed together to a paste consistency, the glue can be worked for about 2 hours. Treat the parts as if you were using white glue: clamp firmly, wipe up excess glue with a damp rag, and let the glue set for about 24 hours.

Fabric Glue

Available at cloth and sewing shops and the sewing sections of variety stores, fabric glues and cements can be used to bond fabric edges, patches, and repairs (with and without backing fabric). Such adhesives are very useful for small-scale repairs to furniture and upholstery.

HARDWARE

Hinges

Hinges are used for cabinet work and many kinds of repairs. Butt hinges are the most common. They consist of two oblong plates (called *leaves*) connected by a pin. The common materials are brass and steel. For general light-duty work a 1½-inch butt hinge will serve nicely.

Surface-mounted hinges are butt hinges with both leaves mounted flat on the work (instead of on the edges as is common). This may be necessary because of thinness of the mounting material or for design considerations. Surface-mounted hinges may be plain butts or decorative hinges with pressed, engraved, or finished leaves.

Pivot hinges are commonly used on modern cabinet doors or other applications where clean design is desired. Pivots mount at the top and bottom of a door and only show a small bit of metal when the door is closed.

Piano hinges (or continuous hinges) are long butt hinges that can be cut down with a hacksaw to fit nearly any situation. They are good for chest lids, thin-walled cabinets, and other situations where maximum strength and resistance to flex is desired.

Strap hinges are utility hinges. Used on outdoor and knockabout furniture, these surface-mounted hinges have long-ish (up to 5 inches) triangular leaves for maximum strength on rough-surfaced wood.

Corner Braces/Brackets

These are very useful in shelf and cabinet construction. Corner braces are prebent and predrilled angles of metal used to support pieces of wood at 90-degree angles. Available with legs from ½ to 4 inches long, these are valuable braces for table and chair legs, small shelves, and furniture and cabinet frames. The smaller corner braces can be hand bent to different angles.

Related to corner braces are *shelf brackets*, which also are prefabricated at 90-degree angles. Shelf brackets are commonly made of stamped steel with raised ridges that prevent you from changing the angle. Holes are drilled in the steel to allow you to screw the brackets to the shelf and the wall. Shelf brackets come with legs from 3 to 16 inches long.

Mending Plates

Made of steel with predrilled and countersunk screw holes, mending plates (or braces) are invaluable repair aids. You can use them to repair and reinforce frames, furniture, and new construction. The common shapes are T, L, and flat oblong.

Shelf Hardware

When constructing a bookcase you might want to be able to adjust the height of the shelves or add more shelves at a later time. The best way to give yourself maximum flexibility is to use shelf standards (often called *pilaster strips*) and support clips. These metal strips are cut with slots that accept small metal clips. The clips support the bookshelf boards. By moving the clips up or down the strips, you can adjust the height of the shelves; by adding more clips and boards, you can add more shelves.

You must buy four pilaster strips for each shelf unit you construct. Get them long enough so that you can run them continuously along the height of the unit. (Cut excess length from the strips with a hacksaw.) Buy four support clips for each shelf board you plan to install. (Clips are cheap and come packaged in boxes or bags.)

The strips are screwed to the inside edges of the shelf unit, two on each side of the piece. The clips are mounted using hand pressure (or pliers if they fit tightly) and indexed according to the reference marks on the strips so that the shelf will be level.

Mirror Hangers

Available at hardware stores and variety stores, these inexpensive plastic hangers are used to hang mirrors on plaster walls. You can adapt the hanger to hold flat art work sandwiched between glass and cardboard sheets. By using hangers,

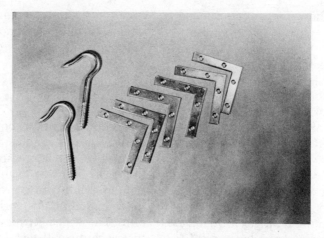

FIGURE 4-9. Mending plates and screw hooks.

glass, and cardboard you can hang and display art for a fraction of the cost of conventional hanging systems.

Screw Eyes and Accessories

Screw eyes and screw hooks are useful for fastening and supporting things. A common screw eye can be driven into a drilled hole by hand, pliers, and cross bar. Screw eyes are available from ½ to 4 inches long. A screw hook is a screw eye with an open body for supporting wires, hardware, and fixtures. A square-bend screw hook is an L-shaped screw device useful for certain hanging jobs, especially where an angular look is desired.

Related to these screw devices are S-*hooks* (available from 1 to 4 inches in length), which are useful for connecting screw eyes to chain links, for hanging pot and utensil handles from a kitchen hanging grid, and other support jobs. A *turnbuckle* is a metal turning piece with two threaded screw eyes attached. When cable, chain, or line is attached to the screw eyes you have a means of adjusting the line's tightness. As the center piece is turned it tightens or slackens the tension the screw eyes exert on the line.

Magnetic and Roller Spring Catches

These are used for repair and construction work on cabinet doors and lids. Magnetic catches hold by means of a magnet and a metal catch plate. The holding power is sufficient for most light-duty doors. Magnetic catches don't wear as much as friction catches do, and they can be a good choice for constant-duty doors.

Roller-spring catches are very secure holding catches. Select a high-quality model with nylon rollers and sturdy springs for long and quiet service. Both friction and magnetic catches are two-piece units; the catch mounts to the frame of the piece, and the strike or catch plate mounts to the door.

Knobs and Pulls

These are available in a great variety of styles and finishes. Perhaps the simplest and sturdiest are still the best for general use. You might select porcelain, glass, or wood knobs with integral bolts and nuts for securing to doors, lids, and drawers. These styles are available in every size and finish and will be durable and inexpensive choices.

Pulls can be simple steel or brass sash lifts and are available at hardware stores. These pulls attach with four screws, and will serve for drawers, doors, large lids, and chests. Other simple pulls are available that bolt through the mounting surface.

In knobs and pulls you should keep in mind that solid, impervious materials will wear better than plated or painted material, even though the latter might look better during the first few months' use.

PAINTS AND FINISHES —————

Polyurethane Varnish —————

A tough, clear finish suitable for use on wood, tile, stone, and other natural products, polyurethane is a plastic product formulated to produce either a high gloss or a satin finish when dry. Buy it in quart or gallon cans, and apply it with a fresh, clean brush. Most porous objects will need two or three coats of urethane to get complete protection.

Enamel ——————————

This is a paint that produces a smooth, hard, and very durable finish. Enamels are often designed for special purposes, so it is well to read the label for full information. Some special-purpose enamels are for wood, masonry, metal appliances, automobiles, kitchen equipment, out-

door furniture, or high-temperature applications. Most enamels can be purchased in gloss, semi-gloss, or flat finishes.

Enamel is an excellent choice for most painting jobs on furniture, fixtures, and other household objects. It is applied with a brush over existing enamel or (when working with raw surfaces) over an enamel undercoater or general-purpose primer.

Primers ——————————

Essential to a good finish, primers provide a good bond to the underlying material and a good surface for the finish paint. Primers usually pay for themselves because they make it possible to use one or two finish coats of paint where two or three might have been necessary. Some primers are slightly resilient and can protect the finish from cracking and flaking due to minor bumps and nicks.

For wood and wood products, a latex-based primer will prepare the surface for finish latex or oil-based paints. For metal and other nonporous products, an enamel undercoater or metal primer will do nicely. Primers can be used over raw material and over paints and finishes in poor condition.

Spray Paints and Finishes —————

Available at hardware stores, paint stores, and auto supply stores, these convenient sprays allow you to finish small objects quickly and easily. They are usually too expensive for large projects but can be perfect for small pieces of furniture, appliances, ornate details, and equipment.

Some spray finishes include enamels (general purpose, appliance, and automobile); epoxy-based (for appliances and fixtures); acrylic flat and gloss finish colors; glass frosting, metal primer, polyurethane, and clear acrylic finishes; rust inhibitor primer; and wrinkle-finish enamel.

Oil Finishes

For refinishing old furniture and finishing new wood, oil finishes—both clear and pigmented—protect and soak into the wood while at the same time bringing out its grain and other natural features. A penetrating oil stain/sealer product is most desirable. This kind of finish will allow you to leave the wood otherwise unfinished (you can rub in some paste wax to bring up a shine), or you can finish over the stain/sealer with polyurethane for a slick, shiny finish.

Waxes

These are used for polishing and maintaining wood furniture. The best product is a thick paste wax that you apply with a rag and then rub and buff to a high gloss. Spray and liquid waxes will also serve but tend to have less wax content than paste products and may not be concentrated enough for older, worn items.

STRIPPERS, CLEANERS, SOLVENTS, LUBRICANTS

Paint Remover

Essential for stripping paint and varnish from furniture, wood, carvings, and other wood products, paint remover is also good for some heavy-duty cleaning jobs. The best remover is a semi-paste, water-wash product. The paste consistency allows the stripper to cling to fancy carvings and vertical surfaces, and the water-wash formulation allows you to remove deep stains and discolorations with water and steel wool.

There are major differences between brands, so you should experiment and ask for advice from your retailer. Paint remover is expensive, so you might want to reserve it for tricky projects or use it for removing the last traces of paint after you have used some other method for the bulk of the paint.

TSP (Trisodium Phosphate)

TSP is a powdered chemical that is very useful for cleaning and preparing dirty items. Simply put 1 cup of TSP in 1 gallon of hot water for cleaning purposes. TSP can also be used to strip paint and varnish from small pieces. You can make a strong solution (nearly a paste) of TSP and hot water and brush it on the surface to be stripped. Use 5 to 6 pounds of TSP to 1 gallon of very hot water. It will soften finishes after 10 to 30 minutes.

You can also prepare a stripping pot of TSP and water in an old metal washtub. Use a hotplate to keep the solution hot, and immerse small objects in the tub to be stripped. TSP and water can be a messy and clumsy method of stripping, but it is much cheaper than paint stripper and is fine if you have the equipment and space to do the job properly.

Buy TSP at paint stores and large hardware stores. You can buy large quantities of TSP (25 pounds and more) very cheaply at supply houses that carry industrial and institutional cleaning goods. Look in the Yellow Pages under "Laundries—supplies and equipment" and "Institutional and commercial cleaning supplies."

Paint Thinner

Often called *mineral spirits*, this is the basic product to have around for thinning oil-based paints and for cleaning and preparing brushes. It is also very useful for cleaning old furniture of wax and other gummy deposits prior to refinishing. For economy, buy inexpensive, generic-brand paint thinner in gallon cans or jugs from your paint store.

Alcohol

Alcohol is a solvent that will melt away old shellac finishes and is used for refinishing old furniture and cleaning small objects. Use denatured alcohol (pure alcohol), *not* rubbing alcohol (which contains up to 80 percent water). You can buy denatured alcohol from paint stores and large hardware stores.

Acetone

Often called the universal solvent, acetone is very useful for cleaning and dissolving many glues, finishes, and deposits. It's the prime ingredient in nail polish remover. Buy acetone from paint stores, hardware stores, or (in small quantities, as nail polish remover) variety stores.

Solvent/Lubricants

Often sold in spray cans for automotive use, these products range from aerosol carburetor and choke cleaner (a very powerful solvent for nearly every kind of deposit) to general-purpose spray lubricants with small amounts of solvents (essentially light oil mixed with a volatile carrier that soon evaporates). These spray products are very helpful in working on delicate mechanical equipment. Often the product comes with a thin plastic tube so that you can introduce solvent/lubricant into tight areas.

Light Oil

Sold in small squeeze cans for household use, light oil can be used to lubricate small pieces of hardware, mechanical equipment, and other light-duty metal parts.

Graphite

Available at locksmith shops and auto supply stores, powdered graphite is a good dry lubricant for equipment that can't accept oil. Graphite can be brushed or blown into small areas to stop squeaks and lubricate moving parts.

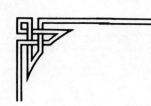

5

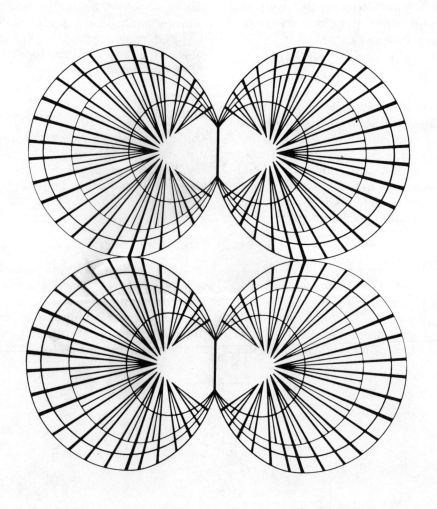

DESIGN AIDS

MAKING A LIGHT BOX

Tools and supplies needed

Circular saw
Electrical tools
Tape measure
Drill and bits
Screwdriver
Medium sandpaper
¼-round wood molding
1 × 12-inch white pine
Double strength glass sheet
½-inch chipboard
Two undercounter fluorescent units
Wood screws
Line cord, switch, plug
Silicone caulk
Glass frosting spray

Procedure

Constructing a light box for pattern transfer; cutting stencils; or working with old photographs, slides, and illustrations is a basic design aid project. A light box is a means for conveniently tracing art work and for working with illustrations you have taken from a number of sources to use on furniture, walls, floors, or other surfaces. The box is simply a means of illuminating a design or illustration from below so that it shows through a piece of paper placed on top of it. Simple as it is, a light box will be one of the most useful design tools you can own.

The most expensive items you will need for the box are two undercounter fluorescent lighting units. These are complete fixtures that are sold for installing under cabinets, countertops, and in other confined areas. Fluorescent (rather than

incandescent) units are employed because they will throw off less heat as they
are used and will not cause the glass surface to become too hot to work with.

These undercounter units typically
come complete with on/off switches,
cords, and lighting tubes. For the box described here it is recommended that you
buy 24-inch units rated at 20 watts each.
You can buy larger or smaller units according to the final dimensions of the
project. Units are available down to 8
inches in length, which are perfect for
constructing a compact box for small-for-
mat work. The total length of the units
must be at least 2 inches less than the
length of the completed light box frame.
The other components of the box are standard materials and are readily available.
The box could be made of any number of
other materials, but the ones described
here will provide a sturdy box at minimum cost.

Begin the project by cutting 1 × 12-
inch white pine into basic lengths. Cut a
piece of white pine to a 28-inch length
and cut another piece 18 inches long.
Take the 28-inch piece, and with your circular saw cut it in half down its length,
giving you two pieces approximately 5⅝

inches wide by 28 inches long. Cut the
18-inch piece in the same way. When you
have the four pieces of the frame, you
should lightly sand any rough edges with
medium sandpaper. Keep all of the edges
square while you sand by tacking or taping a piece of sandpaper to a secure flat
surface and then rubbing the wood pieces
back and forth across the stationary sandpaper, keeping the wood straight as you
sand.

Assemble the frame by drilling pilot
holes and then driving 1½- or 2-inch flat-
head screws. Place the 5-inch-wide
boards on edge (putting the 28-inch
pieces within the 18-inch ones), and attach them with the screws. Use eight
screws, two at each corner of the frame.
You will end up with an open box about
18 × 29½ inches. Stiffen the box by cutting a piece of ½-inch chipboard to fit the
box's outside dimensions. (Measure your
box carefully, and cut the chipboard to fit
flush to the box's outlines.) Attach the
chipboard to the box by drilling pilot
holes and driving eight 1- or 1½-inch
screws.

Now that you have the final dimensions locked in place, it's time to get a
piece of glass cut for the work surface. As

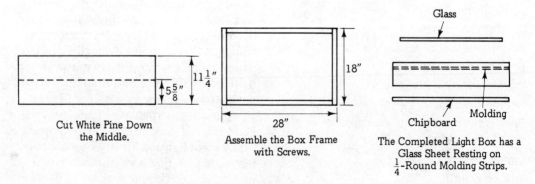

Cut White Pine Down
the Middle.

Assemble the Box Frame
with Screws.

The Completed Light Box has a
Glass Sheet Resting on
¼-Round Molding Strips.

FIGURE 5-1.   How to construct a light box.

a minimum, you should use double strength glass (⅛-inch thick). If you are going to be doing a lot of work or you want to cut stencils on the box, you should use heavy glass (³⁄₁₆- or ⁷⁄₃₂-inch thick). Measure the exact *inside* dimensions of the frame, and specify that you want your glass cut exactly to those measurements.

When you have your glass, you must frost one side of it in order to provide an even, diffused light for the work surface. There are several spray products available to frost glass (check a large paint store, art supply, or auto store). Lay the frosting up in several thin layers, rather than in one thick one. The glass will accept the coating best if it is laid flat on several sheets of newspaper. This way gravity will help even out the layers of frosting.

While the frosting is curing on the glass, mount lengths of molding to the inside of the frame to support the glass work surface. You want the strips of molding to support the glass so that it sits flush with the surface of the frame. That means that the strips will have to sit below the surface of the frame by the exact thickness of the glass that you bought. Carefully measure, cut, and mount the strips (round side of the molding down) to the inside of the frame. Use 1-inch screws to secure the molding.

After the strips have been installed, mount the two lighting fixtures to the unit. You can mount the fixtures to the sides of the frame (if the fixtures are thin enough to fit), or you can mount them to the chipboard base. If you mount the fixtures to the base, center them so that the lighting tubes are an equal distance from each other and the side walls of the box. Secure the fixtures with short wood

screws. Drill a ¼-inch hole near a corner of the box for an electrical cord.

Cut a length of lamp cord and feed one end through the hole in the box. Draw 6 inches of cord into the box and knot the cord so that it can't be pulled out of the box. Bring the cords from the two fixtures near the lamp cord and cut them so that they will mate to the lamp cord. Strip the ends of the cords and attach the wires with wire nuts, or by soldering and then wrapping with electrical tape. Install a line switch on the lamp cord at a convenient place along its length, and finish the electrical work by installing a self-tapping plug on the end of the cord.

Mount the glass in the box (frosting side down) by putting a thin bead of silicone caulk on the support strips. Place the glass carefully on the caulking, and press it down into the frame until it sits flush with the rest of the structure. Allow the silicone to cure for a few hours before using the box. (It will totally cure in 12 to 24 hours.)

Plug the box in and turn on the line switch. The fixtures should provide a brilliant, even illumination under the frosted glass. Leave the unit on for 30 minutes, checking the temperature of the glass and frame frequently. If the unit is overheating you can drill a series of ⅜- or ½-inch ventilating holes in the wood frame to cool the unit. Place the holes in the two short sides of the box near the bottom of the unit. After the holes are drilled remove the chipboard base from the frame to clean out the sawdust before using the unit again.

In brief

1. Decide on the box's dimensions. Obtain fluorescent fixtures to fit.

2. Cut white pine into frame pieces.

3. Sand the rough edges of the frame pieces and assemble the frame with wood screws.

4. Cut a piece of chipboard to the frame's outlines and attach it with wood screws.

5. Get glass cut to the inside dimensions of the frame, and frost the glass with spray.

6. Mount strips of ¼-round molding inside the frame as glass supports.

7. Mount the two lighting fixtures to the long sidewalls or the chipboard with screws. Drill a hole in the box for a power cord.

8. Draw a cord into the box and secure it. Attach the cord and the fixture cords together with wire nuts or solder and tape. Install a plug and line switch on the lamp cord.

9. Put a bead of silicone caulk on the support strips. Install the glass on the strips, and let the caulk cure for a few hours.

10. Test the fixture. If it overheats, drill a series of vent holes in the short side walls of the box.

Tips

If you can't find frosting spray, you can use white spray paint. You must spray white paint very evenly and thinly in order to get a uniform surface. Make sure that you hold the spray head parallel to the glass at all times as you lay thin coatings of paint on the glass. (Move your whole arm as you spray, not just your wrist.)

A worthwhile refinement to the box is to paint the entire inside of the unit with white paint to provide a reflective surface for the fixture's light. While the glass coating is drying, spray two or three coats of gloss white paint into the unit. Let the paint dry for 30 minutes before installing the ¼-round molding strips.

A final refinement to your light box would be to install rubber feet on the chipboard bottom so that you don't mar your furniture when you use the box. Simply buy four hard rubber feet at a hardware store or home center. The feet come complete with short screws that you can drive into pilot holes in the chipboard.

MAKING AN OPAQUE PROJECTOR

Tools and supplies needed

Circular saw

Drill and bits

Adjustable hole drill

Tape measure

Screwdriver

Electrical tools

1 × 12-inch white pine

Lamp cord and plug

Line switch

1½-inch woodscrews

1-foot-square mirror tile

Tin can (approximately 3¼-inch diameter)

3½-inch magnifying glass

Epoxy glue

Two porcelain cleat sockets

Procedure

Commercially available opaque projectors are expensive pieces of equipment. With your own labor and a few inexpensive materials, you can construct a projector that will serve nicely for home projects. An opaque projector can take designs and clippings from newspapers, magazines, and books and show them on a wall. It will also project photographs and other material that you might want to use for designs or outlines. With an opaque projector you can test out the effect of a given design on a wall or other area before you commit to actually tracing, drawing, painting, or stenciling it.

The opaque projector described here will project material up to 6 × 6 inches. Larger original material can be projected in sections. Because you will be using an inexpensive magnifying glass for a projection lens, the color and scale of the enlarged image won't be entirely true—but it should be close enough for copy and testing work. The unit will project an image in a dark room up to about 8 feet from a wall, so you have plenty of distance in which to select a suitable size for the projected image.

The projector housing is constructed entirely of white pine lumber for simplicity. The only optical goods you need are a lens (from a variety store magnifying glass) and a mirror tile (from a hardware store, home center, or tile outlet). In addition to the lumber, lens, and mirror, you need a tin can with a diameter nearly equal to that of the lens (a tuna can or tomato can will probably fit your lens) and electrical goods to mount and supply two light bulbs.

Cut 1 × 12-inch white pine into five pieces. Cut two pieces 11¼ inches square (11¼ inches is the usual width of 1 × 12 white pine). Cut three pieces 11¼ × 12¾ inches.

Take the two square pieces and prepare them to hold the mirror. Adjust the depth of cut on the circular saw until the blade will cut only ½-inch deep. Take both square pieces and mark from one corner 9 and 9¼ inches. Do this on each piece along two adjacent sides of the wood (see the illustration on page 91). Take a straightedge and lay it between the 9-inch marks and draw a line; then move it to the 9¼-inch marks and draw a line. Do this on both pieces of wood.

When the lines are drawn use your circular saw to make cuts down all four lines. When the cuts are made use a screwdriver blade to break out the thin strip of wood from between the cuts. After the cuts are cleared of wood run your circular saw down the channels you have created to remove any burrs from the wood. After this is done you will have two ½-inch deep channels in the wood that will accept the mirror tile and hold it at the proper angle to the lens and design.

Take one of the oblong pieces of wood and draw a line down the middle of the 12¾-inch dimension (6⅜ inches from one side). From one side of the 11¼-inch dimension, draw a line 2¾ inches from the edge of the wood. The intersection of the two lines is the place to put the center bit of the hole drill.

Adjust the hole drill so that it will make a hole exactly the diameter of the tin can that you will be using as a lens barrel. Test the hole drill out on a scrap piece of wood to make sure of the measurement. When you are satisfied, drill a hole in the marked oblong of white pine.

Assemble the projector by first screwing the back piece to the two sides. Take one of the undrilled oblongs and place it next to the two square side pieces so that a box is formed. Be sure that the channels face the inside of the box and that they are parallel with each other (see the illustration on page 91 for the correct orientation of the pieces). Drill pilot holes and drive screws to attach the pieces.

When you have three pieces attached insert the mirror tile into the channels to check the fit. While the tile is in place take the two electrical sockets and place 100-watt bulbs in them. From the front of the projector, place the bulb units into the projector and establish where on the sides the sockets can be anchored. You want the bulbs to be as near the top of the mirror as possible without touching either the mirror or the front of the unit when it is attached. When you have established by trial and error the best position for the sockets, mark the spots and screw the sockets to the sides of the unit.

Remove the mirror tile from the unit and attach the front piece to the sides. Use the piece with the lens hole in it and position it so that the hole is near the bottom of the projector. Attach the front with pilot holes and screws.

Complete the projector frame by taking the last oblong piece of lumber and placing it on top of the unit with its edge flush with the edge of the front piece. This will create a 1-inch gap at the back of the projector top, which will be used to handle the unit and for ventilation. Secure this piece by drilling pilot holes and driving screws.

Drill a single ¼-inch hole in the side of the projector near to one of the bulb sockets. Take a length of lamp cord (8 feet is about right) and use it to connect the two sockets. Strip insulation from the cord and wrap the wires around the connecting screws. Use the single length of cord to connect both sockets. (Don't leave any slack cord between the sockets that might hang down into the projection area.) Establish the point at which the cord will meet the side of the projector on its way out, and tie a knot into the cord at that point. Feed the free end of the cord

out of the hole in the projector side until the knot is drawn up to the hole. Install a line switch at a convenient place on the cord's length, and finish the job by installing a self-tapping plug on the end of the cord.

Turn the unit upside down. Slip the mirror tile into the channels and let it rest against the front of the projector. Take two ¾-inch screws and place one in each channel so that they will prevent the mirror from slipping out of the projector when it is turned right side up. Turn the projector over and gently ease the mirror down the channels until it rests securely on the retaining screws.

Before you can use the projector you will have to mount the magnifying glass lens in a lens barrel. Because you don't know the focal length of the lens that you bought, you will have to experiment to find the proper length barrel. Set the projector up in a darkened room and place some art work under it. Turn the lamps on, and hold your magnifying glass in front of the projection hole. By holding the glass at varying distances from the hole, you will discover the distance for the best focus. (It should be from 1 to 4 inches in front of the projector.) Note that the focal distance will change slightly as you move the projector nearer or farther from the wall. When you have a good idea as to the optimum focal distance you can select a suitable length lens barrel.

A tunafish can with both ends removed makes an ideal short-focus barrel. A longer tomato or sauce can might be used for longer-focus lenses. Other good products for barrels include a length of cardboard tube, copper drain pipe, or PVC tubing.

Once you have selected a barrel simply remove the magnifying glass from its

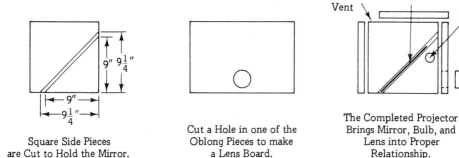

FIGURE 5-2.   Details of opaque projector construction.

handle and rim and attach it to the barrel with epoxy glue. A thin coating of glue on the rim of the barrel onto which you place the lens is sufficient. Let the glue cure for 24 hours, and you are ready to use your projector.

In brief

1. Cut white pine into two squares and three oblongs.

2. Adjust the depth of the saw to ½ inch. Mark 9 and 9¼ inches on the squares and draw cut lines.

3. Cut down the four lines. Break out the thin strip of wood left between cuts. Run the circular saw down the channels to clear out any burrs.

4. Mark a point 6⅜ inches from one edge of an oblong piece and 2¾ inches from an adjacent edge. Place your drill on that point and cut a hole the diameter of the lens barrel.

5. Screw the back to the two sides. Be sure to check the orientation of the pieces with the drawing.

6. Insert the mirror tile and experiment with placement of the bulb

sockets. Screw the sockets to the sides of the projector.

7. Remove the mirror and attach the front piece to the sides. Make sure that the lens hole is positioned at the bottom of the projector.

8. Take the last oblong piece and screw it to the top of the unit. Place it so that there is a 1-inch gap at the rear of the projector.

9. Drill a ¼-inch hole near one of the sockets. Connect the two sockets with a single piece of lamp cord. Knot the cord at the point where it will exit the projector. Feed the cord out of the hole.

10. Place a line switch on the cord and install a self-tapping plug on the free end of the cord.

11. While the unit is upside down, insert the mirror. Install two screws in the mirror channels so that the mirror will not slip out of the projector when it is right side up.

12. Test the focal length of the lens you bought. Select a proper length barrel and attach it to the lens with epoxy glue.

Tips

The projector is designed to be operated for short periods of time. Fifteen minutes is the maximum running time, and then the unit should cool down before being used again. The mirror is positioned so that there is some ventilation of the space around the light bulbs; however, if your unit overheats you should drill ½-inch ventilation holes in each side of the projector slightly below the position of the sockets. Do not attempt to increase the strength of the projector by installing higher wattage light bulbs—this will only cause the unit to overheat, and it will risk fire.

One refinement that you might want to incorporate in the projector is to spray paint inside the lens barrel with flat black paint before gluing the lens to it. This will sharpen the image of your projector by cutting down on any light bouncing off surfaces inside the barrel.

The projector is not going to be under any unusual structural stress, so you don't need to glue joints or use a great number of screws when you assemble it. You should be able to put the unit together with twelve 1½-inch screws—two for each edge that butts together. The mirror is held loosely by the channels and is prevented from slipping out of the projector by the ¾-inch screws at the end of each channel. The lens barrel is designed to be held by friction in the hole cut in the front of the projector. If you are having trouble holding the lens in position, you can wrap the barrel with tape or cloth to take up any slack in the fit.

USING A PANTOGRAPH ——————

Tools and supplies needed

Wood, plastic, or metal pantograph
Drawing board or ¼-inch underlayment

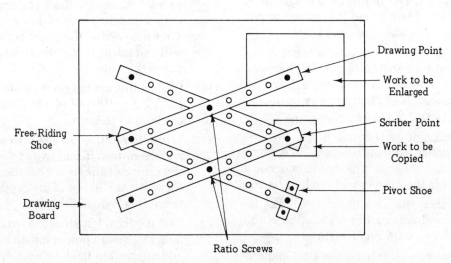

FIGURE 5-3. A typical pantograph set up.

Fine sandpaper
Mechanical pencil drawing leads
Masking tape
Wood screws

Procedure

A pantograph is a drawing and drafting instrument used for enlarging or reducing patterns and designs. The instrument consists of four rigid links that are joined to make a parallelogram shape. The links are drilled along their length and pins are inserted at points to determine the scale that the instrument will produce.

One of the most useful applications of the pantograph would be if you wanted to make a rough pattern of a design for use in stenciling, mural and wall painting, or neon fabrication. A small illustration or drawing could be enlarged via the pantograph to serve as a template for something unusual to decorate your home. For example, neon sign shops will make up neon tubing into any shape that you want so long as you can supply a full-size outline of the design. You could use the pantograph to enlarge a drawing of a horse, a rocket ship, an advertising logo, or an abstract design and have it executed in neon by a local neon fabricator. The pantograph can allow you to create something that no one else has.

A pantograph is a simple enough instrument, and you could make your own with ¼-inch strips of flat wood molding. It's doubtful, however, that you could build as good a one as you can buy very inexpensively at an art supply store. A good medium-priced pantograph is made of hardwood, with metal fittings to trace the design and a special fitting to hold the drawing lead. Typically the pantograph you buy will have links about 20 inches

long with 25 adjusting holes that will allow you to enlarge or reduce from 1⅛ to 8 times.

A pantograph must be securely mounted in order for the links and fittings to work accurately and in concert. It must also have a smooth surface to ride over in order to work properly. The pantograph is usually used on an artist's drawing board—a 1-inch thick surface about 20 × 30 inches. If you don't have an artist's board, you can make a suitable surface by using an inexpensive piece of ¼-inch mahogany underlayment. This product is available at nearly all lumber yards. It is used to provide a very smooth and stable surface for tile and floor products. Buy a 4 × 8-foot sheet, and you can cut it to your needs.

You could mount your pantograph to a smooth floor and provide poster board underlayment for the pattern and tracing area; however, you probably won't want to mar your floor by screwing the pantograph to it. It is possible to mount a pantograph to a wall for tracing and enlarging a design to be painted in later. In this case you would have to anchor the instrument by screwing into the plaster (using anchors or finding solid studs to drive screws into) and then hold the moveable end of the parallelgram with your hand while you trace the pattern. After the pantograph is removed from the wall, repair the screw holes with joint compound or spackling plaster.

To secure the pantograph, you are often given common thumb tacks. These are usually unsatisfactory—they can pull loose and often don't secure the pantograph sufficiently even when firmly embedded. Use ¼-inch wood screws to bite into the drawing board or underlayment and hold the pantograph firmly.

When you are ready to use the pantograph you must first select the desired ratio for reproduction. Decide how large the finished drawing is to be and divide the size of the original into that. If you want the finished drawing to be 12 inches and the original is 4 inches, the ratio you want is 3. Place the screws that connect the two sets of links into all the holes marked 3, and the pantograph will be set up to that ratio.

The work to be copied is mounted with masking tape to the board under the scriber point. The paper you will draw on is taped to the board under the drawing point. It is necessary to experiment to get a good placement for each item in a given ratio.

When everything is set up you can operate the pantograph. Use your dominant hand to guide and press the pencil point to the paper. As you copy, watch and follow the scriber point as it moves over the original design. Don't apply pressure to the scriber point.

It takes some practice and a steady hand to operate the machine successfully. A new machine will have to be loosened up so that it doesn't stick and resist your movements. A beginner will find that the smaller ratios are easier to handle than the larger ones and are a good training ground for more ambitious work later.

To reduce the size of drawings, you must interchange the position of the drawing point and the scriber point. The operation in reduction is the same—apply pressure with the drawing point and follow the pattern with the scriber point.

In brief

1. Find or make a suitable drawing and mounting surface.

2. Use ¼-inch wood screws to secure the pivot shoe to the drawing surface.

3. Select the ratio. Place the ratio screws in the holes marked with the same numbers.

4. Mount the work to be copied and the blank paper to the board with masking tape.

5. Operate the instrument by pressing the pencil point and following the pattern with the scriber point. Do not apply pressure to the scriber.

Tips

Make sure that the drawing lead is adjusted in the holder so that its point is the same distance from the pantograph link as the scriber point is. You don't want a too long or short pencil lead bending or throwing the pantograph links off. Sharpen the pencil lead by using a small piece of fine sandpaper. You can bring the lead to a fine point by sanding back and forth on one side of the lead.

If the pantograph's action gets sloppy or shaky you can try firming the links up by putting flat steel washers under the thumb screws on the pivot shoe, free riding shoe, scriber point, and drawing point.

MAKING A SILKSCREEN PRINTER

Tools and supplies needed

Circular saw
Screwdriver
Drill and bits
Tape measure
Staple gun

2 × 4 lumber

¾-inch chipboard

Screen fabric

Four corner braces (2½-inch legs)

Epoxy glue

Two 2-inch loose-pin butt hinges

Wood screws

Polyurethane varnish

Masking tape (2 inches wide)

Procedure

A silkscreen printing unit is a very useful craft tool. It allows you to reproduce designs on paper, cardboard, and fabrics. With it you can produce your own wallpaper, greeting cards, or even family and gift T-shirts. The unit is easy to construct, and along with a bit of practice and a good book on the subject, you can create a host of products with a few hours of your spare time. Silkscreening is a fascinating hobby, and it can provide you with inexpensive and striking art and decorative items.

You want a printer that is sturdy and has a secure frame, so you can neatly control the application and distribution of ink. This unit uses 2 × 4 lumber cut down to 2 × 2 strips, but you could use larger stock for your model. Select high-quality, clear grade lumber for the frame. It's worth the extra expense to get the best because you will only be buying a small amount and the frame of your printer must be smooth and warp-free. Dimensions for the frame are not critical. The suggested measurements here will give you a unit with a generous printing area, but you are free to go with any size you want—larger or smaller.

Take an 8-foot length of knot-free and perfectly straight 2 × 4 and cut a 30-inch length from it. Cut the remaining length of 2 × 4 into two strips. Simply measure the width of the wide dimension of the lumber, divide it in half, draw a straight line down the center of the lumber, and run your circular saw down the cut line. You will end up with two 5½-foot strips of wood approximately 1¾ by 1½ inches. (The dry size of a normal 2 × 4 is 3½ × 1½ inches.) From the strips, cut four 24-inch lengths.

While you have your circular saw set up, cut ¾-inch chipboard into an oblong 30 × 36 inches. This chipboard (which has a smooth and warp-free surface) will make an excellent base for the printer.

Assemble the screen frame by putting the 24-inch pieces together. Lay the pieces down on a smooth and level surface (1¾-inch dimension face down). Arrange the pieces so that you have a frame with the overall dimensions of 27½ × 24 inches. Apply epoxy glue to each of the four joints, and secure the frame by driving a single 3-inch screw into each joint. Reinforce the frame by installing a metal corner brace to the outside of each corner, using the wood screws that come with the braces. Set the frame aside for the glue to cure.

Work on the base of the printer. Screw the 30-inch 2 × 4 bracing piece to one of the 30-inch edges of the chipboard with four 2-inch screws. Finish the base by applying a coat of polyurethane varnish to the entire surface.

Return to the frame after the epoxy has cured. Attach the screen fabric to the frame with a staple gun, evenly and tightly stretching it over the frame as you work. You will need a pair of wide-jaw canvas pulling pliers (or a friend's assistance) to pull the fabric taut. Staple the fabric directly to the face of the wood

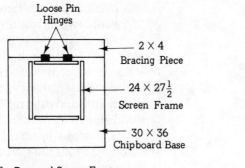

Loose Pin Hinges

2 × 4 Bracing Piece

24 × 27½ Screen Frame

30 × 36 Chipboard Base

The Base and Screen Frame are Aligned to Each Other and Fastened with Hinges.

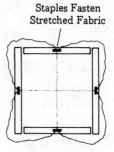

Staples Fasten Stretched Fabric

The Starting Position for Stretching Fabric over the Frame.

FIGURE 5-4. How to construct a silkscreen printer.

frame, not to the sides. Start by stapling the center of the fabric to one side, and then pull and staple the center of the fabric to the other side. After that is done, pull and staple the fabric center to the remaining two sides. After the fabric has been anchored in this way, start pulling and stapling from the center and work to each corner, pulling between each staple. Place your staples near to each other, approximately ⅛ to ¼ inch apart. The fabric should be very taut. Proper tension is when the screen gives about ½ inch when pressed.

After the screen is firmly attached, cut off the excess fabric with a scissors or razor blade. Trim the fabric nearly flush with the staples. Then seal the fabric and frame with tape to prevent ink from getting between the two materials. With the screen side of the frame up, cover the staples and fabric with strips of 2-inch-wide masking tape. Turn the frame over and put strips of tape into the angle formed by the wood and fabric. (You want to cover and seal that area where ink might get caught.) After you have taped these areas, brush urethane over the tape to seal it.

When the screen unit is dry, combine it with the printing base by installing two loose-pin butt hinges. Loose-pin hinges will allow you to remove the screen frame from the printing base for printing on fabrics, furniture, and other bulky objects, and for cleaning the screen. Place the screen frame on the printing unit (screen side down), and butt one of the 27½-inch sides up against the bracing piece of 2 × 4. Center the frame in the printing base approximately 1¼ inches from each side. Install the hinges 4 inches in from the edges of the screen frame, and secure them with screws to the bracing piece and the screen frame.

In brief

1. Select high-quality wood for the frame. Cut a 30-inch bracing piece and four 24-inch frame pieces. Cut ¾-inch chipboard for a base.

2. Assemble the screen frame with epoxy, screws, and corner braces. Allow the frame to cure.

3. Screw the bracing piece to the chip-

board. Polyurethane the entire printing base.

4. Attach the screen fabric with staples. Pull each section of fabric taut between the staples.

5. Trim excess fabric nearly flush with the staples. Seal the fabric and frame with strips of wide masking tape. Coat the tape with polyurethane.

6. Combine the screen frame and the printing base with loose-pin hinges. Make sure the screen side is in contact with the printing base.

Tips

You might want to make a holding device to keep the screen propped up during a run of printing. Simply fasten a 4-inch piece of 1 × 1 lumber to one side of the screen frame with a wood screw. Tighten the screw enough so that the prop moves stiffly and stays where you leave it. Leave the prop in place at the side of the screen frame during printing, and move it down to hold the screen off the printing base when you pause or want to change printing surfaces.

Shop at an art supply store or commercial silkscreen supply house for fabric, inks, an ink squeegee, stencil materials, and other supplies. Ask the store personnel for the best mesh size on the fabric according to the work you plan to do. In general, a number 12 rayon or polyester mesh will serve for most work. Silk fabric is available, but for economy you will probably want to go with a synthetic product.

Silkscreen printing is a simple process, but you will need the guidance of an experienced printer or a good instructional book before you can begin to do

work yourself. A book can give you authoritative information on different inks, masking procedures, design techniques, and tools.

Images are produced by placing a stencil on the screen that blocks ink from being pushed through the fabric and deposited onto the paper, cloth, or item being printed. Stencils can be made of paper, lacquer film, glue, photographic emulsion, and other products. Since stencil preparation is one of the basics of the technique, you will want to study up on how to do this and perhaps use a light box, pantograph, opaque projector, and other tools to design and cut your stencils accurately and quickly.

STENCILING

Tools and supplies needed

Stencil material (paper, mylar, etc.)
Boiled linseed oil
Paint thinner
Stencil knife and blades
Single-edge razor blades
Stencil brush (1½-inch diameter)
Stencil brush (½-inch diameter)
Masking tape
Paint (acrylic, latex, oil)
Newspapers and rags
Glass or hardwood cutting surface

Procedure

As a technique for embellishing and decorating walls, floors, and furniture, stenciling has an honorable history. It was used by homeowners from colonial to Victorian times to add color and interest to plain pine furniture and floors in informal rooms, and to highlight some feature of the building's architecture. Stenciling was often used as a substitute for wallpaper, and it was popular for redecorating since it could be used over an uneven surface.

You might want to use stencils to recreate a period look in an old home, or you might want to decorate a piece of furniture or section of wall with a design that reinforces the look you want to achieve. Stencils can decorate items such as old-style bathtubs, waste baskets, lampshades, chairs, and chests. There are stencil books available that contain hundreds of classic designs and motifs suitable to different periods. These publications make stenciling very easy and are a good starting point. Check a large art supply store for them, and also inquire at a local art museum or historical society for leads on stencil design books. Some of these books have designs printed on quality stencil paper, so all you have to do is cut the stencil out and use it.

You can also make or adapt your own designs to be converted into stencils. The materials for stencil making are readily available and easy to work with. Art supply stores carry sheets of stencil paper, which is a medium-weight stock impregnated with oil. The oil makes the paper easy to cut and allows the stencil to stand up to repeated applications of paint.

Frosted mylar and clear acetate sheets are also used for stencil making. These plastic products make it easy to trace the design and are easy to cut accurately. Both products are durable and will stand up to repeated use.

In a pinch you can adapt nearly any strong paper or card stock to stencil use. Brown kraft paper can be used. (This is the material used for heavy wrapping and for grocery bags.) After the pattern is cut in the paper, brush shellac or urethane varnish on it to seal it. You can also make stencils from bristol board, poster board, or manilla paper. Brush a 50/50 mixture of boiled linseed oil and paint thinner on the stock after you have traced your design onto it. Let the paper dry for 15 minutes. Then cut the stencil with a razor blade or special stencil knife. The oil will make the paper easier to cut and will strengthen the stencil overall.

You need a hard surface to cut stencils accurately. A glass-topped light box is ideal. Short of that, try a plain piece of glass or a length of smooth hardwood. Use single-edge razor blades, an artist's utility knife, a precision craft knife, or a special stencil cutting knife (sometimes called a *frisket*).

You have to cut with care to avoid tearing or weakening the *ties*—the sometimes delicate solid areas of the design that hold the stencil together. If you do damage a tie, reinforce it front and back with masking tape and replace the tape as necessary when you use the stencil.

When the stencil has been cut out, attach the stencil plate to the object or surface to be decorated. Use strips of masking tape on two edges of the stencil plate for this. You want the plate to be secure while you apply paint. The stencil will be blurred by any movement of the plate.

The best all-around brushes for stencil work are stiff-bristled, round brushes available at art supply stores and large paint stores. A large and a small brush should take care of most of your designs. The brush is kept very dry while you work. You only dip the bristles a short way into the paint, and you work out any extra paint on newspaper sheets spread out nearby. Shake and rub the brush on the newspaper, and when you get an even, thin distribution of paint on the paper you are ready to apply the brush to the stencil. You don't want any extra paint on the brush that might run under the stencil plate and ruin the design.

You can apply paint to the stencil by dabbing the brush up and down in the stencil openings or by briskly moving the brush back and forth and around each opening. Whichever method you use, keep the brush in an opening only as long as it takes to fill the area with color. If your brush is as dry as it should be, you will probably have to load the bristles with fresh paint for each new portion of the stencil.

After the stencil has been used, it should be cleaned with a solvent (water or paint thinner) and a rag to keep excess paint from hardening at the edges of the openings and spoiling the lines of the stencil.

In brief

1. Use prepared stencils and designs or draw and cut your own stencils from paper, plastic, or card stock.

2. Treat your stencil with oil to make it easier to cut. Use razor blade instruments to cut the outlines of the designs.

3. Attach the finished stencil to the surface with masking tape. Lightly load the brush with paint and work any excess paint out on a sheet of newspaper.

4. Apply paint to the stencil by dabbing, brushing, or swirling.

5. When the stencil has been used, prepare it for storage by cleaning with solvent and rags.

Precut or Printed Stencils Exist for Nearly Any Period or Style of Decoration.

FIGURE 5-5. Examples of stencils.

Tips

You can use any kind of paint to stencil—oil, latex, acrylic, even fabric paint if you want to stencil on cloth. The trick is in using a thick consistency of paint so that your brush stays dry and the paint doesn't run under the stencil plate (especially when stenciling vertical surfaces). Most latex and acrylic paints are naturally thick and can be used right from the can. Some oil paints are on the thin side. You can experiment and leave a small quantity of oil paint in a cup or saucer for a few hours to thicken it by evaporation. In any case, when you use oil paint you must be extra careful to work out any excess on a newspaper or rag.

You might be tempted to try stenciling with spray paints. It would seem to be an ideal way to avoid tricky work with stencil brushes. Unfortunately, it seldom works out. It is difficult to control the overspray of paint onto surfaces you don't want painted, and it is very difficult to get spray paint to give a sharp outline of the design.

MAKING AND USING PAINT COMBING TOOLS

Tools and supplies needed

Artist's utility knife
Paint brushes
Rubber-bladed window squeegee
Common hair combs and brushes
Latex flat or semi-gloss paint
Acrylic paint
Clear polyurethane varnish
Masking tape

Procedure

An inexpensive method of adding texture and visual interest to flat surfaces such as walls, floors, and simply constructed furniture pieces is to apply vivid acrylic paint over a contrasting undercoat, and then use homemade tools to remove bits of the acrylic and reveal some of the undercoat. The surface is then allowed to dry, and two or three coats of urethane varnish are applied to protect the finish and give it added depth.

The effect is somewhat like the scratchboard drawings that you may have done in school art classes. The method is one way to give some drama to an otherwise undistinguished area or piece of furniture. You might try it on some of the chipboard and plywood platforms and cubes described later in the book.

To start, go to a variety store and browse through the selection of inexpensive hair brushes and combs. You are looking for some devices that you can use to scrape the top coat of acrylic. Good bets include coarse and fine toothed pocket and hand combs, wide spaced combs for teasing and styling hair, and hair detangling combs. Also look at a few hair brushes, especially those with soft plastic or rubber teeth that are ⅛ to ¼ inch apart. While you are at the variety store, buy a common window washing squeegee. A rubber-bladed model about 6 inches wide will do nicely.

At a well-stocked paint store, select a flat or semi-gloss latex color as your undercoat. You might try off-white, gray, or some muted pastel as a good undercoat. Select acrylic paint for the top coat. It comes in very intense, vivid colors and has a stiff, paste-like consistency that makes it perfect for combing with your improvised tools to achieve the texture

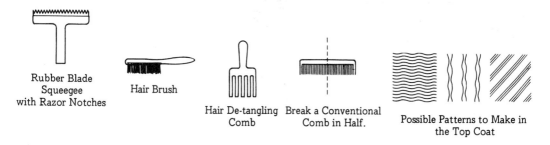

Rubber Blade
Squeegee
with Razor Notches

Hair Brush

Hair De-tangling
Comb

Break a Conventional
Comb in Half.

Possible Patterns to Make in
the Top Coat

FIGURE 5-6. Paint-combing tools and patterns.

effect. For the final protection coat, use a gloss or flat (satin) finish polyurethane varnish.

To apply the technique, paint the object or area with the latex undercoat. Depending on the color and condition of the finish, one or two coats will be needed. Let the paint dry thoroughly. Then use a paint brush to apply the acrylic over the latex. You can cover the latex completely. Use the brush to lay on stripes of acrylic, or brush a special pattern onto the latex. Comb the acrylic to remove some of it, revealing the undercoat and making a texture. You can use the hair combs and brushes to make unique patterns, and you can make your own comb by notching the rubber blade of the squeegee with razor blades and a utility knife. The notches you make in the squeegee don't have to be uniform. Also try breaking off some teeth in the comb for an unusual effect. As you draw your tools through the acrylic they will remove paint and you will have to constantly keep them clean by wiping them on rags or paper towels.

You can try some of the patterns illustrated, or you can invent some of your own. As long as the acrylic is wet, you aren't committed to anything you have done. You can always recoat the area with more acrylic and try combing again.

When you are satisfied, clean up your tools and allow the acrylic to dry. The job is finished by applying two or three coats of urethane varnish with a brush. Allow the urethane to dry for 6 to 12 hours between coats.

In brief

1. Purchase combs, hair brushes, and a rubber squeegee.

2. Select a latex undercoat color, an acrylic topcoat color, and gloss or flat urethane varnish.

3. Brush on one or two coats of latex undercoat and let it dry.

4. Brush on the acrylic, covering the whole area or making a pattern on the undercoat.

5. Comb the acrylic with your tools. Cut notches in the rubber squeegee to come up with your own pattern of teeth. Keep wiping paint from the tools as you work.

6. Allow the acrylic to dry, and finish with two or three coats of urethane.

FURNITURE PROJECTS

FURNITURE REGLUING

Tools and supplies needed

Clamps
Clothesline
Scrap wood
Glues (PVA, resorcinol, epoxy)
Wax paper
Rubber mallet
Knife

Procedure

Inevitably when you are working with "found furniture" and old pieces that have a lot of character but show plenty of wear, you need to repair loose joints, broken legs, or shaky trim. The repairs are straightforward for the most part, but there are some tricks that can save you time and give superior results.

Nearly all joints in old furniture are glued ones. The glues used in very old furniture are animal-based products that are sensitive to moisture, temperature, and physical injury. Modern glues are very superior products, and if your repairs are properly made the reglued joints should be stronger than the furniture itself.

Common white glue (PVA glue) is a good choice for repairs to pieces that stay indoors. It is cheap and it cleans up with water. If the joint is tightly clamped, white glue will provide a very good bond. The glue is water soluble, so it can soak into the fibers of the wood for a tight grip. For even better bonding, use aliphatic resin (often called *tight bond*) glue. It works like white glue but resists moisture better and gives a better bond.

For outdoor furniture and pieces that must have very strong joints, use resorcinol or epoxy glue. Both products are two-part glues that must be mixed together and applied and cleaned up quickly, so you have to have everything prepared and ready to be joined and clamped before you mix the glues. Always follow package directions. Both kinds of glues are expensive, so it pays to use them only for very demanding work.

The key to proper gluing is to thoroughly clean out the joint before applying new glue. If you simply lay a bead of new glue over the remains of the old, you will probably fail to make a strong joint. For one thing, the new glue is prevented from reaching the actual surface of the joint by the layer of old glue. For another thing, the joint probably won't fit tightly because you have the thickness of old hardened glue plus the thickness of the new glue. This will cause the joint to push the new glue out or will make the joint an ill-fitting one because of the extra material.

Always scrape the old glue from the joint surfaces before applying new glue. The old glue will come off easily with the use of a penknife, razor blade, or utility knife. If you are working with a dowel and socket joint, scrape the glue from the dowel and attempt to get as much out of the socket as you can.

Apply new glue to both surfaces of the joint. Allow the glue to sit on the material for 3 to 5 minutes before joining the material. This will let the glue soak into the fibers of the wood. If more glue is needed after this, apply it and then join the surfaces. Clean up any excess glue by scraping with a knife and rubbing with a wet rag.

Once the joint has been reglued you must apply constant pressure to the area until the glue has cured. This pressure is the second key to getting a strong and reliable joint. When working with old, fancy pieces, it can be difficult to clamp the joint. There are some unusual methods that can work in these situations.

If you are gluing a very thin joint, you can apply pressure by wrapping string, sewing thread, or fishing line around and around the joint. First cover the joint with wax paper to prevent the line from sticking, and then wrap it with line to clamp it.

If you have a very large flat area to clamp, you can use scrap pieces of wood to spread the weight and then use bricks, telephone books, and other heavy objects to apply pressure. One of the best sources of heavy weight for this method is a plastic or metal trash can filled with water. Depending on the size of the can and the amount of water you use, you can get just about any degree of clamping you want.

Use clothesline tourniquets to clamp odd and bulky shapes such as chairs, couches, or chests. Simply wrap a length of line around the object, tie it off, and use a sturdy piece of scrap wood to twist the line tightly. It's a good idea to apply soft cloth pads to the edges of the project to prevent the line from digging into the work.

You can cut strong rubber bands from bicycle, motorcycle, and automobile inner tubes. These bands are very useful for clamping medium-sized and odd-shaped objects. The strength of the band will be a function of how wide you cut it.

In brief

1. Select white glue, aliphatic resin glue, resorcinol glue, or epoxy glue according to the strength of bond or degree of moisture resistance needed.

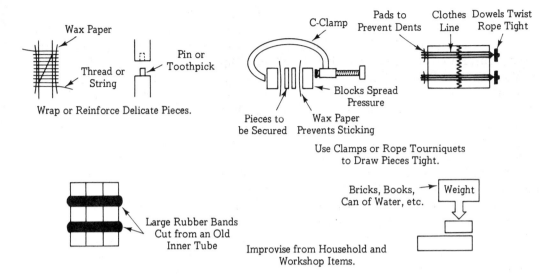

Wax Paper

Thread or String

Pin or Toothpick

Wrap or Reinforce Delicate Pieces.

C-Clamp Pads to Prevent Dents

Clothes Line

Dowels Twist Rope Tight

Blocks Spread Pressure

Pieces to be Secured

Wax Paper Prevents Sticking

Use Clamps or Rope Tourniquets to Draw Pieces Tight.

Large Rubber Bands Cut from an Old Inner Tube

Bricks, Books, Can of Water, etc.

Weight

Improvise from Household and Workshop Items.

FIGURE 6-1. Gluing and clamping techniques.

2. Clean the joint of old glue by scraping with a blade. Apply new glue to both surfaces of the joint and allow it to soak into the wood.

3. Apply more glue if needed, and join the surfaces. Clean up any excess glue.

4. Clamp or otherwise apply pressure to the area until the glue has cured. Use conventional or homemade devices.

Tips

When working with very delicate pieces it is sometimes impractical to clamp the joint while the glue cures. Usually these delicate pieces are not under any severe stress, so they will stay in place with plain gluing. You can reinforce these pieces and make it easier to glue them in place by putting toothpick or straight-pin posts in the joint. Break a round toothpick to a convenient length (1/2 to 1 inch) and drill or punch a hole in the two joint surfaces to receive the toothpick post. If you use a length of straight pin you should be able to force the pin into the two joint surfaces without using holes. These small posts will help strengthen the joints and will hold the pieces in place while the glue cures.

A very useful tool for taking loose joints apart for regluing is a rubber mallet. You can find one at an auto supply store, where they are sold for working on car bodies and installing hubcaps. With a rubber mallet you can safely knock furniture apart without marring the surfaces. If you are working with a simple chest or chair, it may be worth disassembling the whole piece so that you can reglue all of the joints, instead of just securing one or two loose ones.

Related to these joint repairs is the process of filling patches of wood that are burnt, chopped, rotted, or chipped. You can use a powdered latex putty that you mix with water and apply with a putty knife. The putty can be sanded when dry and then stained and finished to be a near match for the surrounding wood.

A quick repair to these damaged sections of furniture is to use auto body filler. You can't use filler unless you intend to paint or otherwise cover the area that you are patching because filler can't be stained to imitate wood. However, it does dry quickly and is a strong and easily formed material that can even (with practice) be used to rebuild curves and complex designs. Select a body filler that uses a putty base to which you add a hardener. Mix only what you can apply and form in 5 to 10 minutes because the material sets up rapidly. Apply the material and smooth it with the plastic tools that come with the filler kit. When it is fully cured (about 30 minutes) you can shape it, carve it, sand it, and prime and paint it. New layers can be put on top of the filler to build up thick patches, and because the filler cures rapidly, you can lay up several layers in an afternoon of work.

REMOVING OLD FURNITURE FINISHES ——————

Tools and supplies needed

Paint thinner
Denatured alcohol
Lacquer thinner
Extra fine (#000) steel wool
Fine (#00) steel wool
Rags
Saucepan

Procedure

The four finishes you are likely to encounter when recycling old wood furniture are wax/oil, shellac, lacquer, and varnish. Each of these finishes must be removed with a different solvent. The first solvent to try on a piece is paint thinner. Dip a clean rag in paint thinner and wash and rub down the entire piece. This treatment will remove wax and oil finishes that have built up over the years from polishing and maintaining, as well as dirt and household grease deposits. If the piece has only a wax or oil finish, this treatment will strip all of it away, and it may be the only thing needed before refinishing proceeds.

If there is still finish on the object after you have washed it down with paint thinner, try wetting a piece of extra fine steel wool with denatured alcohol and rubbing it on a small section of the finish. Use denatured alcohol from a paint store, rather than rubbing alcohol from a drug store, because denatured alcohol is pure alcohol, while rubbing alcohol is up to 80 percent water and is useless as a solvent for furniture finishes. Pour a small amount of alcohol into a saucepan and cover the main container tightly. (Pure alcohol quickly absorbs water from the atmosphere, which weakens it as a solvent.) Work on a small section of the finish at a time since the alcohol will evaporate quickly. As the finish loosens and become liquid, wipe it up with rags. Use fine grade steel wool for tough sections of finish.

If alcohol dissolves the finish, you are working with shellac. Removing shellac with alcohol goes quickly, and the piece will be ready for refinishing as soon as the piece is entirely clean and the alcohol has evaporated. If the finish doesn't dissolve under the application of pure alcohol, you are dealing with either a lacquer or a varnish finish.

Test for a lacquer finish by mixing a cup of denatured alcohol with a quart of lacquer thinner and pouring some into a saucepan. Dip a piece of steel wool into the solvent and rub it on the finish. If the finish loosens and liquefies, proceed as you did for shellac removal—rub with solvent and wipe clean with a rag.

If lacquer solvent doesn't work on the finish, you are dealing with varnish. See the next project, which is on paint and varnish removing, for details on getting this kind of finish off the piece.

In brief

1. Wash the piece down with paint remover to clean wax, grease, dirt, and oil.

2. Test the finish with steel wool and denatured alcohol. If it dissolves, remove it by rubbing and wiping.

3. If the finish doesn't dissolve in alcohol, try lacquer thinner cut with alcohol. If it dissolves, remove it by rubbing and wiping.

4. If the finish doesn't come off with these solvents, it is varnish, which can be removed with commercial paint remover.

Tips

If the finish is shellac, but plain alcohol is not entirely effective in dissolving it, try mixing a cup of lacquer thinner with a quart of alcohol. This mixture is effective on the improved shellacs that were applied to furniture before the advent of lacquers.

Use the sequence of solvents given so that you don't waste time working with solvents that won't work. It's important to wash down an old and dirty piece with paint thinner first so that accumulations of wax and oil are removed. Wax, especialy, can impede the action of alcohol and lacquer thinner in dissolving shellac and lacquer.

Since denatured alcohol and lacquer thinner are very absorbent and volatile solvents, you should take care that they don't get spoiled by excessive contact with the atmosphere. Pour out only what you can use in a few minutes, and keep the bulk container tightly capped. When storing these solvents, load the partially full containers with clean marbles or pebbles to bring the liquid level to nearly cap height.

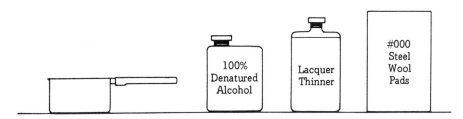

Use a Saucepan or Bowl to Hold
the Solvent and Keep Your
Main Supplies Tightly Capped.

FIGURE 6-2. Some of the supplies needed to remove old finish from furniture.

As you work with the solvents they will tell you roughly when the piece of furniture was built (or at least when it was last refinished, if it has been worked on before). Pure shellac was in use before 1850, improved shellac from 1850 to 1920, lacquer from 1920 to the present, and varnish from 1925 to the present. Varnish is not likely to be found on mass-produced furniture, since it is tricky to apply. It will be found on custom built and hand refinished pieces.

REMOVING PAINT AND VARNISH ————————————

Tools and supplies needed ————————

Saucepan
Paint brush
Putty knife
Wide-blade razor scraper
Wire brush
Steel wool
5-pound coffee can
Wire coat hanger
Goggles
Rubber gloves
Semi-paste paint and varnish remover (water wash type)
Newspapers
Rags

Procedure ——————————————

Stripping paint and removing old, cracked, and discolored varnish is a very common project for restoring furniture and recycling fixtures and other objects. A semi-paste chemical remover usually works best for removing thick coatings of old finish. The thickness of the product keeps it from running off vertical surfaces, and it will stay wet and active through about three layers of finish. Look for a product that can be rinsed with water. (This will speed clean-up and allow you to polish the wood with steel wool to remove stains.)

Before you start work you should build a waste container for the softened finish that will come off the piece you are stripping. Take a 5-pound coffee can and punch two holes in opposite sides of the container near the top rim. Take a straightened length of coat hanger wire (15 inches is about right) and insert it through the holes. Bend the free ends of the wire up and twist them together to form a handle for the container. The piece of wire that stretches across the opening of the can is good for scraping softened finish from putty knives, razors, and other scraping tools.

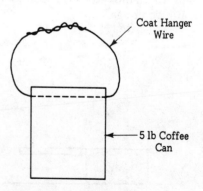

Make a Waste Can
for Cleaning Softened
Finish from Your Scrapers.

FIGURE 6-3.   A paint-stripping aid.

For ease of working, it is best to have the piece that you are stripping disassembled and laid horizontally so that you can apply stripper and scraping tools comfortably. Remove the drawers of any piece and strip them separately. If possible, remove table legs and lay them down on newspapers to strip. Have plenty of newspapers, rags, and clean water on hand to clean up spills and to promptly remove any stripper that gets on your skin.

Chemical strippers will burn and irritate your skin, so it is best to wear rubber gloves to protect your hands. Eye protection is a must. Stripper can fly off in unexpected directions when you are working with scrapers and wire brushes, so wear goggles both to apply and remove stripper. It is important to work in a well-ventilated area to avoid being overcome by the strong fumes that stripper gives off.

Pour out the stripper into a saucepan and apply it to the finish with a paint brush. Use as few strokes as possible, since the stripper forms a wax film immediately to keep the product wet and you don't want to disturb that film. Keep applying remover until it will sit for 20 minutes without drying up. After you have applied the remover don't hang around the project—you will be tempted to start scraping before the stripper has had time to work. Go do something else for a while and come back in 10 minutes to check the wetness of the stripper. If it has dried out, apply more and go away for 20 minutes.

When the stripper has been on the surface for 20 to 30 minutes, come back to the project and start scraping the finish off. Use a razor blade scraper, putty knife, and wire brush. A wire brush is particularly useful for round pieces and tight grooves and corners. Be gentle with the brush so that you don't gouge the surface of the wood as you brush the finish away. Scrape the softened paint from your bladed tools into the waste container and remove softened finish in the wire brush bristles by washing under a strong stream of water.

If any paint remains after scraping and brushing you must repeat the process. Apply the remover, wait for it to work, then scrape and brush. Each application of stripper will take off about three layers of finish. With some heavily coated objects, you will have to apply stripper two or three times.

When you get down to bare wood, apply a thin coat of stripper, let it soak into the wood for 5 minutes, then polish the surface with a piece of steel wool that you keep dipping into fresh water. The combination of water and stripper will draw any residual stain from the wood and will polish the wood so that later sanding will be minimal. Rinse the project with water and wipe it down with clean rags.

In brief

1. Make a waste container for the softened paint with a coffee can and a coat hanger wire.

2. Disassemble the piece to be stripped as completely as possible.

3. Protect your hands, eyes, and lungs by using rubber gloves and goggles and working in a well-ventilated area.

4. Apply stripper to the finish with a paint brush. Keep applying it until the stripper will sit for 20 minutes without drying up.

5. Scrape the softened finish with a razor blade scraper, putty knife, and wire brush.

6. Repeat the process if any paint remains.

7. Apply a thin coat of stripper to the bare wood and polish with a piece of wet steel wool.

8. Rinse the project with water and wipe it clean with rags.

Tips

If you have to strip thin vertical surfaces (such as table legs) in place without being able to lay them down, try putting a catch pan beneath them to hold stripper that runs down. You can use old pie pans or tin cans under table and chair legs, and you can dip your brush into these containers to recycle the stripper.

Chemical paint removers are expensive products, and some people save money by stripping the first layers of finish with an electric heat gun or propane torch and then using chemical products for the final layers. You might try this approach, but you should be aware that it is very easy to damage and char the wood with heat paint removing. The process is best employed with rough pieces that have thick accumulations of paint and varnish. It is *not* recommended for fine furniture and small objects. When using heat stripping techniques, always work in a well-ventilated area (outdoors is best) and have a fire extinguisher ready for any accidents.

To use a propane torch, buy a flame-spreader fitting that attaches directly to the pencil-flame burner that came with the torch. This flame spreader will direct the torch's heat in a 1 1/2- to 2-inch band as you move it over the surface to be stripped. As the paint wrinkles and blisters from the heat of the torch, scrape it off with a putty knife or dull razor blade scraper. The method works well once you get the feel for it, and you can quickly remove thick coatings from flat surfaces. Details in the wood such as carvings, grooves, and moldings must be brought out with chemical stripper once the bulk of the finish is off.

A heat gun is a variation on flame paint removing. It consists of an electric coil mounted in a handle with a reflector to concentrate the heat onto the surface being stripped. It works a bit more slowly than a propane torch, but the action is the same. The heat softens and blisters the finish, and you follow closely with a scraper to remove it.

Some people have experimented with other kinds of products to remove finishes at a cost lower than that of commercial paint strippers. One method is to use trisodium phosphate (TSP). This powdered product has the ability to remove finishes if it is concentrated enough and if the temperature is high enough. Commercial furniture strippers use large tanks of near-boiling TSP to remove finishes quickly from all kinds of wood. It's not practical for you to have your own tank of TSP solution, but you can work with it outdoors on a hot summer day.

Obtain TSP from a large paint store or from a company that deals in industrial and commercial cleaning and laundry supplies. For a typical stripping project such as a table or chest, use 3 pounds of TSP in 2 quarts of hot water to make a supersaturated solution of TSP.

Apply the solution to the piece with a bushy paint brush or old cloth mop. Wear eye and hand protection. Do your stripping outside on a driveway or somewhere you don't want vegetation to grow because the TSP solution will kill most grass and ground cover. Let the TSP work for 15 to 30 minutes. The hotter the day outside, the faster it will soften the finish.

When you test the surface and find that the finish has softened, scrape it with a putty knife, razor blade instrument, and wire brush. A coarse grade of steel wool (#2) is useful for rubbing off sections of softened finish and working on curves. When the finish is off, rinse the whole piece down with a hose and wipe the piece dry with clean rags. Let the piece dry in the sun for the rest of the day.

TSP in a weaker solution (1 cup to 1 gallon of hot water) makes a great heavy-duty cleaner. Use it to clean masonry, tile, painted objects, metal, and just about anything else that you want to get very clean in preparation for refinishing and painting. (You should be aware that TSP will dull shiny paint.)

REMOVING VENEER ——————

Tools and supplies needed

Rags or towels

Water hose

Razor blade scraper

Putty knife

Steel wool

Sandpaper

TSP

Paint remover

Utility knife

Procedure

Veneered furniture is widely available in the used-furniture market. It wears a thin coating of some exotic wood over solid construction of some other, less exotic wood. If you like the look of the veneer, and it is firmly attached to the base wood and the finish can be brought back with cleaning, solvents, or reamalgamation, everything is fine. If however, the veneer is in bad shape—chipped, bubbled, or peeling away in spots—or if you just don't like the idea of a piece of furniture pretending to be what it's not, you can often remove the veneer to expose the honest construction that lies under the surface.

Veneer removal is a risky business, so it should only be used with furniture that you've obtained free or very cheaply. The process of removal could warp the piece, cause it to become unglued, or precipitate other disasters. It's worth taking the risk with a piece that you aren't emotionally or financially attached to. You might come up with a very handsome piece, or you could expose a poor substructure with nothing to offer in the way of aesthetics or utility.

Some brave furniture recyclers have been known to totally immerse a piece in a nearby lake or stream to remove the veneer. This method is not recommended because it's difficult to check on how quickly the veneer is loosening. You could end up ungluing the whole structure, and you might haul your rope up only to find a single stick of wood still attached. The rest of your table would be lying at the bottom of the water.

A good method is to put the piece outside on a hot day and cover it completely with thick, absorbent rags, or better still, towels. Use cord to tie the fabric around the piece and keep it in place. Soak the fabric with water from a hose. Let the heat from the sun and the wet rags work on the veneer to loosen it. Return during the day to soak the fabric again,

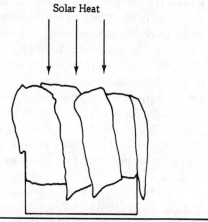

Cover the Piece with Rags or
Towels and Soak With Water.

**FIGURE 6-4. A way to make veneer
removal easier.**

and while you are applying water remove
some fabric to see how the veneer is
doing. Keep the rags wet until the veneer
starts to peel off the base wood. This can
take from 4 hours to 4 days.

When the veneer is loose, remove the
fabric and start to strip the veneer with
scrapers, a putty knife, and steel wool. If
any glue residue is left on the base wood,
strip it off with semi-paste paint remover.
After the piece is cleaned, let it dry thoroughly. If the structure has loosened, reglue the joints and add screws and mending plates as needed. For a simple piece
that has loosened, try knocking all the
joints apart with a soft mallet and then
regluing the whole structure.

When the whole piece has dried and
been reglued, sand the wood with medium and fine sandpaper and then follow
with fine steel wool. Paint or urethane
varnish the wood to provide a final
finish. If you are displeased with the simple lines and uninteresting grain of the
piece, you could use stenciling and other

design techniques to add some visual interest to the wood.

In brief

1. Cover the piece with thick, absorbent
   rags or towels. Tie them into place
   with cord. Soak the fabric with water.
2. Return periodically to check the veneer and to rewet the fabric.
3. When the veneer is loosened, remove
   the fabric and strip the veneer with
   scrapers and steel wool. Use semi-
   paste paint remover to take off glue
   residue.
4. Allow the piece to dry, and reglue
   and reinforce any loose joints. Some
   pieces may need total regluing.
5. Finish by sanding, polishing, and applying paint or urethane varnish. Use
   stenciling or other design techniques
   to add interest to plain surfaces.

Tips

Some veneers will be coated with lacquer
and varnish that will resist the wetting
action of water. You can get the veneer off
faster in these cases by wetting the fabric
with a strong solution of TSP. Use 1
pound of TSP to 1 gallon of water. Keep
applying this solution to the fabric as
needed.

Another trick that you can use for
firmly attached veneers is to score cross
hatches in the finish and the veneer with
a utility knife. This will let the water soak
through and will loosen the veneer more
effectively. Use a razor blade utility knife
and score the surface of the piece with
lines about 1 to 2 inches from each other.
Score the lines about 1/16 to 1/8 inch
deep—this should break the seal of the
finish and cut about halfway into the veneer itself.

REFINISHING OLD SHELLAC AND LACQUER FINISHES IN PLACE

Tools and supplies needed

Denatured alcohol
Lacquer thinner
Extra fine (#000) steel wool
Boiled linseed oil
Paint thinner
3-pound cut white shellac
Cheesecloth or cotton gauze
Lint-free soft cloth

Procedure

Sometimes you will acquire a piece of furniture that has a shellac or lacquer finish that is dull, perhaps powdery looking, but otherwise in good shape. You can quickly recondition these finishes with a couple of simple techniques.

If there is a residue of wax or oil on the finish, remove it by washing and wiping the piece down with paint thinner and rags. Then determine whether the finish is shellac, lacquer, or varnish by testing it with solvents on a hidden area. (See the furniture finishes project.)

If the finish is shellac you can revive its looks by a process known as *feeding the finish*. Take 1 ounce of 3-pound cut shellac (the "cut" refers to its concentration when bought at the paint store; 3-pound is a common concentration), and dilute it with 4 ounces of denatured alcohol. Add 5 drops of boiled linseed oil to the thinned shellac. Dip a piece of extra fine steel wool in this mixture and rub it into the finish with a series of light strokes. When you've worked it into the finish, take a dry piece of steel wool and lightly polish the surface. Let the piece dry for 24 hours before applying a paste wax and giving a final polish with a soft cloth.

A more drastic reviving is called *reamalgamation*, which works for shellac or lacquer finishes that are cracked and crazed, chipped, or thin in spots. To reamalgamate shellac, mix three parts denatured alcohol with one part lacquer thinner. Apply this liquid to the finish with a clean (preferably new) brush. First brush across the grain; then immediately apply another coat brushing with the grain. The old finish will melt, and on the second brushing it will seem as if you are applying a totally new coat of shellac. You are really just redistributing the old shellac that you have dissolved with solvent. Let the job dry for 24 hours, and then polish the surface with steel wool and apply a paste wax.

To reamalgamate lacquer, use straight lacquer thinner and apply it with a new brush. Brush one coat against the grain and immediately apply another coat with the grain. Let it dry, and polish with steel wool and paste wax.

To obtain a high-gloss finish on both shellac and lacquer, there is a process that is a cross between feeding and reamalgamation. There are commercial products available for this work, which are known as *padding lacquers*, *refinishing liquids*, and *one-step refinishers*. You can use these products (which usually have an acetone or ether solvent base) or you can experiment with your own mixtures. A mixture of one part white shellac (3-pound cut) to two parts alcohol with one-half part lacquer thinner is a good start for shellac finishes. For lacquer finishes try a commercially available padding lacquer. (Homemade mixes usually dry out too fast to be useful with lacquer.)

For either lacquer or shellac finishes the procedure is the same. Take a lint-free cloth and place a wad of cheesecloth or cotton wadding in the center. Gather the cloth around the filling to make a soft pad. Dip the pad in your shellac or lacquer product and soak it. Squeeze the excess out and place a few drops of boiled linseed oil in the center of the pad.

Before you even touch the surface with the pad you must start moving the pad in a rapid circular motion. You don't want the pad to stop at any time while it is on the surface because it will stick to the finish you are softening, feeding, and polishing. Hit the surface with the moving pad and keep it moving in a circular pattern as you refinish the piece. When the pad runs out of liquid, remove it from the finish (while still moving it), dip it in the refinishing liquid, squeeze the excess out, and lubricate the pad with a few drops of linseed oil. Any time the pad begins to drag on the surface of the finish, remove it and reload it with more linseed oil.

You have to apply constant pressure and constant motion for this technique to work, so it does require a bit of effort. The pad will stick to the finish the moment you stop moving it and will leave an ugly mark, so always remove the pad before your arm gets tired. The technique produces a brilliant gloss finish, and it can be repeated as often as necessary to build up a thick finish.

In brief

1. Remove any wax or oil from the piece with paint thinner and rags.

2. Test with solvents to determine whether the finish is shellac, lacquer, or varnish.

3. If it is shellac, you can feed the finish with thinned shellac, boiled linseed oil, and extra fine steel wool. Rub it lightly into the finish and let it dry.

4. To reamalgamate shellac, mix three parts alcohol and one part lacquer thinner and brush it on the finish. First brush across the grain, then with the grain. Let it dry, and polish with steel wool and paste wax.

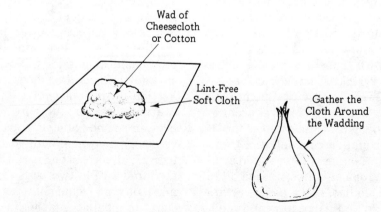

FIGURE 6-5. How to make a pad for one-step refinishing.

5. To reamalgamate lacquer, use straight lacquer thinner. Brush across and then with the grain. Let it dry, and polish with steel wool and paste wax.

6. To obtain a high-gloss renewed finish, use a homemade or commercial refinishing liquid. Make a soft and absorbent pad, wet it with refinisher, add a few drops of linseed oil, and apply it to the finish. Keep the pad in circular motion at all times—before, during, and after it hits the finish. Add more refinisher and oil as required.

PAINTING AND VARNISHING ——————————

Tools and supplies needed

Tin can
Coat hanger
Paint brushes
TSP
Paint thinner
Urethane varnish
Enamel primer
Enamel paint
Newspapers
Rags

Procedure

Once you have stripped the old finish from a piece of furniture or have decided that the old finish should be covered with something, you will be dealing with varnish and paint. The techniques for applying the two materials are practically the same.

The logical choice for a varnish is a polyurethane product. These clear synthetic resin finishes are extremely durable, quick drying, and relatively odorless, and come in gloss or satin varieties. Urethanes will slightly darken the tone of the wood you apply them to. You can get an idea of the final color by wiping some paint thinner on a section of the wood.

The major problem with applying urethane finishes is avoiding brush marks, dust specks, and air bubbles in the final finish. Avoid the dust problem by working in a clean space. Vacuum the area and the piece you are working on. Just before you start to apply urethane, wipe the whole piece down with a rag that you have dampened with a mixture of one part water, one part paint thinner, and one part urethane. Work the mixture into the cloth and squeeze the excess out. This sticky rag (called a *tack rag*) will pick up dust very effectively.

Use a new brush that you have prepared by working and combing the bristles with your fingers for a few minutes to remove all of the loose ones. You don't want any getting in the urethane and lodging in the finish of the piece.

Prepare a clean tin can by punching two holes near the top rim and inserting a length of coat hanger wire. Use this wire to wipe the excess urethane from the brush as you work. Striking the excess will create air bubbles in the urethane, and you want to collect these in a separate can so that they don't get on the piece you are finishing. After the job is done, you can pour the contents of the strike can into the main can.

If it is possible, have the surface you are finishing horizontal. Remove drawers, panels, and doors and lay them down. This way, gravity will assist you in leveling the surface of the finish as you brush it. As you brush the urethane on, use as few strokes as possible—constant brushing will leave brush marks and cause more air bubbles to form.

Brushing with the grain works best. Try laying the urethane on in strips about 1/2 inch from each other. Then use short strokes across the grain to fill in the areas between the strips. This method takes advantage of the extra urethane that builds up on the edges of the brush. After the whole surface is coated, dry the brush on the strike wire and lightly draw the tips of the bristles over the surface, with the grain.

When you come to an edge, don't let the brush go over it. It will deposit extra urethane there. Lift the brush off the surface just as it reaches the edge. Carvings and irregular shapes are best finished with a fairly dry brush. Keep cleaning the brush on the strike wire as you work these areas to avoid laying in so much urethane that it pools in curves and corners.

The key to a flawless urethane finish is to use extra fine steel wool between coats. Wait until the surface has hardened (12 to 24 hours), then lightly buff it with steel wool. The steel wool takes out brush marks and imperfections and gives the surface a good bite on the next coat. Usually two or three coats of urethane are called for. If you are working on totally raw wood, three coats are usually the minimum since the first coat will soak deeply into the wood.

If you want to keep your brush soft between finishing sessions without cleaning it, wrap it tightly in a plastic freezer bag and place it in your freezer. Thaw it out 1/2 hour before using it again. The freezer treatment will keep a urethane or paint brush useable for about 3 weeks—long enough for any number of finishing sessions on your furniture.

When you decide to paint something, the key is proper preparation. Whether the material is wood, metal, plastic, plaster, leather, or masonry, it must be prepared. Use a solution of TSP (1 cup to 1 gallon of water) to clean grease, dirt, scale, and other foreign matter from the old surface. Use a wire brush, putty knife, and sandpaper to clean any loose and flaking finish, and prepare the surface for the new coating. As with varnishing, work on horizontal surfaces whenever possible.

The most logical choice for general-purpose painting is enamel, which provides a shiny, durable, quick-drying finish on most surfaces. Enamels are available in cans for brush applications and spray cans for quick, small jobs.

When you are dealing with raw surfaces it is best to use a primer before applying a finish coat of enamel. A primer seals and conditions the material and prepares it for a good bond with the finish coat. Most enamel primers are resilient and will take minor bumps and shocks without causing the finish coat to flake off. Primers are available in cans for brushing on flat surfaces and in spray cans for use on small projects and complicated surfaces such as carvings or moldings.

Most enamels have been formulated to flow on smoothly and to be self leveling. Brush them as you would for urethane. You can strike excess enamel from the brush right on the rim of the paint can because enamel generally doesn't foam up unduly with air bubbles.

Spray enamels are widely available and are very useful for small projects since they provide an even coating, dry

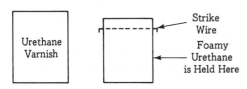

Use a Clean Container with
a Strike Wire for Cleaning
Foamy Urethane from Your Brush.

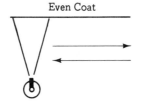

Move Your Whole Arm and
Body Parallel to the Work.

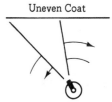

Don't Just Pivot Your
Wrist or Forearm.

FIGURE 6-6. Hints on how to paint and refinish efficiently.

fast, and allow you to work easily with irregular shapes. The main thing to remember about spraying enamel is to keep the can moving constantly and to hold the can at a uniform distance from the project as you spray so that the finish will be the same thickness all around.

Move your entire arm parallel to the surface you are spraying. Don't swing your arm or pivot your wrist to cover the project. Since spray enamel dries very quickly, it pays to lay up your finish in several thin sprayings rather than one thick one. The finish will be much stronger, and the chance of drips and sags will be much reduced if you apply the paint in three applications, waiting about 3 minutes between each.

In brief

1. Apply urethane varnish in a dust-free environment with a clean, new brush. First wipe the object down with a sticky rag to get all the dust from it.

2. Make a strike can by inserting a coat hanger wire into the rim of a tin can. Use this can to keep foamy urethane from contaminating the main container.

3. Apply urethane with as few strokes as possible. Lay down strips of finish with the grain, and then connect them with short cross-grain strokes. Smooth the entire surface with the tip of your dry brush.

4. For extra fine work, buff the finish between coats with steel wool.

5. When painting, always prepare the surface. Clean dirt, loose paint, and grime with TSP and scraping tools.

6. Prime raw surfaces to condition the material and provide a good backing for the final coating.

7. Brush enamel as you would urethane. Strike excess paint off on the rim of the can.

8. Spray enamels and primers by keeping the can constantly moving and holding the can at a uniform distance from the project. Lay the finish up in three thin layers rather than one thick one.

DESKS, TABLES, AND WORK SURFACES

Tools and supplies needed

Drill and bits
Hammer
Circular saw
Tape measure
1-inch chipboard

Terra cotta flue tiles

4 × 4-inch lumber

Epoxy glue

Wood screws

6-inch nails

Procedure

One of the first things you need when furnishing a living or work space is a flat surface for working, dining, or household chores. One of the classics for an ultra simple work surface is to place a smooth-surfaced door over two short filing cabinets. This works fine and is one of the cheapest and most effective ways of quickly setting up a desk. If you don't have filing cabinets and a door, or if you don't like the looks of them, there are a few simple alternatives.

Terra cotta flue tile is a product sold for lining old and new chimneys. It is supplied in 2-foot-long sections at masonry supply stores and is available in a dark red or medium beige color. If you make two stacks of three 8 × 12- or 8 × 16-inch flue liners, you have a perfect base for a work surface. Cut a piece of chipboard to about 3 × 5 feet, place it on top of the liners, and you have a table or desk. The open ends of the liners provide storage for items such as books, office supplies, silverware, or linens. You can urethane the chipboard, paint it, cover it with fabric or some other sheet material, or leave it natural.

The great virtue to this kind of construction is that the flue liners and chipboard aren't pretending to be anything but what they are. The structure and texture of the materials are exposed, and the honesty of the piece is part of its charm. If you need a bit more height for the table top, you can place bricks or pieces of 2 ×

4 under the chipboard to raise it a few inches. You can let gravity keep the liners stacked on top of each other, or you can get more stability by placing dabs of epoxy putty between the liners to secure them.

Another simple system is to build two wooden trestles from 4 × 4-inch lumber. Since you are building the trestles from scratch, you can make them any height you wish (30 inches is a good height for general use). Cut 4 × 4-inch lumber into four 30-inch pieces and four 17-inch pieces.

Arrange the 4 × 4s as shown in the illustration. Drill two pilot holes in each corner of the trestles to receive 6-inch nails. After the holes have been drilled, mix and apply epoxy glue to all joint surfaces. Secure the joints by driving 6-inch-long nails (called *spikes*) into the pilot holes. Make sure the trestles are square, and leave them alone for 24 hours while the epoxy cures.

When the trestles are ready, cut chipboard into a table top. A good size for a dining table is 3 feet by 5 feet. Attach the trestles to the underside of the chipboard (see the illustration for suggested spacing). Epoxy glue and wood screws make a good system for securing the chipboard and the 4 × 4s. You can also try using carriage bolts through the chipboard and into the lumber. Another method is to spread the stress over the underside of the chipboard by gluing and screwing lengths of 1 × 12 lumber to the chipboard and then bolting or screwing the trestles to these.

In brief

1.   Secure six 8 × 12- or 8 × 16-inch terra cotta flue liners. Stack them as a base for a chipboard table top.

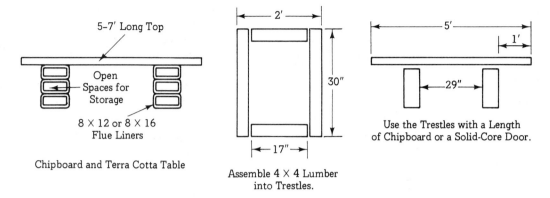

FIGURE 6-7.   Examples of easy-to-make tables.

2. Cut a piece of 1-inch-thick chipboard to approximately 3 × 5 feet and place it on top of the liners.

3. Build trestles from 4 × 4-inch lumber. Cut the lumber into four 30-inch pieces and four 17-inch pieces.

4. Arrange the lumber and drill pilot holes for 6-inch nails. Glue the joints with epoxy and then drive nails into the pilot holes. Make sure the trestles are square and allow the epoxy to cure.

5. Cut a chipboard top. Attach the trestles to the underside of the chipboard. Use epoxy and screws or carriage bolts, or use 1 × 12 lumber to spread the stress.

Tips

Chipboard that is 1-inch thick gives you maximum flexibility in designing a top for your table. You can cut the 4 × 8-foot sheets to any dimension you choose. However, if you want a top with a bit more thickness and some definite wood grain to it, select a solid core wood door. These doors are sold at home centers and lumber stores. It is important to get a solid core door (rather than a foam or hollow core door) so that it will stand up to the pressure and weight placed on it. The door can be finished with two or three coats of urethane varnish to protect it and bring out the wood veneer surfaces.

PLATFORMS, RISERS, AND CUBES ——————————————————

Tools and supplies needed

Circular saw

Drill and bits

Hammer

Tape measure

1 1/2-inch screws

Nails

3/4-inch chipboard

3/4- and 1-inch plywood (smooth on one side)

2 × 4 lumber

White glue

1-inch steel pipe nipples, caps, and flanges

Procedure

Producers in television, film, and the live theater use basic building blocks to form their sets. These basic platforms, risers, and cubes can be combined and recombined, painted, covered with fabrics or other materials, and otherwise adapted to make different shapes and designs. This adaptability is why these pieces are always found around studios and theaters. You can make platforms, risers, and cubes for your home and use them in some of the same ways set designers do. You might use two or three platforms to create a separate area in a large room. A cube might serve as a coffee table, work surface, or display pedestal for a sculpture or a group of decorative articles. You might combine a riser, two platforms, and three cubes to make a stepped seating area for viewing a large-screen TV.

Construction of the units is simple and straightforward. Use plywood for the platforms and risers since they will have to take a lot of weight. Select inexpensive, one-side-smooth plywood since only one surface will be exposed. Chipboard is an excellent material for cubes—it is smooth, easily worked, and takes a nice paint finish.

Dimensions for the units described here are only suggestions. The platform will accommodate a standard single mattress, and it could be turned into a couch by using the mattress and a foam bolster supported by a wall. The riser is dictated by the standard size of plywood sheets. You could build a smaller one or you could combine more than one unit to come up with a larger total surface. The cube is sized to be a convenient seat, table, or pedestal. The dimensions for all of the units can be expanded or contracted as desired. If you expand the size of the platform and cube, you will have to add some extra material to stiffen the large surfaces. For instance, if the platform were expanded to 75 by 54 inches (double bed size) you would need to add two additional braces to support the top surface. If the cube were greatly expanded, you might want to use 2 × 4 frame pieces instead of 2 × 2s.

To build the platform, take four 8-foot lengths of 2 × 4 and cut two 70 1/2-inch pieces, two 37 1/2-inch pieces, four 8 1/2-inch pieces, and one 34 1/2-inch piece. From two 4 × 8-foot sheets of 3/4-inch plywood, cut one 75 by 39-inch piece, two 73 1/2 by 12-inch pieces, and two 39 by 12-inch pieces.

On the two 73 1/2-inch pieces of plywood install the two 72-inch and the four 8 1/2-inch pieces of 2 × 4. Use wood screws and firmly attach the 2 × 4s to the plywood as shown in the illustration. On the two 39-inch pieces of plywood install the 37 1/2-inch pieces of 2 × 4.

Spread white glue on all the joint surfaces of the frame and assemble it with two nails at each corner, driven into the plywood and through to the underlying 2 × 4s. Install the remaining 34 1/2-inch 2 × 4 as a brace in the center of the frame. Secure it with white glue and nails driven from the sides of the frame.

Apply white glue to the surface of the frame and attach the plywood top piece. Secure the top of the platform with nails driven approximately every foot along the edges of the plywood.

Make a riser by purchasing twelve foot-long lengths of 1-inch steel pipe (these 12-inch lengths are called *nipples*). Also buy caps and flanges for the pipe. The plumbing store might not have flanges in stock, but you can usually find

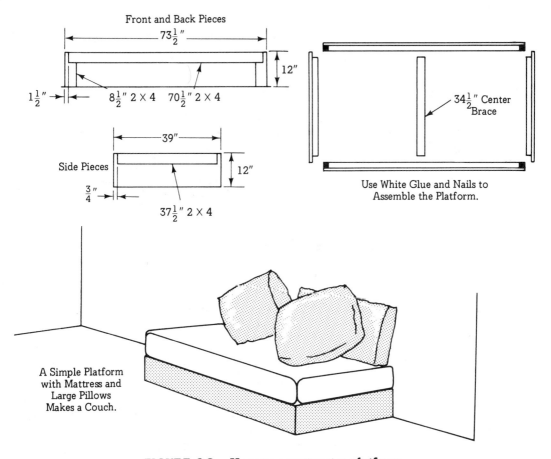

Front and Back Pieces

73½"

12"

1½"   8½" 2 × 4   70½" 2 × 4

34½" Center Brace

39"

Side Pieces   12"

¾"

37½" 2 × 4

Use White Glue and Nails to Assemble the Platform.

A Simple Platform with Mattress and Large Pillows Makes a Couch.

FIGURE 6-8. How to construct a platform.

them at an industrial hardware store or steel supply house. Screw the pipe flanges to the underside of a 1-inch-thick piece of plywood, using the pattern shown in the illustration on page 122. Screw the lengths of pipe into the flanges and screw the caps on the threaded ends of the pipes. Turn the plywood over and you have your riser.

The advantage to this design is that you can quickly unscrew the pipe legs to disassemble and store the riser. You can also put different length pipes into the flanges to raise or lower the platform. The

riser is not the most sophisticated looking piece, but with some carpeting on the platform and some fabric as a border to hide the pipes, it can function as a quick, inexpensive, and portable home stage or elevated seating area.

To make a cube, take two 8-foot 2 × 4s and cut them into four 2 × 2 strips. Cut the strips into four 18 1/2-inch pieces, four 20-inch pieces, and four 22 1/2-inch pieces. Take a 4 × 8-foot piece of 3/4-inch chipboard and cut it into six pieces as shown in the illustration (on page 123)— four 24-inch squares and two 24- by 22

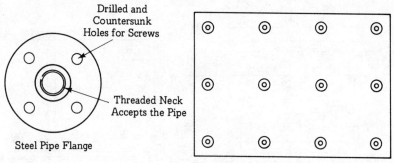

Drilled and
Countersunk
Holes for Screws

Threaded Neck
Accepts the Pipe

Steel Pipe Flange

Screw the Flanges to the Underside
of the Riser in a Uniform Pattern.

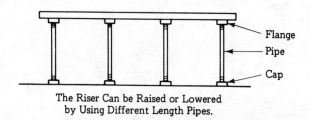

Flange

Pipe

Cap

The Riser Can be Raised or Lowered
by Using Different Length Pipes.

FIGURE 6-9. Details of riser construction.

1/2-inch pieces. Label the chipboard pieces as shown in the illustration.

Take squares A and B and attach the 22 1/2- and the 18 1/2-inch strips as shown in the illustration. Indent all the strips 3/4 inch from the edge of the chipboard. Take squares C and D and attach the 20-inch strips as shown. Indent the long edge of the strips 3/4 inch from the edge of the chipboard and indent the short edge of the strips 2 inches from the edge. Use wood screws to secure the strips to the chipboard. You can apply a bead of white glue to the strips and chipboard for extra strength.

Assemble the cube by fitting the squares together. Use screws driven from the chipboard of C and D into the strips of A and B. Fit the plain chipboard sides (E and F) to the cube by laying them in place

on the strips and driving screws into the strips of A through D. Use white glue on the joints for extra strength.

Finish the cube by applying a dark penetrating stain to the chipboard and then three coats of urethane varnish, or by priming the raw chipboard with a latex-based primer and then applying one or two coats of enamel paint.

In brief

1. To make a platform, cut 2 × 4s into nine pieces and 3/4-inch plywood into five pieces.

2. Screw the frame pieces to the plywood pieces. Assemble the frame by using white glue and driving nails at each corner. Install a 2 × 4 brace in the center of the frame.

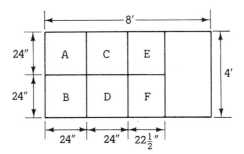

Cut Chipboard into Six Pieces

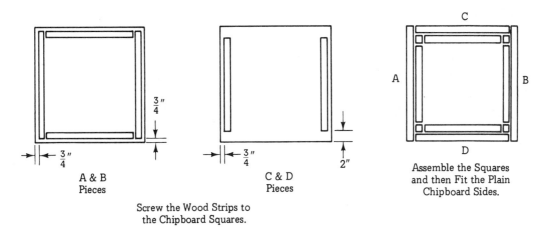

Screw the Wood Strips to
the Chipboard Squares.

FIGURE 6-10. How to make a cube.

3. Attach the plywood top to the frame with nails and white glue.

4. To make a riser, purchase twelve lengths of pipe, twelve caps, and twelve flanges.

5. Screw the flanges to the underside of a 4 × 8 piece of 1-inch plywood. Screw the pipes to the flanges and the caps to the pipes.

6. To make a cube, cut 2 × 4s into 2 × 2s. Cut the 2 × 2s into mounting strips. Cut a 4 × 8-foot sheet of 3/4-inch chipboard into six squares.

7. Install the strips on the squares to provide a frame for the cube. Use screws and white glue to secure the strips.

8. Assemble the cube with screws and white glue. Install the chipboard squares to the open sides of the cube.

9. Finish the cube by staining and varnishing or by priming and painting.

BUILT-IN STORAGE CLOSET

Tools and supplies needed

Circular saw
Level
Tape measure
Screwdriver
Drill and bits
Hole drill
1 × 12 white pine
Aluminum clothes pole
Wood screws
3/4- or 1-inch chipboard
12 corner braces
4 magnetic catches
2 sash handles
6 butt hinges

Procedure

This is a design for a large storage closet for clothes, linens, and other household items. It is set up to accommodate lots of hanging clothes, but it could be adapted to other storage problems. You could eliminate the clothes poles and install more shelves to handle small household goods. The closet must be built up against a flat wall, and it must run floor to ceiling in order for the design to work. The height of your ceiling will dictate the height of the closet. The width of the closet is up to you—it can be any width up to 8 feet (the size of two 4-foot-wide pieces of chipboard, which you will use as doors).

Begin by measuring the height of your ceiling and cutting five pieces of 1 × 12 white pine to fit. The white pine should fit snugly when erected between floor and ceiling. For the side walls of the closet, take four of the white pine pieces and overlap them, two and two, so that you come up with two pieces 18 inches wide. Secure the pine with screws.

Stand the 18-inch pieces up between floor and ceiling as the two side pieces of the closet. Secure them to floor and ceiling with eight 6-inch corner braces, two at the top and bottom of each piece. Use a level to make sure that the pine pieces are installed straight and true as you secure them to the ceiling and floor with corner braces and screws. Position the pine pieces 4 inches away from the wall. This will bring the forward edge of the pine out from the wall 22 inches. Install the single center piece of pine. Attach it floor to ceiling with corner braces. It, too, is set out from the wall by 4 inches.

Take two lengths of white pine and cut them to the width of the closet. Cut these lengths into four strips 5 5/8 inches wide. Install these strips at the top and bottom (front and back) of the closet to stiffen the frame. Use screws and corner braces to secure them to the upright pine pieces.

Now that you have the basic structure of the closet, you can divide it into storage space. One way is to install three aluminum tube clothes poles in such a way as to provide hanging storage for long clothes and shorter clothes. See the illustration for a suggested set-up. Drill the uprights with an adjustable hole drill to accept the clothes poles. Place the poles 11 inches from the wall.

Above and below the clothes poles you can provide white pine shelving for other storage. Cut 1 × 1-inch strips from scrap pieces of white pine to use as supports for the shelves. Install the supports

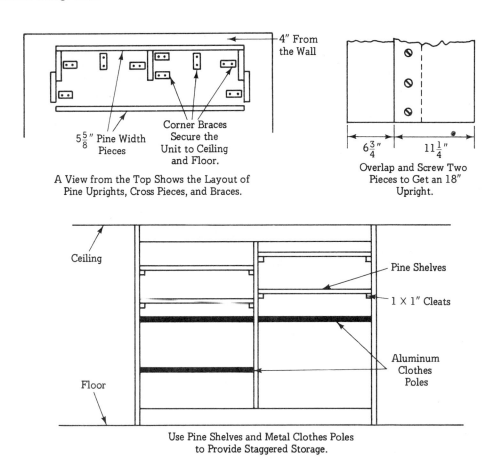

4" From the Wall

$5\frac{5}{8}$" Pine Width Pieces

Corner Braces Secure the Unit to Ceiling and Floor.

A View from the Top Shows the Layout of Pine Uprights, Cross Pieces, and Braces.

$6\frac{3}{4}$" $11\frac{1}{4}$"

Overlap and Screw Two Pieces to Get an 18" Upright.

Ceiling

Pine Shelves

1 × 1" Cleats

Aluminum Clothes Poles

Floor

Use Pine Shelves and Metal Clothes Poles to Provide Staggered Storage.

FIGURE 6-11. Aspects of storage closet construction.

with screws to the pine uprights. Measure and cut lengths of 1 × 12 to fit between the side and center pieces, and secure them to the supports with screws.

To install doors, measure the height of the closet opening from the top of the bottom bracing strip to the bottom of the top bracing strip. Trim 4 × 8-foot sheets of 3/4- or 1-inch chipboard to fit this space. Measure the width of the closet opening and trim the chipboard with a circular saw.

Install three hinges to each chipboard door. Because of the weight of the chip-

board, you will have to secure the hinges with short stove or machine bolts rather than screws. Drill holes through the chipboard to match the holes on the hinge leaf. Put bolts through the holes and secure them to the backside of the chipboard with washers and nuts. Use a hack saw to cut the bolts flush with their nuts.

Place the chipboard doors in the closet frame and attach them to the two end pine uprights with screws. (Use 2 1/2-inch screws and drill deep pilot holes in the pine to prevent splitting.) Finish the doors by installing magnetic catches at the top and bottom of each door half and putting a metal sash handle on each door.

The closet can be painted or varnished with urethane. Perhaps the best combination is to use urethane for the pine uprights and then prime and paint the chipboard doors. The doors can be stenciled with a large design, or an opaque projector or slide projector can be used to project a design onto the doors to be traced and then painted.

In brief

1. Measure the ceiling height and cut five pieces of pine to fit. Overlap four pieces to make two pieces 18 inches wide. Secure the overlaps with screws.

2. Secure the side pieces to floor and ceiling with corner braces. Place the rear edges of the uprights 4 inches away from the wall. Install the single center piece with corner braces as well.

3. Install four strips of pine as top and bottom braces for the closet. Use screws and corner braces to secure them.

4. Divide the closet with clothes poles and pine shelving. Drill the uprights to accept the poles, and install pine strip supports for the shelves.

5. Trim sheets of chipboard to fit the closet opening. Install three hinges on each chipboard door. Use stove bolts to attach the hinges to the chipboard.

6. Attach the hinges to the closet with 2 1/2-inch screws. Finish the doors with magnetic catches, top and bottom, and install sash handles on each door.

Tips

Additional security can be provided for the closet by using corner braces to attach the top bracing strips to the ceiling. This can be a way for you to catch the joists below the plaster that may not occur at the right places for you to use them as supports for the uprights. Use a magnetic stud finder to locate all of the joists that occur along the length of the top braces. Install 2 1/2- or 3-inch corner braces at these points to secure the pine braces and provide extra stability for the closet as a whole.

An alternative method of securing the aluminum clothes poles in the closet is to use 2 × 4 or 2 × 3 mounting blocks. Set your hole drill to the diameter of the clothes pole and drill holes in six 4-inch lengths of lumber. Place the drilled lumber pieces on the ends of the clothes poles, place the poles in between the pine uprights, and drill and screw the lumber pieces to secure them.

PVC FURNITURE ————————————

Tools and supplies needed

Hand saw or hack saw
Tape measure
Miter box
Level
PVC pipe and fittings
PVC solvent cement
Masking tape
Sandpaper

Procedure

One of the most interesting materials for use in building furniture is polyvinyl chloride (PVC) pipe and fittings. This plastic plumbing material is used for fresh water supply and for drain, waste, and vent purposes. The pipe is fairly rigid, and when used with the standard angle fittings it can be made into strong and durable furniture frames. Commercial furniture companies make PVC pipe furniture, and some models can be found at your local retail store (a great place to check the design and construction of a piece that you might want to construct on your own). Pipe furniture is ideally suited for outdoor use since plastic doesn't rot, rust, need painting, or otherwise deteriorate in the elements. The honest and clean looks of PVC pipe can also be adapted to certain pieces that you might want to use inside your house. Because it's an industrial material complete with plumbing code markings and embossed trademarks and brand names, it fits in perfectly with interiors that use other raw building materials such as flue tiles, steel ducts, or unfinished lumber.

The pipe and fittings are best bought at a professional plumbing supply house. Plastic pipe is sized by its outside diameter (OD). Common sizes are 1/2, 3/4, 1, 1 1/2, 2, 3, 3 1/2, and 4 inches. The common colors for the pipe and fittings are white, cream (or tan), and gray. Since PVC can't be painted you will want to specify the color you want, and you should make sure that the supplier gives you matching color fittings.

The pipe and fittings are put together with PVC solvent cement. This product actually melts the PVC a bit and then bonds it. A joint made with cement will be permanent. Some pipe furniture builders simply let friction hold the joints together so that the piece can be disassembled for moving or storage. This can work well for simple nonstressed

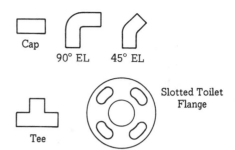

FIGURE 6-12. Common PVC fittings.

items such as small table bases. You can also make semi-permanent joints by drilling pilot holes in the PVC joints and driving screws. Use self-tapping sheet metal screws to fasten the joints.

A very simple project that can be constructed with PVC is a table pedestal. This pedestal would be suitable for mounting a medium sized (about 36 inches) round or square wood table top. The project uses a single length of 4-inch (OD) PVC drain pipe and two toilet flanges.

Decide on the height of the table (30 inches is about right) and cut a length of 4-inch PVC drain pipe to that dimension. Use a crosscut hand saw and a miter box to make an accurate cut. If you don't have a miter box, wrap a piece of masking tape around the pipe at the cut line to serve as a guide for your saw so that you make a straight cut.

Clean the cut end of the PVC with a piece of sandpaper, removing the burrs and crumbs of plastic left by the saw blade. Rough up both ends of the pipe with the sandpaper so that they will be ready to be cemented to the toilet fittings. The sandpaper removes the plastic glaze from the pipe and prepares it for a good bond.

Bring one of the toilet flanges close to the pipe. Wipe PVC cement onto one end of the pipe. Use the applicator on the cap of the cement to apply an even coat of cement to the end of the pipe. Immediately insert the pipe into the flange. Drive the pipe as far down as it will go into the fitting and twist the pipe one-eighth turn. Set the fitting down on a level surface and check with a level to make sure that the pipe is seated squarely in the fitting. Hold the pipe square for a minute or two while the cement sets.

Repeat the process for the other end of the pipe. Coat the pipe end with ce-

ment, insert it into the fitting, seat the pipe, then check for squareness and allow the cement to set. After both fittings have been secured to the pipe, let the assembly sit undisturbed for 2 to 4 hours for the cement to harden fully.

When the pedestal is cured, screw or bolt a table top to one of the flanges. The flanges have holes and slots cut in them that you can use to secure the table top. Suitable tops would be a circle of 3/4-inch plywood or chipboard (cut with a sabre saw) or a square of wood that you

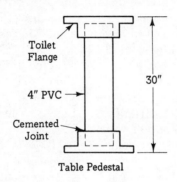

Table Pedestal

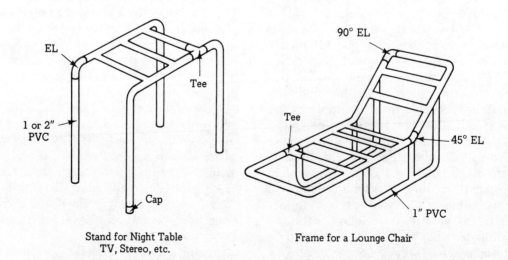

Stand for Night Table
TV, Stereo, etc.

Frame for a Lounge Chair

FIGURE 6-13. Furniture that can be made from PVC fittings.

have constructed from 3/4-inch-thick pieces.

For additional stability, you can screw a circle of plywood to the lower flange to act as a flat base for the table. The lower flange could also be bolted directly to a secure surface (patio, wood deck, etc.) for a permanent mount. One other option for additional stability would be to weight the lower half of the table base. Before installing the table top, pour gravel mix concrete into the PVC pipe until it comes one-third to one-half the way up the pipe. Let the concrete harden into place and you have a table pedestal that resists tipping. You would have to provide some method for securing the concrete in the tube— perhaps installing one or two stove bolts through the PVC pipe to hold the mass of hardened concrete.

In brief

1. Cut a length of PVC to the length you need. Use a miter box or piece of masking tape to guide your cut.
2. Clean the cut end with a piece of sandpaper. Use the sandpaper to rough up the ends of the pipe that will go into the fittings.
3. Wipe PVC cement onto the end of the pipe. Insert the pipe into the fitting, drive it down, twist one-eighth turn, and check to make sure that the pipe is square in the fitting.
4. Repeat the procedure for the other end of the pipe. Let the assembly cure for 2 to 4 hours.
5. Screw or bolt a round or square table top to one of the flanges. For additional stability you can attach a small circle of wood to the lower flange, attach the flange directly to a floor, or weight the base with concrete.

Tips

If you don't like the colored printing that is painted on the side of the PVC pipe, you can remove it with solvent. Try acetone (nail polish remover), or liquid carburetor cleaner (from auto stores). Put a bit of solvent on a rag, wipe it over the printing, and take the softened printing off with a clean rag.

To cut accurate circles in plywood or any other material that you might use for a table top, use a 4-inch nail, a length of string, and a pencil. Cut the string to half the diameter of the intended circle. Tie a small loop in each end of the string. Place the nail in one loop and the pencil in the other. Place the nail in the center of the stock and hold it there. The pencil will now describe a perfect circle around the nail as you move it over the stock, keeping the string taut at all times.

Your imagination and observation will give you plenty of ideas for PVC furniture that you can make. It is ideal for making stands for electronic equipment or for creating frames for glass-topped tables or shelves. One of the great things about PVC is that you can custom make a frame to fit some piece you have found that you might not otherwise be able to use. If you find an odd set of cushions, a slab of metal or glass or marble, or a nice piece of wood, you can design a PVC support system for it.

FURNITURE FROM UNEXPECTED SOURCES

Tools and supplies needed

Pressure-treated 2 × 4 lumber
Decorative concrete blocks

2 1/2-inch galvanized roofing nails
Epoxy auto body filler
Circular saw
Hammer
Tape measure

Procedure

You have to stay constantly aware of opportunities for constructing furniture from inexpensive and easily available products and supplies. Decorative concrete blocks from a masonry supply store can be the basis for attractive and durable outside furniture. These blocks are generally 1 foot square and come in a variety of geometric patterns.

Select pressure-treated 2 × 4-inch lumber to combine with the blocks because it will stand up to weather and moisture. Pressure-treated lumber usually has a greenish tint to it, but be sure to check for a stamp on the lumber that says pressure-treated to make sure that you're getting true outdoor lumber.

Bench. To make a bench, first cut two 8-foot 2 × 4s into four 4-foot-long pieces. Cut another length of 2 × 4 into two 13-inch pieces. Lay the 4-foot-long pieces down on a smooth surface. Butt the pieces closely together and square the ends. Lay the two 13-inch pieces over the others as shown in the illustration. Nail

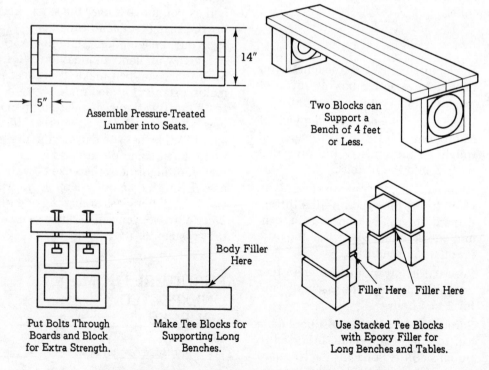

14"

5"

Assemble Pressure-Treated Lumber into Seats.

Two Blocks can Support a Bench of 4 feet or Less.

Put Bolts Through Boards and Block for Extra Strength.

Body Filler Here

Make Tee Blocks for Supporting Long Benches.

Filler Here   Filler Here

Use Stacked Tee Blocks with Epoxy Filler for Long Benches and Tables.

FIGURE 6-14.   How to make a block bench.

the boards together with 2 1/2-inch galvanized nails.

Arrange two decorative blocks about 36 inches apart. Place the bench seat down across the blocks. Test the seat, and if it's secure enough as it is you have your bench. If the seat is not secure enough you can bond the lumber to the blocks by using epoxy body filler from the auto supply store. Lay a bead of filler on the top surface of the blocks. Press the wooden seat on to the filler and apply pressure for 1/2 hour using a trash can full of water or some more concrete blocks.

A more secure bond can be made between the blocks and the boards by drilling holes in both materials (using regular and masonry bits) and installing carriage bolts through them. Use a hack saw to cut the bolts down so that they don't spoil the design of the blocks.

Table. A table can be constructed of blocks and boards in a similar manner. This time arrange four blocks into two T formations about 36 inches apart. Use epoxy putty to secure the blocks to each other. Apply putty to the top surfaces of the first T formations and place a second set of four blocks directly on top of this.

Secure the second set of Ts with putty. This gives you two 24-inch block pedestals. While the putty cures, work on the lumber table top.

Construct the top as you did for the bench, but cut eight 4-foot lengths of 2 × 4. Cut two 27-inch cross pieces. Lay the lumber down and fasten it with galvanized nails. When the top is complete lay it on the block pedestals.

If the table is secure enough without any extra bond, fine. If not, use body putty or carriage bolts to give it extra stability.

In brief

1. Use pressure-treated 2 × 4s and foot-square decorative blocks. Cut 2 × 4s into 4-foot pieces and two cross pieces. Lay the boards down on an even surface and secure them with nails.

2. Lay the top on the block pedestals. Use epoxy or bolts to give extra stability if needed.

3. When building tall block pedestals, use epoxy to secure blocks in T shapes and to secure one set of blocks on top of another.

7

WALLS

WALL-HUNG SIDE BOARDS

Tools and supplies needed

Circular saw
Hammer
Tape measure
Hack saw
Level
Drill and bits
Stud finder
½-inch wood dowel
White glue
8- or 12-inch-wide stair tread
Wood screws
1 × 2-inch smooth furring strips

Procedure

Here are two designs for shelf sideboards that you mount to the wall for use as storage, display, and utility space. If the shelf is mounted in a dining room or living room, it can function as a serving sideboard. If the sideboard is mounted in a hall or foyer, it can be a place to put items such as letters, keys, or handbags. These shelves can replace bulky chests and cabinets that people often use for such purposes. The space below the shelves can be used as storage for small chairs, umbrellas, and other infrequently used items.

The designs use stair tread lumber. This is wood that is specially cut and milled to resist flexing. It is often of yellow pine, which has a dense and even grain that takes a nice finish if urethaned. The advantage to using stair tread as shelving is that it won't bend under heavy weight and generally won't warp. It has a rounded nosing milled into one edge of the board, which makes a pre-finished edge for the shelf.

Sideboard. One design uses a wall and two corners. Measure the distance between the two corners and cut a single length of stair tread to fit. Also cut 1 × 2-inch furring strips to fit the same space. Cut two more furring strips to the width of the stair tread minus 2 inches; for example, cut them to 10 inches if you are using 12-inch tread.

Decide on a height for the shelf (25 to 35 inches is recommended). Mark that height on the wall at several places. Use a level and a straightedge to draw a continuous line across the wall from corner to corner at the desired height. Place the level at each corner and draw short continuations of that line onto the two adjacent walls. Move a magnetic stud finder along the line and mark the places where studs occur.

Place the furring strips on the wall, putting their top edges even with the line. Mark the stud positions on the strips and drill and screw them to the wall. Place the long strip along the main wall and the two short strips on the adjacent walls. When the strips are in place, lay the cut length of stair tread onto the strip cleats you have created. The shelf should be secure without any further screws. If you want the shelf to be rock solid you can drive a few screws into the shelf and through to the cleats below.

This design is good for a long, continuous sideboard. You might want to mount it at one end of a dining room or living room. The cleats and walls give the shelf enough strength to take heavy dishes, sculptures, or stereo components.

Floating Shelf. Another design is not as strong, but it is useful for a relatively short shelf (18 to 36 inches) that you can mount to the wall without any visible support. Decide where the shelf is to be. Use a stud finder to determine where the hidden studs are, and mark them on the wall. You need at least two studs to be able to mount the unit.

When you've found the studs, decide how long the shelf is to be and cut a piece of stair tread. Mark the spacing of the studs onto the flush edge of the stair tread. Be sure to center the spacing of the studs along the length of stair tread so that the shelf will be balanced. If, for example, you have three studs 16 inches apart on a 36-inch shelf, you would place the marks at 2, 18, and 34 inches along the stair tread.

Drill holes 4 inches deep in the rear edge of the shelf. Start the holes exactly in the center of the stud marks and midway in the shelf's thickness. Use a ½-inch diameter drill bit with a ⅜-inch shank (available at a large hardware store or electrical supply store). Be sure to purchase a bit that has enough length to drill deeply.

Cut 8-inch lengths of ½-inch wood dowel with a hack saw. Cut one length for each stud along the shelf's length. Coat half the dowels' length with white glue and drive the dowels into the holes in the shelf with a hammer. Let the glue cure for 12 hours before installing the shelf in the wall.

When the shelf is ready to be installed, drill holes through the wall to the studs with the ½-inch drill bit. Place

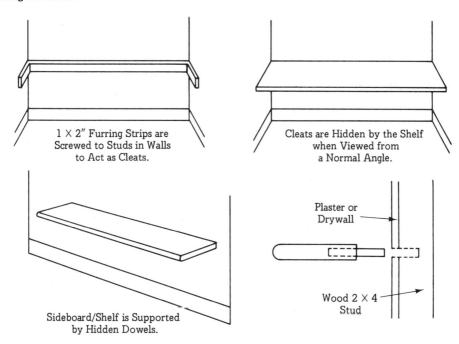

1 X 2" Furring Strips are Screwed to Studs in Walls to Act as Cleats.

Cleats are Hidden by the Shelf when Viewed from a Normal Angle.

Plaster or Drywall

Wood 2 X 4 Stud

Sideboard/Shelf is Supported by Hidden Dowels.

FIGURE 7-1. How to make sideboard shelves.

the holes so that they will mate with the dowels at the back of the shelf, using the dowels as a guide. Use a level to make sure that the drill marks are level to each other and the floor.

Coat the exposed dowels with white glue and drive the shelf into the wall. Use a hammer and a scrap block of wood or a rubber mallet to drive the shelf firmly against the wall without marring its front edge. Clean up any excess white glue with a damp cloth and allow the glue to cure for about 12 hours.

In brief

1. For a sideboard, cut a length of stair tread to fit the space between two walls. Cut furring strips to act as cleats for the shelf.

2. Mark a line using a straightedge and level across the wall and onto the two side walls. Use a stud finder to find and mark the position of all the studs along the line.

3. Place the strips on the wall and drill holes for screws to secure them to the studs. Secure the long strip along the main wall and the two short strips on the side walls. When the cleats are in place, lay the stair tread on them.

4. For a floating shelf, find all the studs in the general area of the wall. Mark at least two studs convenient to the shelf position.

5. Determine the length of the shelf and cut stair tread. Mark the spacing of the studs on the flush edge of the tread. Center the stud marks to balance the shelf.

6. Drill holes with a ½-inch drill bit to accept dowels. Cut 8-inch lengths of ½-inch dowel with a hack saw. Coat the dowels with glue and drive them into the shelf. Let the glue cure.

7. Mark and drill matching holes in the wall for the dowels. Use a level to make sure that the holes are straight and true to each other and the floor.

8. Coat the exposed dowels with glue and drive the shelf into the wall. Use a hammer or mallet to seat the shelf firmly in the wall. Allow the glue to cure before using the shelf.

Tips

Many people like the look of unfinished stair tread. If you do want to finish it, however, urethane varnish is the best method. Use two or three coats of gloss or satin urethane to give the shelf a low-maintenance finish.

BUILT-IN STORAGE UNIT

Tools and supplies needed

Circular saw
Drill and bits
Screwdriver
Tape measure
Stud finder
Level
1 × 12-inch white pine
1½-inch wood screws
4-inch corner braces

Procedure

One of the best ways to organize your possessions neatly is to build wall-mounted storage units. These can provide the organization and access you crave for books, records, tapes, electronic equipment, games, and other small household goods. By getting these items out of the living area and onto shelves, you create more room for furniture and you organize the items so that they can be quickly found.

The design here is a simple one utilizing 1 × 12-inch white pine uprights that run from floor to ceiling. The basic unit consists of two uprights 36 inches apart, with white pine shelves running between them. A single upright can be shared by two shelf ends when you construct a unit that runs over 36 inches long. The broad white pine gives you enough depth to store bulky objects such as stereos and TVs. The entire unit is very simply constructed of pine, screws, and corner braces.

Cut white pine into two uprights the exact distance from floor to ceiling. Cut two pieces of white pine the length of the intended unit, and cut these pieces in half to come up with four strips, 5⅝-inches wide.

Erect the upright pieces of pine, and use the 5⅝-inch strips to fasten the uprights into the proper position in relation to each other. Use strips at the top and bottom of the uprights and at the front and back of the unit. Fasten the strips with screws, or use corner braces to tie everything together. Use a level to check that everything is square and true. Once the strips and uprights have been attached, push the unit into position near the wall and any corners that you are using. Secure the unit to the floor and ceiling by using corner braces. Use a magnetic stud finder to locate and mark the stud positions on the ceiling so you can screw corner braces to them. Recheck everything with a level as you work to make sure that the unit is square.

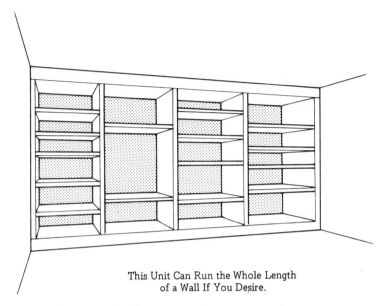

This Unit Can Run the Whole Length
of a Wall If You Desire.

FIGURE 7-2. A homemade storage unit.

When the unit is fastened securely to floor and ceiling, decide how many shelves are required and cut them from white pine with your circular saw. Install the shelves directly to the uprights with 1½-inch wood screws. Stagger the position of the shelves between the uprights so that you always have room to drive screws from the sides of the uprights. The shelves and screws will stabilize the uprights and firm the entire unit.

The unit can be left natural or finished with primer and enamel or a clear urethane varnish. Three coats of urethane will bring out the grain in the pine and will provide a durable, easily cleaned finish.

In brief

1. Cut uprights to the height of the ceiling. Cut two pieces of pine to the length of the unit. Cut these pieces in half to come up with four 5⅝-inch wide pieces.

2. Erect the uprights and fasten them together with the pine strips. Use screws or corner braces to tie the lumber together. Use a level to check for straightness while securing.

3. Push the unit flush to the wall and to any corners you are using. Secure the unit to the ceiling and floor with corner braces. Use a stud finder to position the ceiling corner braces. Use a level while working to ensure that everything is true.

4. Cut shelves to fit between the uprights. Secure them by driving screws from the sides of the uprights. Stagger the position of the shelves to give yourself room to drill and fasten.

5. Finish the unit with urethane or enamel, or leave it unfinished.

Tips

The unit can be constructed to any length required. The maximum distance between uprights should be 36 inches (the longest distance that white pine should be asked to bridge). Just keep adding uprights at regular intervals to go across the entire wall if desired.

Don't be tempted to attach the strips to the uprights before the uprights are erected—once the strips are in place you won't be able to tilt the unit to a vertical position because there won't be enough head room. Use a ladder and a helper while you fasten the strips to the upright pieces.

HANGING SYSTEMS FOR ART ————————————

Tools and supplies needed

Hand saw or hack saw
Tape measure
Hammer
Drill and bits
Level
Stud finder
Utility knife
1 × 2-inch smooth furring strips
Glass
Cardboard
Roofing nails
Finishing nails
Screw eyes and hooks
Monofilament fishing line
Wood picture molding
Metal molding hooks
Plastic mirror hangers

Procedure

There are many different systems for hanging paintings, graphics, photos, fabrics, and other flat objects. The four meth-

ods described here are good ones from the standpoint of flexibility, economy, and ease of installation. There are many variations to the ideas behind these projects, but the procedures described here will get you started, and you can adapt from there.

Banner-style Hanging. Often you will want to hang a colorful fabric or weaving from the wall as an art object. You can hang it very simply as a banner. Take the top 5 inches of the piece and double it over to form a 2½-inch channel at the top of the piece. Sew a continuous seam to close the channel edges. (You might be able to use a hot glue gun to secure the channel if the fabric has a tight weave.) Cut a smooth furring strip 4 inches longer than the width of the fabric. Insert the strip into the channel and center the ends of the strip. Drill a hole in the center of each strip end or drill and drive a 1-inch screw eye into each strip end. Tie one end of a length of clear fishing line (40 to 60 pound test) to each hole or screw eye, and the piece is ready to be hung banner-style from a nail or peg in the wall.

Fastening a Hanging to the Wall. If you are working with a bigger, heavier piece of weaving you might want to fasten it to the wall so that it doesn't sway or get knocked around. You can also secure the material to a furring strip so that the fabric doesn't pucker or gather unattractively.

Take a long furring strip and cut it to the length of the top edge of the piece. Lay the strip down and arrange the top edge of the piece along the strip, placing it even with the top edge of the strip. Drive a series of ½-inch galvanized roofing nails (so the fabric doesn't get rust stains) into the fabric and through to the furring strip. Stretch the fabric taut between the nails so that it lies smooth.

Mark the places on the wall where the studs are. Draw a line across the wall where you want the strip to be and use a level to make sure that it's straight. Mark the stud locations on the top edge of the strip. Drill holes and drive 1-inch screw hooks into the strip. Drill holes and drive 2-inch screws into the wall and through to the studs. Let ½ inch of screw stick out of the wall. Take the strip and hanging and secure it to the wall by placing the hooks over the screws. Tighten the screws, if necessary, when the hanging is in place.

Picture Molding System. Another good system for hanging art, especially framed photos, paintings, and graphics is to use a picture molding. A molding system allows you to change pictures and positions very easily without marring the walls or finish of the room. Picture moldings are often used in galleries so that new exhibits can be installed efficiently. If you like to rotate and change your wall art, or if you want to hang things without nails or screws, it's worth the effort to install molding.

For maximum flexibility, install molding around the entire perimeter of the room. With your tape measure calculate the running footage along all the walls of the room. Go to a large lumber store and ask to be shown a catalog or sample board of moldings. A good picture molding will have a deep groove or carved space that will accept a metal hook. Purchase enough molding for your room and install it with finishing nails. Buy nails long enough to penetrate the molding and plaster and go at least 1 inch into the wood studs.

The best place for the molding is about 1 foot below the ceiling. Use a stud finder and pencil to mark the location of the studs below the surface. For long runs of wall, once you have established the spacing of the studs, it will usually hold true for the whole wall, so you can use your tape measure to mark studs. When the wall has been marked for studs, drive finishing nails to secure the pieces of molding. Butt pieces of molding to make long, straight runs. Use a miter box or free-hand hack saw cuts to make neat 45-degree angles for fitting molding to the corners of the room.

When the molding is installed, you can leave it natural or you can paint it to match or contrast with the walls of the room. Art is hung by taking a length of monofilament fishing line and attaching it to a steel molding hook. The hook is attached to the molding at the location where the picture is to be placed. The line is cut at the length necessary to hang the picture at a desired height. The line is tied to another steel hook, and that hook supports the art by holding the frame's edge or the hanging wire on the backside of the frame.

"Sandwich" Systems. Yet another method of securing flat art to a wall is to make a glass and cardboard "sandwich" and secure that to a wall with inexpensive mirror hangers. The method requires you to drill and screw to the wall, so it is not a very flexible method of display. (You would have to remove the sandwich, plaster the holes, and drill new holes to move the art elsewhere.) However, the method does provide an inexpensive way to eliminate a frame, mat board, picture wire, screw eyes, and all the other trappings of conventional art display.

Use the sandwich only for flat work such as photos, posters, graphics, or prints. Do not use this method for very expensive art, since the edges of the art are unprotected and the acids in the common cardboard backing can attack fine art and cause it to disintegrate. The sandwich is for fun art such as inexpensive silkscreen prints, mass-produced posters, or photographic reproductions.

Begin by obtaining a quantity of corrugated cardboard. If you are working with small pieces of art you can use flat pieces from liquor boxes, grocery boxes, and so forth. For larger, poster-sized pieces you will have to go to an appliance or furniture store and ask for the boxes that couches, chairs, and refrigerators are shipped in. These large boxes are free for the asking, and with a utility knife you can quickly cut the panels free and come up with enough flat cardboard to sandwich 10 or 12 large posters.

Buy one package of mirror hangers for each piece to be displayed. They are available in variety stores. The hangers are sold complete with screws and plastic anchor shields (for hollow walls). Most pieces can be hung with four hangers; six might be needed for very large pieces to keep the sandwich tight to the wall.

Measure the exact dimensions of the art you want to display. Go to a glass store and have a sheet of single-strength glass cut to those dimensions. Be sure to tell the cutter that you need a piece in those exact measurements—often cutters will intentionally undersize a piece of glass by fractions of an inch to make fitting it to a window frame easier.

Take the cut piece of glass and lay it on a piece of cardboard. Using the edges of the glass as a guide, cut the cardboard with a utility knife to the exact outline of the glass. When the cardboard is cut, remove the glass and clean it thoroughly with window cleaner and a lint-free cloth. Set the glass aside until you are ready to hang the art.

Take the cut cardboard and place it on the wall to find the proper position for the art. Use a level to make sure that the cardboard is level to the floor and square to the walls. Hold the cardboard in position and place a mirror hanger at the bottom edge of the cardboard about 1 inch in from its corner. Use a pencil through the hole in the hanger to mark the wall. Move the hanger to the other corner of the cardboard and mark the wall. Now place the hanger at the top left hand corner of the cardboard and mark the wall. Move the hanger to the top right hand corner and mark the wall there as well.

Remove the cardboard from the wall and use a drill to make holes in the wall for the hanger screws. Use a bit large enough to accommodate the plastic anchor shields that come with the hangers and screws. Insert the shields in the holes and loosely attach the hangers to the wall with screws.

Place the art between the cardboard and the glass sheet. Carefully square all the edges. Carry the sandwich to the wall and place the unit into the mirror hangers. When the unit is in place, tighten the screws to the wall to draw the hangers up to the sandwich.

In brief

1. To hang fabrics, sew or glue a channel across the top of the piece, insert a piece of furring strip, attach a length of clear line, and hang from a nail or peg.

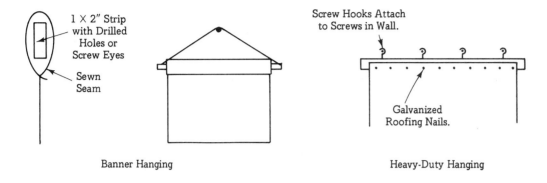

Banner Hanging

Heavy-Duty Hanging

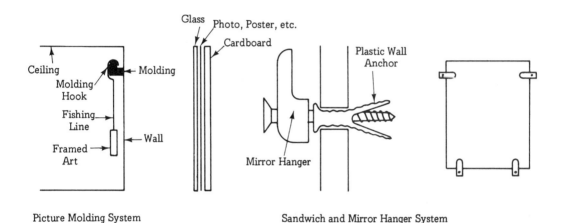

Picture Molding System

Sandwich and Mirror Hanger System

FIGURE 7-3. Various ways to hang art.

2. For larger, heavier fabrics, secure the top edge of the piece to a furring strip with roofing nails. Hang the strip from screws driven into the wall by installing screw hooks to the top of the strip.

3. A continuous picture molding gives ultimate flexibility. Install it with finishing nails. Hang the art by using a metal hook on the molding, a length of clear line from that, and a hook at the back of the art piece.

4. Flat, inexpensive art can be sandwiched between cardboard and glass. Purchase mirror hangers and glass cut to size. Use cardboard from grocery or furniture boxes.

5. Cut the cardboard using the glass as a guide. Position it on the wall and mark the places for hangers. Drill holes and loosely install the hangers.

6. Sandwich the art and place it in the hangers. Tighten the hangers to the wall with a screwdriver.

RECYCLING FRAMES ————

Tools and supplies needed

Miter box
Back saw
Hack saw
Drill and bits
Razor blades
Wire brush
Putty knife
Hammer
Flat corner braces
Glue (white or epoxy)
⅛-inch-thick hardboard
Screw eyes
Picture framing wire
Mat board
Spray art-mounting adhesive
1-inch brads

Procedure

There are plenty of old picture frames to be found in junk shops, flea markets, and attics. Many of them have handsome and detailed carving or molding. Still other frames are damaged but can be restored by cutting down, reinforcing, or stripping until only the basic structure shows.

Another rich area is using old window frames, glass cabinet doors, and damaged mirrors as picture frames. It requires a creative eye and some unusual techniques to recycle these materials into frames for art work, but some great effects can be achieved and the price is right.

One of the easiest methods of recycling inexpensive junk shop plaster frames is to remove the damaged plaster ornament from the basic structure of the frame. You can take the plaster off by chipping it with a hammer, screwdriver, putty knife, and wire brush. You can also soak the frame in a tub of water to loosen the plaster from the wood. The wood will swell and break the seal it has with the plaster, and you should be able to peel the ornament off by hand.

By taking off the damaged and sometimes gaudy plaster, you have revealed the simple lines of the base wood. If you sand and finish the wood with stain, paint, or urethane, you have a nice frame from a junk shop throwaway. If necessary, reinforce the frame corners by installing flat mending plates on the backside of the frame, and reglue the joints with epoxy or white glue.

If you like the ornament on an old frame that is damaged at the corners (the most common site for damage), you can often recycle the frame by cutting off the damage in a miter box and rejoining the corners of the frame. Disassemble the frame, lay the damaged pieces in a miter box, and cut new 45-degree angles with a back saw. The frame you reassemble with glue and corner braces will be shorter and thinner than the original, but it can still be serviceable.

Another option is to use old mirrors and their frames. Often you can find beautiful beveled glass mirrors that have damaged silvering. These mirrors can be used as picture frames by simply scraping off the silvering with a single-edged razor blade. When the glass is clean, you can sandwich flat art between the glass and a cardboard or hardboard backing. Use 1-inch brads driven into the backside of the frame to secure the sandwich.

You can also use glass cabinet doors, common window frames, and just about any glass and wood frame that you come across. Using chemical paint stripper to take old paint and varnish from these frames often reveals beautiful wood and interesting details that will complement whatever you mount within the piece.

Regardless of where you find frames and how you recycle them, you will have to mount your art securely to ⅛-inch hardboard backing before installing it in the frame. The easiest way is to use a spray adhesive available at art supply stores. The product is often called *art-mounting adhesive.* Spray the product on the smooth side of the backing, let it dry until it becomes tacky, and then position the art on the backing and press it into place. Be sure to position the art accu-

rately from the start because the spray adhesive is very strong and won't let you do much shifting after you have touched it with the art.

Mat Board. Sometimes you have a piece of art that is too small to fill the entire frame you wish to use. In this case you can use mat board to take up the slack space between the edges of the art and the frame. Mat board is available at art stores in a variety of colors and textures. Select a board that will provide a smooth visual transition from the frame to the art.

Mat board is cut with a utility knife, razor blade, or hobby knife. Draw reference marks for the cut-out that you will

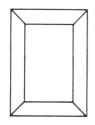

Strip Damaged
Plaster Ornament
to Reveal Simple Lines.

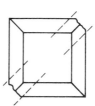

Cut Damaged Corners
in a Miter Box
and Rejoin the Frame.

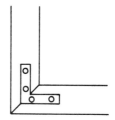

Use Glue and Metal Corner Braces
to Reinforce Corners.

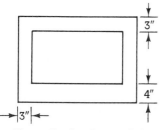

Always Cut the Mat Board More
Generously at the Bottom to
Give the Illusion of Stability
to the Art.

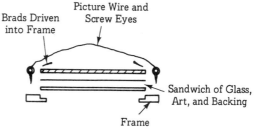

If a Mat is Used, it Should be
Placed Between the Glass
and the Art.

FIGURE 7-4. How to work with old frames.

make on the backside of the mat board. As a general guide, the side and top edges of the mat should never be less than 2½ inches wide and the bottom edge of the mat should never be less than 3 inches wide. The bottom edge of the mat is always cut more generously than the sides and top because our eyes require this optical illusion to give stability to the art work. When you are ready to cut, lay a straightedge across the reference marks and cut the board with a sharp razor blade tool.

The cut mat is installed in the sandwich between the art and the glass sheet. It not only proportions and sizes the art to the frame, but it performs a practical preservation function by keeping the art from touching the glass. Finish any recycling job on a frame by installing two screw eyes in the backside of the frame and attaching a length of picture wire to them. The wire should have only enough slack in it to allow you to hang the frame—not so much that the frame sags forward from the wall.

In brief

1. Recycle damaged plaster frames by removing the plaster entirely or by cutting damaged corners off in a miter box. Reassemble the frames with glue and corner braces.

2. Recycle damaged mirrors by scraping the silvering off with a razor blade. Sandwich the art and backing against the clean glass and drive brads into the frame to secure it.

3. Use other glass and wood frames that you come across in the same way as conventional frames. Use stripper and urethane to bring out the natural details in these unorthodox frames.

4. Use ⅛-inch hardboard as a backing for art, and mount the art to the backing with spray adhesive. Spray, let dry until tacky, then carefully place and press the art onto the backing.

5. Use mat board to proportion art to an oversize frame. Cut the mat from the rear with a straightedge and sharp razor tool. Always cut the bottom edge of the mat more generously than the sides and top to create the illusion of stability for the art.

6. Finish the job by installing two screw eyes in the frame and attaching a length of picture wire.

FRAMELESS PICTURE HANGING

Tools and supplies needed

Circular saw
Straightedge
Tape measure
Glass cutter
Goggles and gloves
⅛-inch-thick hardboard
Single-strength glass sheets
Light oil or kerosene
Art supply corner clip system

Procedure

Art supply stores carry a number of inexpensive and effective systems for framing and hanging flat art. Most of the systems use plastic or stainless steel clips or brackets that hold a sandwich of glass, art, and rigid backing. Any one of these systems will work nicely, and which one you select is up to you. These clip systems require more money and material than the mirror hanger system described earlier. However, you have greater flexibility in positioning and moving art work with commercial corner clip products.

To prepare for using one of the clip systems, you have to provide a secure backing for the art and glass. Art stores sell a rigid but lightweight product called *foam core board*. This product, which cuts with a utility knife or razor blade, is a sandwich of thick paper over plastic foam. Foam core is a good choice for backing small projects, but the product is expensive for use with poster-size art work. A good, inexpensive substitute for foam core is common ⅛-inch hardboard.

Buy 4 × 8-foot sheets of tempered hardboard at the lumber store. Use a tempered product because it will resist moisture in the atmosphere better than an untempered board and will be less likely to warp. Use a plywood-cutting or fine-toothed crosscut blade in your circular saw to cut hardboard accurately.

Cut the hardboard to the exact dimensions of the art piece you want to sandwich. Cut single-strength glass to the same dimensions. To cut glass, lay the sheet on a smooth and secure surface. Make measurement marks on the edge of the sheet with a felt tip marker. Lay a wooden straightedge between the marks as a guide for the glass cutter.

Dip the wheel of your glass cutter in light oil or kerosene to lubricate it. Draw the cutter lightly down the straightedge to score a line in the glass from edge to edge. The cutter should make a sound like tearing tissue paper when you use the proper pressure. Use a uniform pressure to make the score line, and draw the cutter only once down the glass. Going over and over the line with the cutter makes a rough line that will cause the glass to break unevenly.

Remove the straightedge and bring the score line to the edge of your work surface. Use the ball on the end of the glass cutter to tap a starting crack in the glass. Tap the ball firmly on the underside of the glass, directly on the score line, until you see a small fault formed in the glass under the score line. Grip the waste piece of glass and press it down gently to accomplish the break. The glass

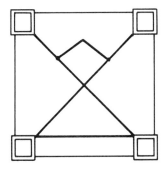

Plastic Corner Clips with
Nylon Tension Cords

Metal Wire Clips with
Fishing Line Tensioners

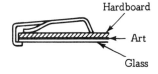

Steel Clips that Grip
the Backing Board
to Secure the Sandwich

FIGURE 7-5. Commercial clip systems for "frameless framing."

should break evenly along the score line starting from the small fault you created with tapping.

Clean the cut piece of glass with lint-free cloth and commercial window cleaner. Lay the art down on the smooth side of the hardboard, place the glass on top of the art, and then apply the corner clip system you purchased from the art supply store.

In brief

1. Cut a piece of hardboard with a circular saw to the dimensions of the art.
2. Cut single-strength glass to the same dimensions. Lubricate the glass cutter with oil or kerosene. Lightly draw it down the glass to score a thin, smooth line. Move the line to the edge of the work surface. Tap the underside of the line with the ball of the cutter to start a crack. Press down on the waste piece of glass to complete the cut.
3. Lay the art down on the smooth side of the hardboard and cover the art with the cut glass. Apply the corner clip system to secure the sandwich.

ADAPTING PRINTED MATERIALS FOR WALL COVERING

Tools and supplies needed

Plastic bucket
Paste brush (3 to 6 inches wide)
Utility knife
Scissors
Single-edged razor blades
Paint brush
Paint roller and handle
Roller pan
Household sponge
Wallpaper smoothing brush (12 inches wide)
Dry or prepared wallpaper paste
Polyurethane varnish

Procedure

The standard wall coverings are paint, texture paint, wallpaper, wood paneling, tile, plastic laminates, and various printed vinyl products. Some adventurous decorators use fabrics and natural materials such as grass matting, bamboo, and cork in an attempt to escape the ordinary. One inexpensive way to achieve an unusual effect for a wall is to cover it with printed material from another time and place. You can paper your wall with old sheet music, magazine photographs and illustrations, foreign newspapers, or movie posters. Practically anything that appeals to you and is flat enough to paste to a wall can be used.

The technique is perfect for one wall in a large room or for several small walls, perhaps in a hallway or foyer. You want the wall to be a large piece of art—a homemade mural that you create by selecting the material that goes into it.

For printed material you need at least three times the square footage of the wall you intend to cover. You are going to be applying the sheets of material in layers with considerable overlapping, so you need enough to make two to three layers plus what will be wasted at the edges of the wall. Collect your material from flea markets, paper drive and recycling centers, libraries, used book and magazine stores, and the classified ad publications.

Buy wallpaper paste (dry or prepared), a wide brush for applying the paste, and an even wider brush for smoothing the pasted sheets to the wall and eliminating bubbles and lumps from the covering. You are going to seal the wall with urethane varnish, so you should buy enough gloss or satin urethane for two or three coats over the entire wall.

When you are ready to begin, prepare a flat surface to paste and cut the sheets on. Spread newspapers or plastic sheeting on the surface to protect it from moisture and paste. Mix the paste or pour the prepared paste into a plastic bucket.

Lay a piece of sheet material face down on your work surface and apply a coat of paste to it with a brush. Coat the entire surface of the sheet. Pick the sheet up with your hands, carry it to the wall, and apply it. The sheets should be small enough for you to handle easily.

Start working from the center of the wall and work out to the edges. Apply the sheets any way that pleases you—sideways, upside down, or cockeyed. The idea is to overlap and lay up an interesting overall pattern. You aren't going for precision. Apply full sheets until you reach the edges of the wall. Then trim the sheets before pasting them, to finish the pattern to the edges.

The wall is built up of single sheets that you paste, apply, and then smooth out with a broad smoothing brush. Press the sheet to the wall so that the edges don't curl under. Then use a smoothing brush to stick the sheet to the wall and to drive out air bubbles and pockets. Work from the center of each sheet out to the edges. Don't be too concerned with wrinkles and imperfections. Since you are working with old and sometimes flimsy material, part of the charm of the finished wall will be the texture of the paper.

As a rule, overlap the sheets by about a third as you work. This should provide enough depth of paper to hide the original wall, and it will let you apply more interesting sections of material over less interesting ones—a picture over a long section of type, for example. Apply the sheets crazy-quilt style until you come to within a foot of the edges.

At the edges, test unpasted sheets to see how they could be trimmed with scissors to complete the design and match the corners. Cut the sheets and then apply paste, using the smoothing brush as usual to stick the sheets to the wall and remove trapped air. Precut sheets that have to fit around windows, switchplates, and other irregularities. Use a utility knife or single-edged razor blade to make final corrections to the paper when it is in place. Because the sheets are overlapped in a random pattern, it is easy to cut the paper to fit around objects. Simply cut the required shape in one edge of the paper and then apply it to the wall. You don't have to worry about matching seams or patterns exactly.

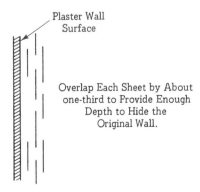

Plaster Wall
Surface

Overlap Each Sheet by About one-third to Provide Enough Depth to Hide the Original Wall.

FIGURE 7-6. A wallcovering technique.

When the wall has been covered, let it dry for 24 hours. Come back and seal the surface by applying urethane varnish. Pour urethane into a roller pan; install a clean, thick nap roller onto a handle; and coat the wall with varnish. You can install a mop handle on the roller handle to make it easier to roll urethane high on the wall. Use a 2-inch brush to urethane the edges and tight places on the wall.

The urethane will soak into the paper and darken it somewhat. Allow the first coat to dry for 12 hours and apply a second coat with a roller. Let the second coat dry for 24 hours and apply a third coat, if desired. Three coats are usually necessary to put a washable surface on the paper—one that you can wipe and scrub down with a cloth and a mild household cleaner.

In brief

1. Collect enough sheet material to cover the wall at least three times. Buy wallpaper paste, a paste brush, and a wide smoothing brush.
2. Prepare a flat working surface, protecting it with newspapers or plastic sheets. Lay a piece of sheet material face down on the work surface and apply paste to it with a brush.
3. Apply the sheet to the wall in any way that pleases you. Apply the smoothing brush to the sheet and work out any trapped air.
4. Start applying sheets from the center of the wall and work to the edges. Overlap sheets by about one-third.
5. When you reach the edges, cut sheets

before pasting them to complete the design and match the corners. Precut sheets to match windows, switches, and so forth.
6. Let the completed wall dry for 24 hours. Apply two or three coats of urethane to the wall with a roller to seal the surface and make it washable.

Tips

You can apply this treatment over old, firmly adhered wallpaper, but it is better to do it over a bare plaster wall or one that has only one or two coats of flat latex paint on it. The problem with old wallpaper is that it may come loose when fresh, wet paste is applied. Another problem is that the extra weight of the new sheets may cause the old paste to fail soon after the installation is completed.

The choice of paste is up to you, but you should avoid wheat paste formulations and use a synthetic-based product for maximum strength. Since the sheets you will be using will cost you little or nothing, it is worth it to buy the very best paste you can find. A vinyl-based liquid paste is a good choice, since it is premixed and can stand up to the extra weight caused by multiple layers and urethane varnish.

This method will also work on furniture, trunks, tables, doors, folding screens, and other large objects. Pasting curious and old printed material on a surface and then protecting it with multiple coats of urethane varnish is a good way to add interest and intrigue to a common or plain object at low cost.

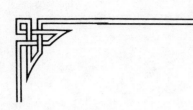

LIGHTING

REWIRING OLDER LAMPS AND FIXTURES

Tools and supplies needed

Knife
Needlenose pliers
Screwdriver
Lamp cord
Self-tapping electrical plug
Threaded lamp socket with switch

Procedure

Renewing the electrical components of old floor and table lamps is one of the easiest recycling jobs you can accomplish. The work is simple, the parts are cheap, and the results can be very satisfying. Old lamps that you find in junk stores, in attics and basements, and at flea markets are inexpensive but provide a nice touch in any decor. If you have an old house, they will fit right in with the architecture. If you have a newer house, old lamps will provide a touch of the antique to any area they occupy.

You should definitely rewire any old lamp that you come across, even ones that are working well. The electrical components in these old lamps are usually getting ready to fail. The cords are frayed, the insulation rotted and crumbling, and the sockets and switches unreliable. For safety and ease of operation you should invest a few minutes and a few dollars in new components to renew the heart of these lamps.

If the lamp needs to be refinished or painted, you should remove all the old electrical material from it before going to work. Cut off the old plug, unscrew the socket from the lamp pipe, and pull the cord and socket out of the lamp. Remove the harp, if the lamp has one, by moving the harp sleeves up and squeezing the harp wires to remove them from the slots in the harp wing. Old lamps may need to be cleaned, wire brushed, sanded, buffed with steel wool, stripped with paint remover, and refinished with urethane or paint.

When the lamp has been cleaned and finished to your satisfaction, proceed with the rewiring. If you know where the lamp is going to sit in your house, measure the distance from that spot to an outlet and cut a length of 18-gauge lamp cord sufficient to reach the outlet. If you don't know exactly where you will put the finished lamp, cut at least 5 feet of cord for a table lamp and at least 10 feet for a floor lamp. It would be advantageous to have enough cord coming out of the lamp to reach an outlet without having to use an extension cord.

Begin by pushing the cord through the lamp so that a free end comes out of the top of the lamp pipe. If the lamp is to have a harp supporting a shade, screw a harp wing over the threaded lamp pipe until it seats against the main stalk of the lamp. Follow the harp wing with the metal socket base. Remove the base from the socket by pressing the corrugated slip joint with your finger and pulling the two pieces apart. Screw the socket base onto the lamp pipe.

Pull the free end of the lamp cord until at least 6 inches extend above the socket base. Split the two conductors apart about 6 inches down the cord with a knife blade. Tie an underwriter's knot in the lamp cord to prevent any strain on the cord from pulling the conductors from the socket. Place the knot about 3 inches from the end of the cord. Tie the knot by making two loops with the wires. Hold both loops with your thumb and forefinger. Pass the free end of one wire through the loop made by the other wire and vice versa. Tighten the knot by pulling on the free ends of the wires.

Strip one-half inch of insulation from the ends of the wire. Twist the exposed conductors with your fingers to secure the individual wires of each conductor. Form clockwise loops in the conductors with a pair of needlenose pliers.

Remove the socket from the metal and cardboard shells that surround it. Place the loops of the wires over the terminal screws of the socket and tighten the screws down on the wires. Make sure that the screws cover the ends of the wires. Use a screwdriver to push any stray bits of wire under the screws as you tighten them.

Pull gently on the lamp cord from the bottom of the lamp to draw the knot against the socket base. Assemble the socket by slipping the cardboard sleeve over the socket, and follow that with the metal socket shell. Clip the socket shell and the socket base together by securing the corrugated slip joint between them.

Complete the installation by putting a self-tapping plug on the free end of the lamp cord. Make sure that the end of the cord is cut off flush with the conductors, using a pair of wire cutters if necessary. Open the plug unit, push the cord into the body of the plug, and secure by reassembling the plug unit. The design of the plug is such that the insulation of the cord is pierced by conductors inside the plug, which makes an electrical and mechanical connection to the lamp cord.

Install a harp, if required, by fitting the wires into the slots on the harp wing, and secure it by slipping the harp sleeves

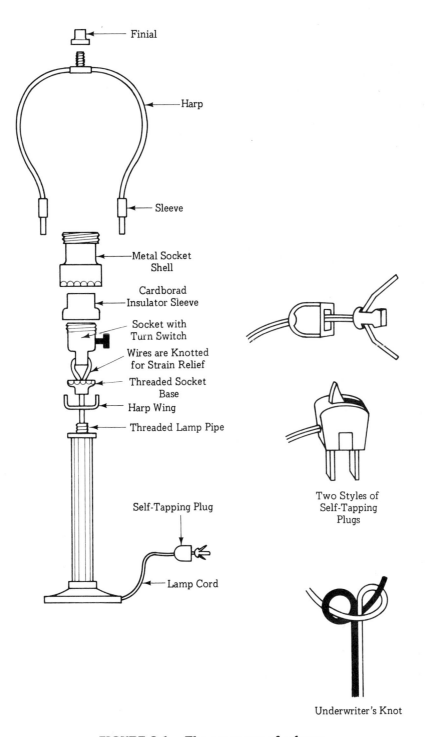

Finial

Harp

Sleeve

Metal Socket
Shell

Cardborad
Insulator Sleeve

Socket with
Turn Switch

Wires are Knotted
for Strain Relief

Threaded Socket
Base

Harp Wing

Threaded Lamp Pipe

Self-Tapping Plug

Lamp Cord

Two Styles of
Self-Tapping
Plugs

Underwriter's Knot

FIGURE 8-1. The anatomy of a lamp.

153

over the slots. A shade can be installed by placing it over the center threaded post at the top of the harp and screwing the finial piece onto the post.

In brief

1. Remove all of the old electrical components from the lamp. Cut off the plug, unscrew the socket, pull the cord from the lamp, and remove the harp. Clean and refinish the lamp before installing new electrical components.

2. Cut a length of 18-gauge lamp cord sufficient to reach from the lamp to an outlet on the wall. Use at least 5 feet for a table lamp, 10 feet for a floor lamp.

3. Push the cord through the lamp until one end comes out of the lamp pipe. Install a harp wing on the pipe if necessary. Remove the base from the new socket and screw it to the lamp pipe.

4. Split the two conductors on the lamp cord with a knife blade. Tie an underwriter's knot about 3 inches from the end of the cord. Strip 1/2 inch of insulation from the ends of the cord.

5. Twist the exposed wires tightly together. Form each conductor end into a clockwise loop. Attach these loops to the screw terminals on the socket. Tighten the screws. Make sure that any stray wires are tucked tightly under the screws.

6. Pull the cord from the bottom of the lamp until the knot seats. Assemble the socket, cardboard insulator, and socket shell. Secure the socket to the socket base.

7. Install a self-tapping plug to the free end of the lamp cord. Open the plug, insert the end of the cord, and then close the plug. Install a harp if required by clipping and securing it to the harp wing.

Tips

Lamp pipe diameters vary with the age and size of the lamp you are working on. The common sizes are ⅜-inch and ½-inch outside diameter (OD). You might encounter ⅝-inch OD pipe when working with old gas lamps and archaic fixtures that you are recycling into electric lights. A good electrical supply store will be able to give you adaptors and sleeves to fit any of these size pipes so that you can fit standard electrical components to them.

Sometimes when working with commercial or industrial lamps and fixtures you might come across very heavy-duty porcelain sockets that are larger than those used for standard incandescent bulbs. The thing to do is to clean these sockets by removing dirt and corrosion from their insides with steel wool. Then buy a porcelain threaded adaptor that will allow you to run a standard incandescent bulb in the larger socket. Run new lamp cord to the terminals on the old porcelain socket and you're in business. The reason that you preserve the old socket is that it is more rugged than household sockets (so it ought to function with just a cleaning), and often these sockets are integral parts of the design of the lamp. You wouldn't be able to install a new common socket without modifying a portion of the lamp or its housing.

WIRING A HANGING LAMP

Tools and supplies needed

Needlenose pliers

Screwdriver

Pliers

Adjustable wrench

Knife

Porcelain electrical socket with nipple fitting

Heavy-duty line switch

Screw terminal plug

Strain relief electrical cord

⅜-inch steel pipe nipple

Nuts and washers to fit nipple

Procedure

Nearly anything can be made into a lamp or lighting fixture once you know the basic elements that you need to combine. Nearly any lamp needs these features: a power cord and plug, a switch, a bulb socket, and a shade or light diffuser.

Since there are so many common objects that can be made into lamps or fixtures, it's worth coming up with a basic design that can accommodate just about anything that has a hole in it or can be drilled. The design described here can be used for making a hanging lamp or fixture. It uses a reinforced lamp cord that can stand the weight of a sizeable shade and a porcelain bulb socket that accepts a threaded steel pipe (also called a nipple) for securing the socket to whatever you are using for the body of the lamp.

First select what you are going to use for the body of the lamp. It could be a clay flower pot, a large tin can, a stainless steel bowl, a glass jug with its bottom removed—whatever can stand the heat of a bulb. The only requirement is that the object either have a hole in it to accommodate the ⅜-inch OD threaded steel nipple, or that it be made of a material that can have a suitable hole put in it.

Take a length of strain relief cord (often called *pendant lamp cord*), and cut it long enough to reach from the outlet on the wall, over a hanging bracket or post, and down to the position where you want the lamp to hang. Place these items on the cord in the order given: a threaded nut to match the steel nipple, a steel washer, the lamp body, another steel washer, and the 2- to 3-inch steel nipple.

On the end of the cord nearest the steel nipple, cut with a knife until you have separated the two conductors and split them down the cord about 4 inches. Unscrew the top of the porcelain socket from the main body and slip the socket top and its fiber washer over the end of the cord. Screw the socket top to the steel nipple. Tie an underwriter's knot in the cord about 3 inches from the end. Strip one-half inch of insulation from the conductors and form the bare wires into clockwise loops. Attach the loops to the screw terminals on the socket.

Reattach the socket top to the socket body. Pull on the free end of the cord to draw the socket, nipple, and washers tight with the lamp body. Secure the lamp by screwing the nut down on the nipple and applying a pliers or wrench to the nut while you hold the socket with your hand to keep it from turning.

At the free end of the cord install a standard rubber or plastic screw terminal plug. You can't use a self-tapping plug on the strain relief cord because of its shape and thickness. Separate the conductors and split them about 3 inches down the cord. Remove the cardboard insulator from the base of the plug, and place the plug on the cord. Tie an underwriter's knot in the cord about 2 inches from the end of the cord. Strip one-half inch of insulation from each conductor, and form the wires into clockwise loops with a needlenose pliers. Attach the loops to the screw terminals. Reinstall the cardboard insulator piece to the base of the plug so

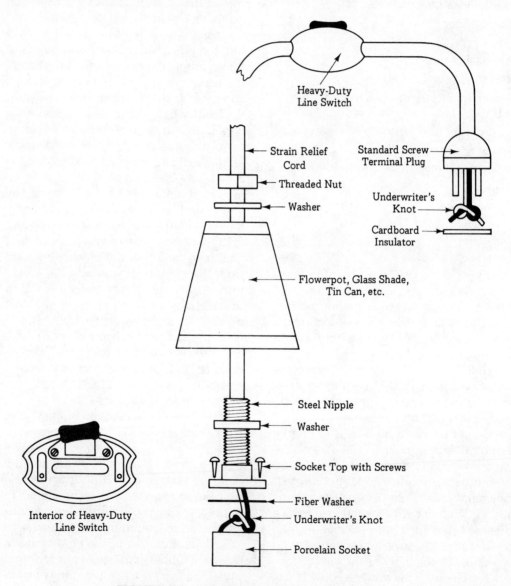

FIGURE 8-2. The anatomy of a hanging lamp.

that it covers the screw terminals and cord wires.

Finish the lamp by installing a heavy-duty line switch at a convenient place on the cord. You need a heavy-duty switch to accommodate the strain relief cord. Split the conductors where the switch will be. Cut one conductor and strip the ends of the wires. Open the switch and attach the wires to the screw terminals. Leave the other conductor undisturbed and place it in the plain molded channel of the switch. Reassemble the switch and screw it tight so that it grips the two lengths of cord and provides strain relief to the connections inside.

In brief

1. Select a suitable lamp body. The object must have a hole for the steel nipple or be capable of being drilled or punched.

2. Cut a length of strain relief cord long enough to hang the lamp and connect it to a wall outlet. Place on the cord a threaded nut to match the nipple, a washer, the body of the lamp, another washer, and the steel nipple.

3. On the end of the cord near the nipple, split the conductors about 4 inches down the cord. Unscrew the top of the socket and slip the top and its fiber washer over the cord. Screw the socket top to the nipple. Tie an underwriter's knot in the cord about 3 inches from the end. Strip insulation from the conductors and attach them to the socket terminals.

4. Reattach the socket top to the body. Draw the assembly up tight to the lamp object. Secure by screwing the nut to the nipple.

5. Install a standard screw terminal plug to the free end of the cord. Slip the plug over the cord, split the conductors, tie an underwriter's knot, strip the conductors, and secure them to the plug. Place the cardboard insulator over the base of the plug to cover the terminals and wires.

6. Install a heavy-duty line switch. Split the conductors, cut one conductor, strip the ends, and attach them to the screw terminals in the switch. Leave one conductor undisturbed. Reassemble the switch and tighten it so that it grips the cord and provides strain relief.

DIMMERS AND SWITCHES

Tools and supplies needed

Pliers
Needlenose pliers
Knife
Screwdriver
Solid state dimmer switch
Turn switches
Toggle switches
Line switches
Wire nuts

Procedure

One of the basics of lamp and fixture wiring is the use of control devices to turn lamps on and off and to dim them if desired. If you are building a light fixture from scratch, you need to know the options available so that you can select and install the proper device. For example, you might want to replace an outmoded device with a newer one that will fit in the space or hole left by the old one. The switches and dimmers described here are the standard inexpensive devices available from any good electrical supply store. If you want you can buy several of each to have on hand to handle projects that come up.

Solid state dimmer switches are designed to be installed in wall-mounted switch boxes to replace common light switches. These dimmers can only be used with incandescent lights and fixtures (fluorescents require a constant current flow to function), and they must be selected to match the load of the fixture. Dimmers are commonly available to handle 200-, 300-, 600-, 750-, and 900-watt loads. Most installations can be handled with the 600-watt model. Simply add up the number of bulbs and their wattages to come up with the load for the circuit. A 600-watt dimmer could handle up to four 150-watt, six 100-watt, or ten 60-watt bulbs.

Dimmers allow you to adjust the intensity of your lights from very dim to full bright. However, using a dimmer will cause the lights to give off a redder and redder glow as they are dimmed. This effect is caused by the characteristics of the tungsten filaments in the lamps as less and less current is passed through them. Use of a dimmer may cause some lamps to give off a soft buzzing sound as they are dimmed. This, too, is a natural phenomenon that may be bothersome but is not a cause for worry. Solid state dimmers won't reduce the life of bulbs and they won't waste electricity. In fact, use of dimmers will reduce the amount of electricity used (the lamps are fed only

what is required for a given level of illumination), with a corresponding increase in filament life.

To install a dimmer switch in an existing switch box controlling a wall or ceiling fixture, first shut off electricity to the fixture by removing the appropriate fuse or throwing the proper circuit breaker to "off." Remove the switch plate from the wall box. Unscrew the switch from the wall box. Carefully pull the switch from the box and unscrew the wires. Remove the switch from the box and attach the wires from the dimmer to the wires from the box, twisting them together and securing them with wire nuts. It doesn't matter which wire goes to which—you are simply installing the dimmer so as to interrupt one pole of a two-pole circuit.

Place the dimmer into the wall box and secure it with the two screws that used to hold the switch in place. Remove the dimmer knob by pulling it off the shaft of the dimmer. Place the old switch plate over the dimmer shaft and secure it to the wall box with screws. Replace the knob on the dimmer shaft. Turn on the electricity to the circuit.

A dimmer can be installed directly on a fixture that you rewired or built from scratch (a concealed lighting channel, an adapted lamp, or a fixture that you have designed and built from found materials). Simply install the dimmer so that it interrupts one side of the electrical circuit. Also make sure that there is sufficient space to mount the dimmer so that its mounting plate is flush with a flat surface. Secure the dimmer to the mounting surface with wood or sheet metal screws. Cover the dimmer with a common metal or plastic switch plate.

For fixtures that need simple on/off control there are several options. If you

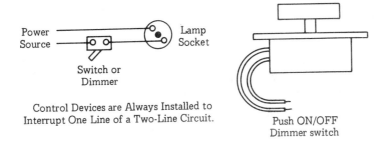

Power Source — Switch or Dimmer — Lamp Socket

Control Devices are Always Installed to
Interrupt One Line of a Two-Line Circuit.

Push ON/OFF
Dimmer switch

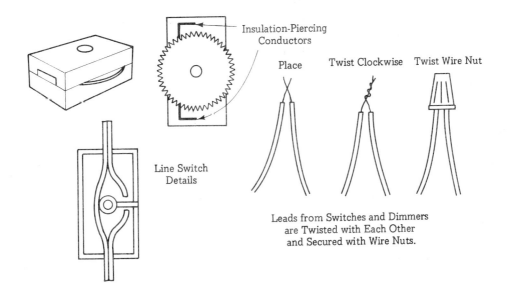

Insulation-Piercing
Conductors

Place   Twist Clockwise   Twist Wire Nut

Line Switch
Details

Leads from Switches and Dimmers
are Twisted with Each Other
and Secured with Wire Nuts.

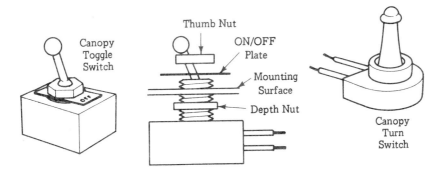

Canopy
Toggle
Switch

Thumb Nut

ON/OFF
Plate

Mounting
Surface

Depth Nut

Canopy
Turn
Switch

FIGURE 8-3. Control devices and tips on installing them.

need a small switch that can be installed in an existing hole in the fixture, use a canopy toggle or canopy turn switch. These canopy switches are designed for tight installations. They have wire leads coming out of their bodies for connection to the lamp's wires with wire nuts.

To install, remove the old defective switch from the hole. Remove the thumb nut from the top of the new switch. (If the switch has an on/off plate remove that too.) Place the new switch in the hole and test to see if the depth setting nut is properly adjusted. If it is not, adjust it until the proper amount of thread shows from the mounting surface. Reinstall the indicator plate and thumb screw and tighten.

Connect the leads from the switch to one side of the lamp circuit with wire nuts and complete the electrical wiring of the lamp. If the switch has an indicator plate, test the switch and adjust the position of the plate so that it indicates properly; then tighten the thumb nut securely.

The simplest switch for fixtures that have a cord is an in-line rotary switch. This can be installed any convenient place along the power supply cord. The switch is installed as shown in the illustration on page 159. One conductor is cut and is laid in a special compartment of the switch body. When the switch is reassembled, two special insulation-piercing conductors connect the switch with the cut conductor. The other conductor is undisturbed and passes through the plain side of the line switch.

In brief

1. Use a solid state dimmer to replace a wall switch to control an existing wall or ceiling fixture. Select a proper dimmer for the wattage load of the fixture or light. Turn off the electricity to the circuit. Remove the wall switch. Connect the dimmer wires to the wall box wires with wire nuts.

2. Attach the dimmer to the wall box with screws and remove the knob from the dimmer shaft. Place the old switch plate over the dimmer shaft. Secure the plate with screws. Reinstall the dimmer knob and turn on the electricity to the circuit.

3. Use a dimmer in adapted lamps or homemade fixtures if you have enough space to mount it. Use screws to attach the dimmer, and cover it with a common switch plate.

4. Use a canopy toggle or turn switch for tight spots. Remove the old switch, remove the thumb nut and indicator plate from the new switch, and install it in the hole. Check to make sure that the depth nut is adjusted properly.

5. Reinstall the indicator plate and thumb nut. Wire the switch into the lamp circuit with wire nuts. Check the operation of the switch, adjust the indicator plate, and tighten the thumb nut securely.

6. Use a line switch for convenient control along a cord. Disassemble the switch, separate the conductors, cut one conductor, lay the cord in the switch, and reassemble. The special piercing conductors in the switch will make electrical contact with the cut conductors.

TRACK AND GRID LIGHTING SYSTEMS

Tools and supplies needed

Circular saw
Tape measure

Tubing cutter

Hack saw

Drill and bits

Level

Stud finder

Electrical tools

1 × 3-inch smooth furring strips

PVC or copper pipe and fittings

Screw eyes

Galvanized steel picture wire

Electrical supplies

Procedure

Track Lighting System. The basic idea behind track lighting systems is to give you a permanent lighting system that has maximum flexibility. Ceiling tracks are installed that have continuous electrical conductors running in them. Individual small lighting instruments (usually 75-, 100-, or 150-watt flood or spot lights) are placed in the tracks, and their light is directed wherever it is needed— up (to wash the ceiling), *down* (to light a piece of furniture or a work area), *to the walls* (to highlight some detail or art work), or a *combination* (letting each instrument light a different area to provide good general lighting).

You can make your own adaptable lighting system using clip-on or screw-on lamps and lamp holders that are available from discount stores, electrical supply outlets, department stores, and other retail shops. These inexpensive lamps can give you the same effect as the instruments in conventional track lighting but are a good deal less expensive. Many lamps are simply designed and made of colorful plastic. Others are utility models made of steel and aluminum.

To make a simple track system, cut a piece of smooth 1 × 3-inch furring strip to the length you want to cover with lights. Use a magnetic stud finder in the general area of the ceiling where you want the track. Find and mark the hidden studs. Place the strip near the stud marks and mark places on the strip to install screw eyes. Drill and screw 2-inch screw eyes into the ceiling studs and into one of the thin edges of the strip. Install lengths of picture wire between the screw eyes to hang the strip from the ceiling. A good distance from the ceiling is about 2 feet, but use your own taste. The strip must at least be out of reach of people's heads if they are going to be passing under it. Use a level to make sure the strip is installed parallel to the ceiling. Wrap the ends of the wire around the screw eyes and twist them to secure.

To supply power to the lights you will be hanging on the strip, install an outlet strip on the ceiling parallel to the furring strip. Buy a strip long enough and with enough outlets to conveniently supply all the lights you plan to use on the track. Strips commonly have four to ten outlets. Mount the strip to the ceiling using screws through to the joists or using plastic anchors or steel molly bolts to hold the strip to the ceiling plaster. The power supply cord that comes out of the strip should be wired into a source of power in the ceiling (an old ceiling fixture box perhaps), or it can be run along the ceiling and wall to a nearby outlet. (The wire can be cemented to the wall and painted to match.)

Once the outlet strip is in place and connected to electrical power, you can clamp lamps onto the wood strip, plug their cords into the outlet strip, and adjust the lamps to get the desired effects. Choose lamps that have curly, telephone-style cords. They will stay neater and look better than straight, uncoiled lamp cords. If the outlet strip is wired into an old ceiling box, you can control the lights by a wall switch or dimmer. If the strip is plugged into a wall outlet, you can install a line switch on the power cord or you can turn individual lamps on and off by hand.

Grid Lighting System. To make a pipe grid lighting system you should use 1½- or 2-inch copper or PVC tubing. A good size for a pipe grid for a room 12 by 20 feet would be about 4 by 6 feet. Use four lengths of pipe and four 90-degree elbows to make the grid. Solder the joints if you are using copper; cement the joints with solvent cement if you are using PVC. Assemble the grid on a flat surface and check to make sure that all the joints are square as you secure them.

If you work with PVC, make sure that all the printing on the pipes is turned up-

wards so that when the grid is hung you won't see it. If you use a copper grid, clean the metal with fine steel wool and copper polish and spray it with clear acrylic or urethane finish to protect the looks of it.

Wire the grid with common lamp cord (or heavy-duty parallel cord for 600-watt and greater loads) and triplex outlet blocks. Lay the cord along the perimeter of the grid and place the outlet blocks midway between each corner of the grid. Strip the wire and connect it to the blocks. Wire the blocks in series (one after the other, using one continuous run of cord). Make sure that you leave a generous length of free cord to serve as the supply source when you install the grid.

Use contact cement to attach the lamp cord and the outlet blocks to the top of the pipes. Apply contact cement to

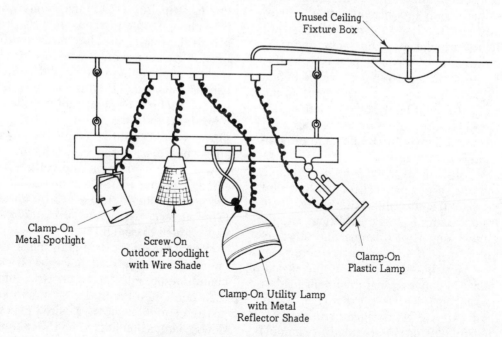

Unused Ceiling Fixture Box

Clamp-On Metal Spotlight

Screw-On Outdoor Floodlight with Wire Shade

Clamp-On Utility Lamp with Metal Reflector Shade

Clamp-On Plastic Lamp

FIGURE 8-4. Track lighting options.

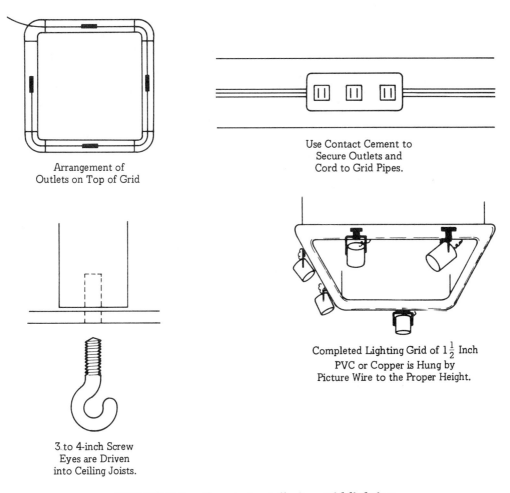

Arrangement of
Outlets on Top of Grid

Use Contact Cement to
Secure Outlets and
Cord to Grid Pipes.

Completed Lighting Grid of $1\frac{1}{2}$ Inch
PVC or Copper is Hung by
Picture Wire to the Proper Height.

3.to 4-inch Screw
Eyes are Driven
into Ceiling Joists.

FIGURE 8-5. How to install pipe grid lighting.

each surface, let it dry until tacky, then press the surfaces together. Make sure that you position the wires and blocks carefully because contact cement bonds immediately and you won't be able to do much shifting.

When the grid is wired, use a tape measure on the ceiling to mark its proper position. Use a stud finder to mark the spots where you can drive screw eyes in to hang the grid. You are looking for four secure places to suspend the grid by its corners. The screw eyes don't have to be exactly on the outlines of the grid, but try to get them as close as you can. When the screw eyes are installed, attach lengths of picture wire to them.

Get someone to help you hold the grid in position near the ceiling as you wrap picture wire from the ceiling to each of the four corners to secure it. Use a level to check for proper installation of the grid as you work. Run the supply cord from one corner of the grid up one picture wire and to the ceiling. Attach the cord to an electrical box in the ceiling or else run it across the ceiling and down a wall to an outlet near the floor.

Install clamp-on lights to the grid and attach their plugs to a convenient outlet block on the top edge of the grid. By adjusting the lamps' position on the grid and using the individual lamp's range of motion, you should be able to throw light to any position of the room.

In brief

1. Cut a track from a length of 1 × 3-inch furring strip. Locate the studs on the ceiling and drive screw eyes into them. Drive matching screw eyes into the wooden strip. Secure the strip to the ceiling with lengths of picture wire.

2. Install an outlet strip to the ceiling with screws, anchors, or molly bolts. Place it parallel and near to the wood strip. Run its cord to an electrical box in the ceiling or to a wall outlet.

3. Clamp lamps to the wood strip and plug their cords to the outlet strip. Select lamps with telephone-style coil cords to make the installation neat and attractive.

4. Make a pipe grid with 1 ½- or 2-inch copper or PVC pipe. Use four lengths of pipe and four elbows. Solder the copper; use cement on the PVC.

5. Turn all the printing on the PVC toward the ceiling to hide it. Clean the copper and spray it with clear varnish to protect it.

6. Wire the grid with lamp cord and four outlet blocks. Lay the cord along the perimeter, attach it to the outlets, and cement the system to the top of the grid with contact cement.

7. Use a stud finder and tape measure to find suitable places on the ceiling for screw hooks. When the hooks are installed, attach lengths of picture wire to them. Hold the grid near the ceiling and attach one wire to each corner of the grid.

8. Run the cord up one wire to the ceiling. Attach it to a ceiling electrical box or run it to an outlet near the floor. Install clamp-on lamps and plug them into the outlet blocks to the top side of the grid.

HIDDEN LIGHTING SYSTEMS

Tools and supplies needed

Circular saw
Drill and bits
Tape measure
Hack saw
Tin snips
1 × 12-inch white pine
Wood screws
Sheet metal screws
Epoxy putty
Metal corner braces
Galvanized steel strapping
Single-tube fluorescent fixtures
Colored gelatin light filters
Flush-mount porcelain or plastic sockets
Lamp cord
Plug and line switch

Procedure

Apart from the conventional options of using ceiling fixtures, floor and table lamps, and wall-mounted lamps, it is possible to install hidden light sources. There are a number of effects you can use concealed light for. It can be used to wash a wall with light, to illuminate a large hanging or art work; it can be mounted to give the illusion of extra depth to a wall; or it can be used to wash a wall with a different color, using colored filters.

Two easy ways to make lighting channels that will conceal light sources are to use white pine or prefabricated round or square gutter. Either method is a fast and inexpensive way to mount and position light where you want it.

There are two options for light sources. If you can come across some used single-tube fluorescent fixtures (from commercial or public buildings) you can mount them in white pine channels. These fixtures often come on the market, so if you find them at an inexpensive price, by all means use them. Fluorescent light is not a very warm light (meaning that it lacks the red and orange hues that sunlight and incandescent lights have). Although it's fine for utility or commercial use, this distorted light is not very flattering to people and furniture at home. However, you can still employ used fluorescents as hidden light if you wrap the bulbs in colored gelatin filters to give a warmer light.

If you can't find cheap fluorescents, or if you prefer to use naturally warm incandescent light bulbs, you can mount them in metal gutters or in white pine channels. You will need to buy flush-mount bulb sockets (often called *cleat sockets*) in order to mount and secure the bulbs to the channel. Use one cleat socket for each 2 feet of channel.

Plan where the channels will be. If they will run floor to ceiling, measure the distance and cut wood or metal to fit. If they are to run along the floor or ceiling, measure that distance and cut the materials to fit. To make up a pine channel, cut each length of 1 × 12-inch board down the middle into two 5 ⅝-inch strips. Cut enough wood to have three strips for each channel that you want to make. Assemble the strips as shown in the illustration on page 166. Use 1 ½-inch wood screws to secure the strips to each other.

To make a channel out of gutter, simply cut 10-foot lengths of gutter with a hack saw and tin snips into the length required. If the run of channel is over 10 feet long, use slip joints (available at the roofing store) to connect lengths of gutter. Use either round galvanized or square aluminum gutter. The square gutter will provide an easier mounting for bulb sockets than a round style, but either style will do.

To wire the channels, simply screw the fluorescent units to the white pine, using ½-inch wood screws. Fluorescents have mounting lips or holes built into their cases. Use lamp cord to connect the terminals on the fluorescent lighting fixtures to a source of power, either through a plug or directly to an electrical box in the wall or ceiling.

To wire an incandescent channel, place flush-mount sockets every two feet along the length of the channel. If the channel is wood, use screws to attach the sockets. If it is metal, use an epoxy putty to glue the sockets to the channel. When the sockets are secure, use lamp cord to connect the terminal screws on the sockets to a power source.

Secure the channels to the mounting surface. If the channels run floor to ceiling, use a 4-inch corner brace at the top and bottom of the channel to secure it to the floor and ceiling. Aim the channel at the wall and place it about 6 to 12 inches

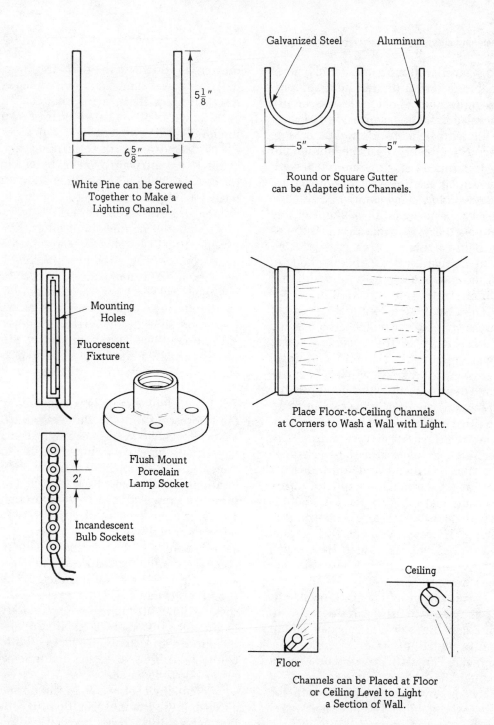

5 1/8"

6 5/8"

White Pine can be Screwed
Together to Make a
Lighting Channel.

Galvanized Steel   Aluminum

5"   5"

Round or Square Gutter
can be Adapted into Channels.

Mounting
Holes

Fluorescent
Fixture

2'

Incandescent
Bulb Sockets

Flush Mount
Porcelain
Lamp Socket

Place Floor-to-Ceiling Channels
at Corners to Wash a Wall with Light.

Ceiling

Floor

Channels can be Placed at Floor
or Ceiling Level to Light
a Section of Wall.

FIGURE 8-6. How to create lighting channels.

166

from the wall. If you use a channel across a wall at floor or ceiling height, you will have to tilt the channel to the proper angle for the effect that you want. Use corner braces that you bend to the proper angle, or else try galvanized steel strapping (sold at plumbing stores as pipe hanger material). The strapping is perforated and flexible, so you should be able to improvise a proper bracket and attach it to the channel and mounting surface with screws.

In brief

1. Decide on the light source. Use single-bulb fluorescents if you can find them at a good price and you don't mind the cool light they give. Use incandescents for warm light and economy when building from scratch.

2. Measure the height or length required for the channels. Cut the material to fit. For pine, cut lengths of 1 × 12 in half to come up with three 5 ⅝-inch-wide strips for each channel. Fasten the pine with screws.

3. For metal gutter channels, simply cut galvanized or aluminum gutter to fit. If the channel is longer than 10 feet, use slip joint connectors to tie the lengths of gutter together.

4. To wire, simply screw the fluorescent fixture to the pine. Screw or glue flush-mount sockets, depending on the material the channel is made of. Use lamp cord to connect the fixtures or sockets to a power source.

5. Secure the channels to the mounting surfaces. Use corner braces or perforated steel strapping to improvise brackets to hold the channels.

Tips

If you want to use colored gelatin filters to color the light from the channels, you can buy them from a theatrical supply house. Consult a big-city phone directory for addresses and numbers of supply houses. Many large-scale suppliers will send catalogs and handle mail orders if you can't get to their showrooms. Colored gels are actually gelatin or plastic films that are formulated to resist heat and stress from hot lamps. If you use a gel for a fluorescent tube, you can wrap it directly on the tube and attach it with tape. If you use the gel over an incandescent bulb, attach it to the edges of the channels so that the gel isn't touching the bulb. Use tape or tacks to secure it.

You will have to experiment with incandescent bulbs of various wattages to come up with the effect you want. Usually, 60-watt bulbs will give the best effect. You can also connect a dimmer to the circuit to give infinite control over the brilliance of the lights. With fluorescents, you have less flexibility. The brightness of the light will be determined by the used fixture you buy. Depending on the length of the fixture, the tube will probably be rated at 75, 40, 30, or 20 watts.

Be sure to guard against overheating of the wood or metal channels. You don't want to risk fire or burns by using high-wattage bulbs. The risk of overheating is increased by the use of colored gel material over incandescent bulbs. Cut small holes or slots in the gel to promote ventilation. If the openings are evenly spaced over the gel, they won't radically affect the colored light of your fixture.

ADAPTING LAMPS
FROM UNEXPECTED
SOURCES ————————————

Tools and supplies needed

Tubing cutter

Drill and bits

Needlenose pliers

Screwdriver

Knife

Adjustable hole drill

Lamp cord

Plug and electrical tape

Line switch

Standard lamp socket

2¼-inch lamp fitter

Glass lampshade

Keyless lamp socket

⅜-inch flexible copper tubing

⅜-inch threaded nipples

Chromed tailpipe extension

White pine scrap

Glue

Procedure

Lamps can be constructed of so many materials that it is impossible to cover here all of the possible adaptations. Here are two simple designs that use cheap parts from auto and plumbing supply stores.

Tailpipe Lamp. The first lamp is a small table model that could be used to throw a spotlight on some small art object, a print on the wall, or wherever a small, low-wattage light beam is desired.

Go to an auto supply store and buy a chromed tailpipe extension. These pieces are sold to dress up the ends of mufflers on custom cars. Select an extension with a slanted tip and an overall length of 7 to 12 inches.

Drill a ¼-inch hole in the bottom of the extension near the plain end, on the opposite side of the pipe from the slant tip. Measure the diameter of the plain end of the pipe and with a hole drill cut a matching piece from a scrap piece of white pine. In the center of the pine circle, drill a ⅜-inch hole.

Screw a 1½-inch-long threaded lamp nipple into the hole on the pine. If there is too much clearance in the hole for the pipe to thread securely, coat the nipple with epoxy glue and insert it. When the nipple is secure in the pine, screw a keyless bulb socket to the free end of the nipple. (A keyless socket is a standard bulb socket except that it doesn't have a built-in on/off switch.)

Remove the socket shell from the socket base to reveal the terminals on the socket itself. Thread a length of lamp cord through the nipple and up into the socket base. Split the cord about 4 inches and tie an underwriter's knot in the cord for strain relief. Expose ½ inch of conductor from each end of the cord and form them into clockwise loops. Place the loops on the screw terminals and secure them with a screwdriver. Then reassemble the socket shell to the socket base.

Push the socket and pine piece up into the tailpipe extension, past the hole you drilled. Thread the free end of the lampcord through the hole and pull it out of the pipe. Position the socket and pine plug in the pipe and secure it with a bead of epoxy glue. Allow the glue to cure.

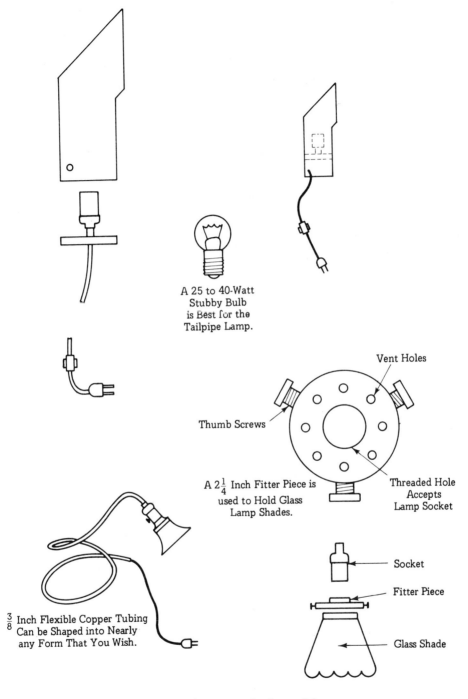

A 25 to 40-Watt
Stubby Bulb
is Best for the
Tailpipe Lamp.

Vent Holes

Thumb Screws

A $2\frac{1}{4}$ Inch Fitter Piece is
used to Hold Glass
Lamp Shades.

Threaded Hole
Accepts
Lamp Socket

$\frac{3}{8}$ Inch Flexible Copper Tubing
Can be Shaped into Nearly
any Form That You Wish.

Socket

Fitter Piece

Glass Shade

FIGURE 8-7.   Aspects of adapted lamps.

Finish the lamp by installing a line switch on the lamp cord and a self-tapping plug on the free end of the cord. Install a low-wattage bulb (a 25- to 40-watt appliance or sewing machine bulb) in the socket. The lamp will produce a directional light that you can aim by turning the slanted tip.

Tubing Lamp. An entirely different kind of lamp can be constructed by taking ⅜-inch flexible copper tubing and bending it into a desired shape. Happily, a threaded lamp nipple will screw into the inside of ⅜-inch copper, so this material is just asking to be made into a lamp.

For your first attempt at bending, try working with about 4 feet of copper tube. Longer lengths can be handled, but it's best to play with a short length to get a feel for it. The material comes coiled, so it is best to work up a design loosely based on the coil shape. Simply pull the tubing into shape with your hands—avoid very sharp bends so that you don't kink the copper. The illustration on page 169 shows a very basic design: You keep the coil shape for the first foot and a half, lift and separate the tubing for the last footage, and end up with a small curve for the last 6 to 8 inches.

When the shape has been made, you can wire the lamp by pushing a length of lamp cord through the tubing. It will go through very smoothly. Take a 1½-inch nipple and thread it into the end of the tubing where you want to mount a socket. Use a pliers to twist the nipple into the soft copper of the tubing. If the nipple won't thread, try flaring the end of the copper slightly with a handle of the pliers.

When the nipple is threaded about halfway into the tube, stop twisting the nipple and thread the socket base onto the free end of the nipple. Push the lamp cord through the nipple and into the socket base until 6 inches show. Split the conductors about 4 inches and tie an underwriter's knot into the cord. Expose ½ inch of conductor at each end of the cord and form them into loops. Fasten the loops to the terminals on the socket. Then reassemble the socket.

Install a 2¼-inch lamp fitter to the threads on the end of the socket. Install a thin glass lampshade to the fitter piece, securing it with the thumb screws on the fitter. Install a self-tapping plug on the free end of the lamp cord to complete the project.

In brief

1. Drill a hole near the bottom of a tailpipe extension. Measure the diameter of the pipe and cut a piece of pine to fit. Drill a ⅜-inch hole in the center of the pine.

2. Screw a nipple to the pine piece. Use epoxy glue if the hole won't hold the nipple securely. Screw a keyless socket to the free end of the nipple.

3. Thread lamp cord through the nipple and socket base and tie a knot for strain relief. Attach the cord to the terminals on the socket and reassemble the socket.

4. Push the socket and pine into the tailpipe. Thread the free end of the lamp cord through the hole. Position the socket and pine and secure it with epoxy.

5. Install a line switch and a self-tapping plug on the lamp cord. Install a 25 to 40-watt bulb in the socket.

6. For a tubing lamp, use ⅜-inch flexible copper tube. Work it with your hands until the shape pleases you.

7. Push lamp cord through the tube. Thread a 1½-inch nipple to the tubing. If it won't thread, flare the tubing slightly with a pliers handle. Thread the nipple halfway into the tubing.

8. Thread a socket base on the free end of the nipple. Push 6 inches of lamp cord past the socket base. Split the cord, tie an underwriter's knot, and attach the conductors to the socket.

9. Install a fitter to the socket and a glass shade to the fitter. Install a self-tapping plug on the free end of the lamp cord.

Tips

To avoid fraying the lamp cord on the raw edge of the hole in the bottom of the tailpipe lamp, use a length of electrical tape wrapped around the lamp cord. You can also install a rubber or plastic grommet (from a hardware store) to protect the lamp cord from any sharp edges as it exits the tailpipe lamp.

One of the factors that will limit the kind of design you can work the flexible tubing into is the weight of the glass lampshade you use. A light glass shade will allow you to form the tubing into quite long curves. Shop at a large electrical supply store and ask to be shown the full selection of thin glass shades that will mate to the fitter piece. Some shades are reproductions of classic shapes from the early days of electric light with cut, pressed, and etched designs in clear and colored glass.

You can give your tubing lamp extra strength and stability if you apply solder to any place along the lamp where tubing touches. In the design illustrated on page 169, solder could be applied at the first

coil and at the second, smaller one. Simply apply flux to the area, heat it with a propane torch, and apply wire solder. After the joint is made, clean the area with detergent and fine steel wool.

To protect the bright finish of the copper tubing you should spray lacquer or urethane finish on the completed tubing lamp. First clean off dirt and oil from the forming operation by applying a liquid copper polish with a soft rag. Then apply two or three coats of clear finish from a spray can. Lay the finish up by moving the can quickly over the whole project and staying as parallel to the surface as you can.

ADAPTING FIXTURES FROM COMMON OBJECTS

Tools and supplies needed

Circular saw

Drill and bits

Hole drill

Tape measure

Screwdriver

Knife

Paper parasol

White pine

Stove and carriage bolts

Flush-mount porcelain sockets

Lamp cord

Screw hooks

Plug and line switch

½-inch link chain

Epoxy glue

Spray paint

Glass fish bowl

Procedure

Here are two lighting fixtures—one for the ceiling and one for the wall—that you can build from an oriental parasol and a common glass goldfish bowl.

Parasol Fixture. For the parasol fixture, select a paper and wood oriental design parasol from a gift shop, import shop, or museum shop. These hand-designed parasols are widely available and are perfect objects to base lighting fixtures on. The inverted parasol is a natural light diffuser, and the parasol handle is a good base for hanging and wiring the fixture.

Select the place where you will hang the fixture and determine whether or not the handle of the parasol will have to be cut down. Use a hack saw to shorten the handle if necessary to get the parasol to the proper height. If the ceiling is very high and you want the parasol to hang lower than the handle will bring it, simply buy a length of ½-inch link chain from an auto supply store or hardware store. The chain can be used to adjust the final height of the fixture.

The key to wiring the parasol is to build a clamp-on base for mounting sockets on the parasol's handle. Do this by cutting two pieces of scrap white pine to 8 × 4 inches. Stack one piece on the other and hold them firmly together as you drill two holes through them at each end. Place the holes about 1 inch in from the ends of the wood. Drill the holes to take 4-inch long stove bolts.

Attach flush-mount porcelain cleat sockets to each piece of pine. Center the sockets on the boards and drill and screw them to the pine. Place the stove bolts through the boards and twist a nut on the end of each bolt. Slip the assembly over the end of the parasol handle and slide it to within 4 inches of the parasol's center. Tighten the stove bolts to secure the sockets to the handle.

Mount Sockets on a
Clamp that Secures
to the Handle

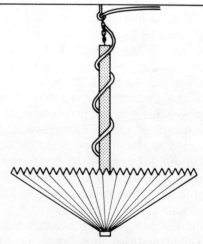

The Completed Fixture is
Hung From the Ceiling
with Screw Hooks and a Chain.

FIGURE 8-8. Details of a parasol light fixture.

Drill a hole in the center of the parasol's handle and install a 1½-inch screw hook. Wire the parasol by taking a length of lamp cord and attaching it to the bulb sockets. Wrap the cord loosely around the parasol's handle.

Mount the parasol to the ceiling by installing a screw hook into the plaster and through to a joist. If you can't find a joist in a suitable position, use a toggle bolt to mount a hook to the ceiling. Hang the parasol directly by the two screw hooks or use a length of chain to bring the parasol to the desired height. Run the lamp cord to an electrical box in the ceiling or to a wall socket. Use a line switch and plug on the cord if you run it to a wall socket.

Fish Bowl Fixture. To make a wall-mount fixture that you can use to provide utility light in the various rooms of your house, buy a common glass fish bowl. Coat the inside of the bowl with white paint from a spray can by holding the fish bowl in one hand and directing the spray from the can into the interior of the bowl with your other hand. Lay the coating up in several thin layers rather than in one thick one. When the bowl is coated with an even layer of paint, let it dry while you work on the mounting boards.

Cut mounting boards from white pine scraps. Depending on the size of the fish bowl you use, your boards should be about 11 × 11 inches. Cut two boards exactly the same size. Lay them on top of each other and drill four holes. Place the holes 1 inch in from each corner of the boards. Drill the holes large enough to accommodate the 2½-inch long carriage bolts you plan to use.

Cut two 8 × 1-inch spacer pieces from white pine. Glue them to one of the mounting boards, centered between the corner holes. Take the other mounting board and drill a hole exactly in the center of it. Use an adjustable hole drill to make it the exact diameter of the fish bowl opening. Put epoxy glue on the inside surface of the hole, and put more glue on the outside surface of the fish bowl opening. Press the fish bowl and the mounting board together and allow the glue to cure.

When everything is secure, mount the porcelain pull-chain socket to the plain mounting board. Drill a ⅜-inch hole in the center of the board. Feed a length of lamp cord through the hole to the side of the board with the spacer pieces on it. Tie a strain-relief knot on the cord to prevent it from being pulled out of the fixture. Split the conductors and expose ½ inch of wire from each end. Fasten the wires to the screw terminals on the underside of the socket. Center the socket on the board and drill and screw it to the board.

Screw a 75-watt bulb to the socket and assemble the fixture. Place carriage bolts in the four holes of the socket board. Place the fish bowl board over the bolts and press the two boards together until the spacer pieces contact both boards. Screw nuts to the bolts to secure the fixture.

The fixture can be mounted to wall surfaces by drilling and screwing the socket board. The fixture is then assembled and secured by screwing nuts onto the carriage bolts. The spacer pieces allow enough air to circulate through the fixture to keep it cool as the bulb burns. The lamp cord can be connected to a box in the wall or can be connected with a plug to a wall socket. (You should carve a channel in the back of the socket board to feed the cord out of the fixture if you plan to run the cord down the wall to a socket.) The pull chain provides on/off control.

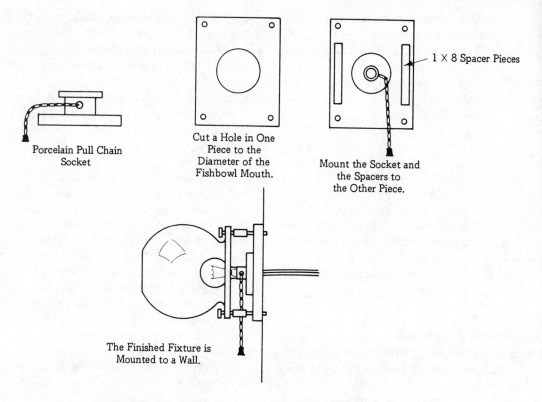

Porcelain Pull Chain Socket

Cut a Hole in One Piece to the Diameter of the Fishbowl Mouth.

1 X 8 Spacer Pieces

Mount the Socket and the Spacers to the Other Piece.

The Finished Fixture is Mounted to a Wall.

FIGURE 8-9.   How to construct a fish bowl light fixture.

In brief

1. Buy a paper and wood parasol. Cut the handle down with a hack saw if necessary to fit the object to the ceiling you intend to use. Make a clamp-on base to mount the sockets. Cut two pieces of pine, stack the pieces, and drill two holes 1 inch from each end.

2. Attach flush-mount sockets to each pine piece. Center the sockets and screw them in place. Connect the pieces with stove bolts and slip the clamp over the handle of the parasol. Tighten them into place.

3. Drill a hole to mount a screw hook in the end of the handle. Wire the sockets with lamp cord, and wrap the cord loosely around the handle of the parasol.

4. Mount the fixture to the ceiling with another screw hook. Use a length of chain to adjust the height. Run the cord to a wall socket or ceiling box. Use a line switch and plug if the cord runs to a wall socket.

5. Coat the inside of a glass fish bowl with white paint. Lay the coating up in several thin layers. Cut two mounting boards from pine. Stack the

pieces and drill holes in all four corners.

6. Cut 1 × 8-inch spacer pieces and glue them on one board between the corner holes. Take the other board and drill it to the diameter of the fish bowl opening. Use epoxy glue to attach the board to the bowl.

7. Drill a ⅜-inch hole in the center of the plain board. Feed lamp cord through the hole and tie it off. Prepare the end of the cord for the screw terminals. Connect the cord to the socket terminals. Then center the socket and screw it to the board.

8. Screw a bulb to the socket and assemble the fixture. Put bolts in the socket board, place the fish bowl board over the socket, and secure the fixture with nuts over the bolts.

9. Mount the fixture to a wall by drilling and screwing the socket board. Connect the cord to an electrical box or to a wall outlet.

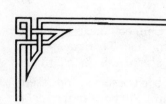

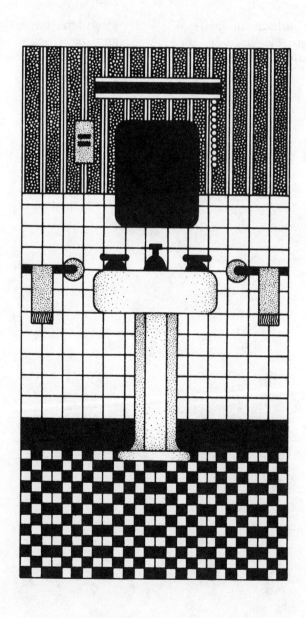

FIXTURES

ADAPTABLE STORAGE UNIT

Tools and supplies needed

Tape measure
Circular saw
Drill and bits
Hammer
Screwdriver
Level
2 pieces of 1 × 12 × 72 inches
2 pieces of 1 × 12 × 29 inches
3 pieces of 1 × 12 × 27 ½ inches
2½-inch wood screws
8 L-shaped mending plates

Procedure

This project will give you a basic unit to use for a variety of storage problems. It can act as a bookcase, cabinet, closet, or wall-mounted storage fixture. The unit is constructed of 1 × 12-inch white pine for simplicity.

Begin by cutting the white pine into the proper lengths. Assemble the 29-inch pieces and the 72-inch pieces by using the eight mending plates. Place the two 72-inch pieces within the two 29-inch pieces. This will make the distance between the two long pieces 27½ inches (the length of the middle shelves). Screw the mending plates to the corners of the box you have formed.

To stiffen the box, drill holes and drive three wood screws into the edges of the 29-inch pieces and through to the edges of the 72-inch pieces. This should strengthen the box enough to allow you to stand it upright.

Decide where the three middle shelves should be placed. Mark their positions on the edges of the box. Drill three holes for each side of the shelf through the sides of the box and through to the edges of the shelf board. Secure the shelves with wood screws. The wood should be soft enough to set the heads flush without using a countersink. Use a level to make sure that the shelves are straight and true as you secure them.

The wood can be left unfinished or it can be stained, painted, or urethaned. The only important thing is to cut the wood precisely and assemble the unit with a level and a measuring tape to make sure it's straight.

This simple unit can be used to store many items such as books, kitchen supplies and tools, linens, and toiletries. You should look at this design as one that can be adapted freely. You can space the shelves differently or adjust the overall dimensions of the unit up or down. You can set the unit on the floor or mount it on the wall with shelf brackets.

In brief

1. Cut the lumber to length—two 72-inch pieces, two 29-inch pieces, and three 27½-inch pieces.
2. Assemble the sides, top, and bottom of the unit with L-shaped mending plates.
3. Stiffen the box by screwing three wood screws into each corner of the box.
4. Place the middle shelves within the box and mark their proper positions.
5. Drill holes and screw three screws into each side of the middle shelves. Use a level to check for trueness.

Tips

This unit can be constructed of 1 × 8-inch wood, which would make it slimmer and more conventionally sized. The deep storage that 1 × 12 pine provides can be very useful, however, especially if you need to store and organize kitchen equipment, stereo equipment, or linens and towels.

You can omit the mending plates from this design and assemble the unit with nothing but wood screws. However, the mending plates make the assembly easier (especially if you are working alone), and they tend to keep everything square and even as you work.

One possibility for this design is to turn it into a cabinet by mounting two doors on the front of it and placing it against a wall. You could salvage or buy a light-duty (1-inch-thick or less) solid wood door and build the shelf to the door's dimensions. Cut the door in half down the middle and mount it to the surface of the shelf with 1½-inch butt hinges. Install wood or porcelain knobs and two magnetic catches.

Another variation would be to buy two louvered white pine doors. Build the shelf to their combined dimensions and mount them to the surface of the unit with hinges. The louvered doors would be especially appropriate for linen or household supply storage where good ventilation is important.

A smaller sized version of this unit (24 × 12 inches, for example) would be perfect for bathroom storage. There is always a storage problem in the bathroom, which is even worse if you have free-standing fixtures that have no cabinet storage space. Mount the unit on the wall (about 5 feet high) with steel shelf brackets. In even the smallest bathrooms there is usually room above the toilet for such a fixture.

Another option is to install the unit on its side about 5 feet high on a wall. The shelf then becomes an open kitchen-style

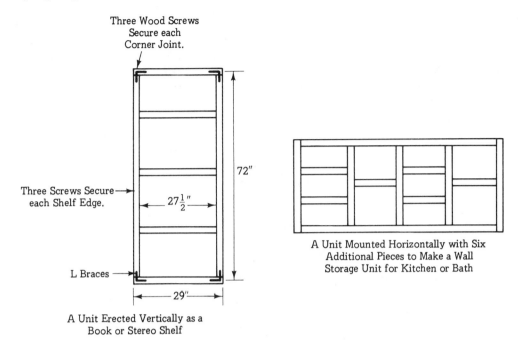

Three Wood Screws
Secure each
Corner Joint.

72"

Three Screws Secure→
each Shelf Edge.

$27\frac{1}{2}$"

L Braces →

←— 29" —→

A Unit Erected Vertically as a
Book or Stereo Shelf

A Unit Mounted Horizontally with Six
Additional Pieces to Make a Wall
Storage Unit for Kitchen or Bath

FIGURE 9-1.   Construction of a storage unit.

cabinet. In this case you would build the shelf to cover the length of a kitchen wall or to match your present kitchen cabinets on the floor. The shelf is installed with steel shelf brackets screwed to the wall studs. Additional pieces of wood could be added to the unit to subdivide the space enclosed by the box and the cross pieces. If the unit is installed in the kitchen the wood should be urethaned or painted for a low-maintenance finish.

RECYCLING OLD GAS STOVES

Tools and supplies needed

Adjustable wrench
Wire brush
Putty knife
Toothbrush
Straight pins
Paint brush
Liquid dishwashing detergent
Cleaning supplies
Pipe tape or compound
Flexible appliance connector
Variety store oven thermometer
Spray solvent/lubricant

Procedure

Gas cooking stoves and ranges from the late 19th and early 20th centuries are very simple appliances, usually consisting of a cast or stamped iron or steel body with steel and iron pipes, fittings, and valves. Stoves built before the mid 1930s are generally free of sophisticated electrical thermostats, thermocouples, automatic gas valves, and pilot light devices. Some of these vintage stoves are very beautifully made, with fancy castings and multi-colored porcelain finishes.

If you have gas service in your area, it is worth considering the purchase and restoration of one of these near-antiques. There is very little to break on them, and the gas burners provide the same speedy and infinite heat adjustments that more modern units do. The only real drawback to these old stoves is that the ovens are not regulated by automatic gas valves to keep the temperature constant. This means that you must buy an oven thermometer and learn by trial and error where to set the oven knobs to get a given heat.

Because these stoves have few moving parts and no sophisticated ones, generally all that is necessary is to give the stove a thorough cleaning, testing, and adjustment before it is put into service. Use your favorite cleaning products to work on the stove body. TSP, household detergent, spray oven cleaner, and scrubbing cleansers all work well on the various surfaces of the stove.

Cleaning. Disassemble the burners from the stove and clean them individually. The burners will slip out of slots or pins in the stove and disconnect from the gas valves by simply pulling. Soak the burners in soapy water and use a wire brush, toothbrush, and putty knife to clean the rust, scale, and dirt from them. Straight pins and small-diameter twist drills work well for clearing the holes in the burners. Rinse the burners thoroughly with fresh water and allow them to dry. Apply solvent/lubricant to the set screws on the air shutters.

Clean the valves carefully while they are still on the stove, using a weak detergent solution and a toothbrush. Wipe the valves dry immediately with a soft cloth. You can apply a bit of high-temperature grease (from an appliance supply or auto store) to the exposed moving surfaces of the valves to lubricate them. Sticky or stiff valves may be freed by applying spray solvent/lubricant. Let the liquid penetrate for a few minutes, and then gently work the valve by hand to loosen it up. Unscrew or pull off the knobs and soak them in detergent to clean them.

Clean and check the thread surfaces on the inlet pipe to the stove. Make sure that the pipe threads are in good shape to receive a new appliance connector. Most antique gas inlet pipes have a ¾- or 1-inch diameter. Go to a plumbing supply store and purchase a flexible appliance connector complete with adaptors that will mate to the stove on one side and the gas supply pipe on the other side.

Appliance connectors are specially constructed corrugated brass tubes that allow you to move an appliance (for installation, cleaning, and maintenance) without unhooking the gas supply. Buy only the length of connector you need, since they are expensive and you don't want any excess tubing to get caught behind the stove. The store will sell you appropriate adaptors with the tubing to handle the inlet and supply pipes. You will need pipe joint tape or pipe joint compound to make gas-tight joints when you connect the adaptors to the pipes. The pipe joint tape is neater to apply than compound, but either method is acceptable as long as the product specifically states that it can be used on gas pipes.

Testing. When the stove has been completely cleaned, reassemble all the parts and prepare the stove to be connected. Make sure that the gas supply pipe you will connect the stove to has a shut-off valve so that the gas flow can be cut off quickly if the stove malfunctions during testing or operation. Attach the adaptor piece to the end of the gas supply pipe. Use compound or tape and secure it with a wrench. Attach the other adaptor to the inlet pipe on the stove using tape or compound. Attach the appliance connector to both adaptor pieces. Do not use

compound or tape for these joints—the fittings are beveled to mate tightly by pressure only. Secure the fittings with a wrench.

When the connector has been installed, check all the valves on the stove to make sure they are closed. Before opening the shut-off valve on the supply pipe to pressurize the stove, prepare a leak-testing solution. Mix a few drops of dishwashing detergent with 3 ounces of

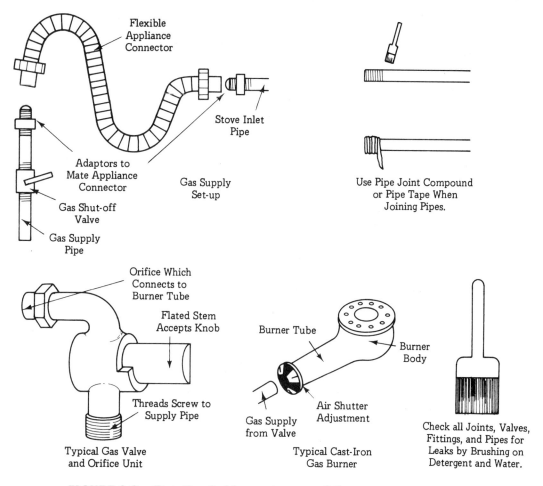

FIGURE 9-2. Details of old gas stoves and tips on gas stove restoration.

water. Put a paint brush into this solution and have it ready to brush on joints, fittings, and valves. The detergent solution will make bubbles if there are any gas leaks in the stove.

Turn the shut-off valve on the supply pipe to admit gas to the stove. Listen carefully for the sound of escaping gas. If everything seems tight, brush on the detergent solution to test for pinhole leaks. Be very methodical and test every joint in the system. Work from the gas supply pipe to the last valve on the stove.

Adjusting. If no leaks show up during the testing routine, you can adjust the burners. Wipe off all the detergent solution from the joints. Work on the surface burners first. Turn on a valve and let the trapped air in the system escape. Then touch a match to the burner and light it. Unscrew the set screw on the air shutter located on the burner tube. Turn the air shutter until a soft blue flame appears. Gradually close the shutter until yellow appears at the top of the flame. Then open the shutter just until the yellow flame tip disappears. The burner is now adjusted for maximum efficiency. Secure the set screw to hold the air shutter at the proper position. Repeat this process with all the remaining burners, including the oven burners.

In brief

1. Clean the stove with detergent, solvents, and household cleaning products. Disassemble the burners and clean them separately. Use a wire brush, toothbrush, and putty knife. Lubricate the set screws on the burner air shutters.
2. Clean the valves with detergent and a toothbrush. Lubricate them with a high-temperature grease. Use solvent/lubricant to free sticky valves.
3. Purchase a flexible appliance connector and adaptors to mate the stove with a gas supply pipe. Use pipe tape or compound to make gas-tight joints.
4. Reassemble the stove and connect it to the gas supply. Pressurize the stove and test for leaks with a detergent solution.
5. Adjust the burners by turning the air shutters to get an optimum mix of air and gas. Get a soft blue flame, turn until yellow appears, then reverse until the yellow just disappears. Lock the settings with the set screws on the shutters.

Tips

If leaks occur during testing, turn off the gas supply immediately. The problem could be loose or poorly fitting joints. Tighten everything you can with a wrench. You can even try disassembling all of the pipes and valves and reassembling them with new tape or compound. If a valve is leaking from its body and tightening doesn't work, it is usually not possible to rebuild the valve. A large appliance store might be able to give you a replacement valve if you remove the bad valve and take it in.

If the burners won't adjust properly for clean and efficient burning, you might have a stove that was designed to operate on a different kind of gas than you have available (natural gas and manufactured gas have different burning characteristics). It is possible to use the stove by replacing the old orifices in the valves with new ones suited to your fuel supply. Remove the orifices with a wrench and take them into a large appliance store. The counter person should be able to advise you on the proper new replacements to match the local fuel type.

BICYCLE WHEEL HANGER UNIT ——————

Tools and supplies needed

Drill and bits
Stud finder
Hack saw
Bicycle wheel
S hooks
½-inch link chain
Screw hooks
Coat hangers

Procedure

One of the best projects for creating storage space in the kitchen is to install some sort of hanging pot and utensil grid. These grids are used extensively in commercial kitchens, where efficiency and cleanliness are important. With cooking vessels and utensils in plain sight and easy reach, you can go for the right item every time. Many people spend a lot of money on high-quality pots and utensils, and a hanging grid can show these well-designed items off to their best advantage. Having everything in sight becomes a design and decorating choice—the look is one of efficiency and functional beauty.

A bicycle wheel with its chromed rim and wire spokes can become a nice grid. You should be able to find a wheel at a flea market or junk store for a few dollars. You might even get a free one by asking for a bent or broken one at a local bike shop. The wheel doesn't have to be functional to serve as a pot grid.

Remove the tire and tube from the wheel and discard them. Clean the wheel with a spray degreaser from the auto store or use brush-on oven cleaner. Wash off the cleaner and rinse the wheel with water from a garden hose.

Take the clean wheel and place it near the ceiling where you want it to hang. Mark reference points on the ceiling with a pencil. Remove the wheel and hunt with a magnetic stud finder to find suitable studs. You are looking for three points from which you can hang the wheel. They don't need to be exactly on the outline of the rim, since some slack can be taken up with lengths of chain. Because the wheel will have a fair amount of weight on it, you should anchor only to solid wood studs—hollow wall anchors won't hold.

When you have marked the studs, drill and screw three 2½-inch screw hooks to the ceiling. Cut lengths of ½-inch link chain to hang from the hooks. Decide how far from the ceiling you want the wheel to hang and cut the chain accordingly. Attach the chain to the ceiling hooks. Hold the wheel near the chains and attach the wheel rim to the chains with three S hooks. Arrange the hooks on the wheel rim so that the wheel is supported evenly by the chains.

Using the spokes and rim of the wheel you can hang pots and utensils with S hooks or with wire hooks that you fashion from lengths of coat hanger wire. Simply clip the wire from coat hangers with a pair of cutting pliers and then bend the wire by hand.

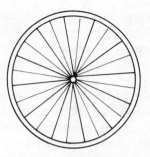

Find or Buy a Bicycle Wheel.

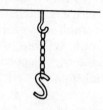

Hang the Rim from the Ceiling
with Three Sets of "S" Hooks,
Chain, and Screw Hooks.

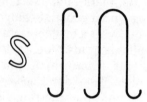

Use "S" Hooks or Hooks Fashioned
from Coat Hanger Wire to Hang Pots
and Utensils from the Spokes
and Rim of the Wheel.

Alternative "Lazy-Susan" Mounting
Using Central Wheel Hub and
Threaded Steel Rod

FIGURE 9-3.   How to construct a bicycle wheel kitchen rack.

In brief

1. Find or buy a bicycle wheel. Remove the tire and tube and clean the wheel with degreaser or oven cleaner.

2. Hold the wheel near the ceiling and mark its outline. Use a magnetic stud finder to mark suitable studs for fastening three screw hooks.

3. Drill and screw the hooks into the ceiling and hang lengths of chain from them. Bring the wheel near to the chains and attach it to them with S hooks.

4. Use S hooks or homemade coat hanger hooks to hang kitchen equipment from the spokes and rim of the wheel.

Tips

A hanging grid can be constructed from almost anything that has a number of surfaces that can accept wire or S hooks—an auto grille, auto bumper, salvaged refrigerator shelving, a length of ornate iron fence, or a piece of heavy steel screening. You can even fabricate your own grid from rigid copper tubing and fittings or 1 × 2-inch furring strips.

An alternative mounting method might appeal to you. The bicycle wheel could be hung from a single threaded steel rod anchored to a plate that is screwed to a ceiling joist. The hanging rod would have a threaded sleeve that would accept the threaded axle coming out of the wheel's central hub. This set-up would allow the wheel to revolve lazy-susan style on its hub. The wheel could be turned to make it easier to reach an object on the far side of the rack. With this method you must take care not to load the wheel up with too many heavy objects. You don't want the single steel mount to have to resist the force of a grossly unbalanced load.

STEMWARE HANGING FIXTURE

Tools and supplies needed

Adjustable hole drill

Drill and bits

Sabre saw

Circular saw

Hack saw

Tape measure

Paint brush

Stud finder

¾-inch plywood (both sides smooth)

Screw hooks

½-inch link chain

Polyurethane varnish

Procedure

This glassware hanging rack is modeled after commercial racks in bars and restaurants. The rack holds goblets, wine glasses, beer and highball glasses, and smaller pony and cordial glasses. Just about anything that has a stem and a circular base can be stored. It's an efficient design because the glasses hang upside down in slots and can be drawn individually by

hand to a circle cut in the hanger that is slightly larger than the base of the glass, allowing the glass to be removed.

If you have a home bar or if you use stemware for daily dining and drinking, this rack will come in handy. Glasses stay clean because they are stored upside down, and they don't break easily since only one kind of glass can come out of the rack at a time.

The model described here is for general use with three basic sizes of glassware. Use the dimensions here as a guide only. You must know what size and type stemware you are going to use before you build the rack. Adjust the size of the rack accordingly. You should allow at least a 1-inch space between glasses and at least 2 inches of solid wood margin around the cutouts.

Cut a piece of ¾-inch plywood to 36 × 24 inches. On the cut piece arrange the glassware that you are going to be hanging. Leaving the recommended space between glasses and around the margins of the rack, plot the best positions for the cutouts. For a rack of six cutouts to accommodate three sizes of glasses, use two identical cutouts for each size glass and place them in descending order from left to right across the board.

Make the cutouts with a hole drill and sabre saw. Cut the holes about ½ inch wider than the bases of the glasses. First make the holes with the hole drill. Then draw slots onto the board with a straightedge and pencil. Make the slots about ¼ inch wider than the diameter of the stems of the glasses. Cut the slots with a sabre saw and a combination or plywood blade. First cut the two parallel slot lines and then use the tight turning radius of the saw to cut out the remaining wood at the end of the slots.

When you finish you will have your plywood cut like the pattern shown in the illustration. Use a piece of sandpaper to smooth the edges of the cutouts. Apply two or three coats of polyurethane varnish to seal the unit.

Hang the unit from the ceiling with chains and screw hooks. Plot the position of the unit on the ceiling and hunt with a stud finder to locate likely mounting studs. Drill and screw four to six hooks to the ceiling. Determine how low you want the rack to be (it should be just above head level when it is loaded with glassware), and cut lengths of chain to fit. Hang the chain from the ceiling hooks.

Drill and screw hooks to the top of the rack and hang the rack from the chains. To secure the unit, use a pair of pliers to close the screw hooks around the links of chain so that the rack can't be knocked free of the hooks accidentally. Load the rack with stemware by placing the base of each glass through the hole in the board and sliding the glass to the limit of the slot.

In brief

1. Cut a ¾-inch piece of plywood into a rectangle 36 × 24 inches. Arrange the glassware to be hung on the plywood. Space the glasses properly and mark where the cutouts should be.

2. To drill cutouts in the wood use a hole drill set ½ inch wider than the base of the glasses. When all of the circular cutouts have been made, draw slots with a straightedge. The slots should be ¼ inch wider than the stem of the glasses.

3. Use a sabre saw to cut the slots. When the cutouts are completed use a piece of sandpaper to smooth the wood. Apply urethane varnish to the whole unit.

4. Hang the unit from the ceiling with screw hooks, chains, and more screw hooks into the plywood. Close the hooks over the chain links after the unit is hung to provide extra security.

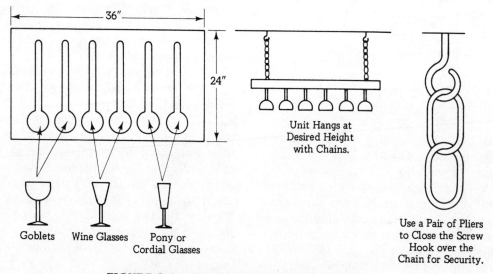

Goblets   Wine Glasses   Pony or Cordial Glasses

Unit Hangs at Desired Height with Chains.

Use a Pair of Pliers to Close the Screw Hook over the Chain for Security.

FIGURE 9-4. Details of a stemware hanger.

Tips

Since this rack is modeled after units found in restaurants and taverns, it makes sense to use restaurant-style glassware. You can buy inexpensive and durable stemware from a local restaurant and bar supply house (check the Yellow Pages for locations). In general you must buy a minimum of a case (12 glasses) at a time of each style of glass. The price break you get for buying in quantity generally makes up for the need to purchase in volume, and you will always have more glasses on hand to replace broken ones.

It makes sense to know what kind of glasses you are going to be using before you build the unit. One of the reasons to buy restaurant glassware is that you can almost be guaranteed to find the same size and style of glassware at a later date to replace pieces or expand the set. You can't always be sure of this kind of consistency when using glasses purchased at regular consumer outlets.

KITCHEN KNIFE RACK ——————

Tools and supplies needed

Circular saw
Drill and bits
Tape measure
Level
Screwdriver
Scrap white pine
Scrap hardboard or paneling
2½-inch-long screws
Plastic wall anchors
Sandpaper

Procedure

This is an ultra-simple knife rack for the kitchen. It is held together and fastened to the wall with two screws long enough to go through the wood and into the wall. The rack can be sized to hold any number

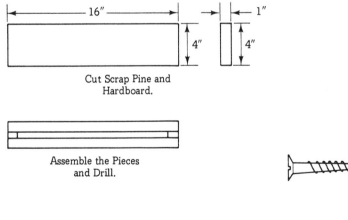

Cut Scrap Pine and
Hardboard.

Assemble the Pieces
and Drill.

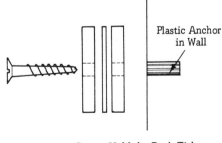

Plastic Anchor
in Wall

Screws Hold the Rack Tight
and to the Wall.

FIGURE 9-5. How to construct a knife rack.

of knives, but the suggested length here should be sufficient to hold the usual kitchen assortment.

Begin by cutting two 4 × 16-inch oblongs of scrap white pine. Sand the edges of the wood with medium sandpaper. Cut two spacer pieces of scrap ⅛-inch-thick hardboard or paneling. Make the spacer pieces 1 × 4 inches. Assemble the rack on a flat surface by sandwiching the two spacer pieces between the oblongs of pine. Place the spacers at the edges of the pine as shown in the illustration. Hold the sandwich tightly together and drill two holes through the rack. Make the holes large enough to accommodate the diameter of the 2½-inch-long screws you are going to use. Place the holes ½ inch in from the edges of the pine and center them 2 inches from the top and bottom edges of the pine.

Take one of the drilled oblongs of pine and place it on the wall where you want the rack to be. Use a level to get it straight on the wall. Mark the wall with a pencil through the two holes in the wood. Remove the pine from the wall and drill two holes in the wall to accommodate plastic anchors. Insert the anchors in the holes, reassemble the rack, put screws through the rack, and fasten the rack to the wall. As the screws grab the wall anchors they will draw the rack up tight to itself and the wall.

In brief

1. Cut two pieces of pine 4 × 16 inches. Cut two ⅛-inch spacer pieces 1 × 4 inches.

2. Sandwich the spacers between the pine pieces. Place the spacers at each end of the pine oblongs. Hold the sandwich and drill two holes through the pine and spacers.

3. Hold one of the pine pieces to the wall and level it. Mark the wall for drilling. Drill and insert plastic anchors in the wall.

4. Reassemble the rack, insert the screws, and fasten the rack to the wall by tightening the screws to the anchors.

PVC WINE RACK ————————————

Tools and supplies needed

Hand saw
Miter box
Circular saw
Drill and bits
Tape measure
4-inch PVC pipe
1 × 12-inch white pine
2-inch wood screws
Medium and fine sandpaper

Procedure

The proper way to store wine bottles is on their sides so that the wine will keep the corks wet. A constantly wet cork will remain swollen and will provide a tight seal to prevent the wine from going bad. Here is a simple rack for storing wine bottles that you can build from lengths of PVC pipe and a few pieces of white pine.

Cut PVC into fourteen 1-foot lengths. Use a miter box and a back saw to get square cuts. If you don't have a miter box you can wrap masking tape around the pipe to guide your free-hand cutting. You

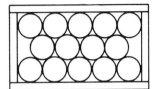 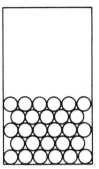

Screw the Pine Frame
Together to Hold
1-Foot Lengths of PVC.

PVC Tubes are Packed
so that they are Flush
with the Front of the
Rack and Stick out about 1 Inch
from the Back of the Rack.

Stack Lengths of
PVC in a Closet
for Mass Storage
of Wine.

FIGURE 9-6. Two wine racks made from PVC pipe.

can use just about any kind of PVC pipe. Thinwall drain, waste, and vent pipe (DVW) is a good choice, but any 4-inch pipe will do.

Use sandpaper to take off the burrs left from cutting the pipes. It is not necessary to take the printed lettering off the pipes because it will be hidden when the rack is assembled. On a flat surface, arrange the fourteen pipes as shown in the illustration. Make sure the pipes are touching each other and that the group is square. Use your tape measure to determine the exact dimensions of the group. You will be cutting white pine to enclose the group.

Cut two pieces of white pine the exact width of the group. Cut two pieces of white pine the exact length of the group plus the thickness of two pieces of white pine (usually 1½ inches). You add the extra measurement to these length pieces so that you can drill and screw into the ends of the width pieces.

Lay the pine pieces next to the pipe group and check for the proper fit. When everything is right, attach the pine pieces by placing wood screws through the

length pieces and into the ends of the width pieces. You can add white glue to the joints to further stiffen the frame if you want.

When the frame is assembled, place the PVC tubes in it. The fit should be so tight that the tubes and frame are under tension when everything is in place. Position the tubes so that their edges are flush with the front edges of the frame. The tubes will stick out by about an inch at the back of the frame.

In brief
_____

1. Cut PVC into fourteen 1-foot lengths. Use a miter box or masking tape to guide your cuts. Smooth the ends of the tubes with sandpaper.

2. Arrange the tubes in a tight group on a flat surface and measure the dimensions of the group. Cut white pine to make a frame. Cut two width pieces the exact width of the group and cut two length pieces the exact length of the group plus the thickness of two pieces of pine.

3. Assemble the pine pieces, check them for fit, and secure them with screws. When the frame is complete, fit the PVC tubes by hand.

Tips

If you want to create an extra-secure rack you can cement the PVC tubes together before building and fitting a frame. Simply wipe PVC cement along the mating surfaces of the tubes and place the tubes together. It is best to work with groups of three tubes at a time and then assemble the modules together to create the whole group. You will have to allow the tubes about 30 minutes to bond securely before you handle them. Full curing takes place in 12 to 24 hours.

You can experiment and perhaps create a PVC grouping that is so strongly bonded by cement that it doesn't need a frame. Such a scheme might work for a small, five-tube rack. Any rack will be under strong tension when you load it with full wine bottles, however, so you will probably want to make the pine frame for safety. PVC does have some flex to it, so it often needs reinforcement or framing.

The design shown here is adaptable. You could easily expand the number of tubes to make a larger rack. If you have a closet that you want to devote to wine storage you could simply lay up as many lengths of PVC pipe as you desire to get the storage you need. Lay the pipes dry and use the sides of the closet as a frame to keep them in place. For very large storage racks, you should get thick-wall PVC pipe (walls at least ¼-inch thick) so that the extra weight won't deform the tubes.

BACKSPLASHES FROM OLD DOORS

Tools and supplies needed

Circular saw
Tape measure
Hammer
Stud finder
Paint stripping tools
Paint brush
Chemical paint stripper
Salvaged wood doors
1 × 12 white pine
2- and 3½-inch finishing nails
Polyurethane varnish

Procedure

If you install a free-standing cast iron tub or wash basin near a wall, you will probably want some kind of backsplash on the wall to protect the plaster from water. Modern free-standing and built-in tubs use tile or plastic panels to serve as backsplashes. Most modern sinks and basins also incorporate some sort of built-in backsplash. You can create an effective and handsome backsplash that is in tune with an old house by simply mounting a wood door on the wall.

Find or buy a solid wood door that is roughly the length of the tub or sink and about 2½-feet wide. Strip the old paint off one side of the door and all of the edges. Do an extra careful job of stripping the door to bring out the detail of the panels and any carving it might have.

Use a magnetic stud finder and mark the position of the studs with a pencil high on the wall. Position the door on the wall next to the tub or sink with the bottom edge nearly flush with the rim. Nail the door to the wall with long finishing nails. Avoid nailing through the panels on the door. Next, cut a 4-inch strip of wood from some 1 × 12 pine. Cut it the length of the top edge of the door. Sand the edges of the strip and nail it to the top edge of the door, making a 4-inch-wide shelf. Use finishing nails to nail straight through the top of the white pine and into the top edge of the door. The white pine should be butted tightly against the wall.

You now have a backsplash with a narrow shelf on top to hold soap, shampoo, and grooming items. Complete the job by finishing the wood with urethane. Use three coats to provide a thick, glossy surface that will resist moisture and water.

You can make this backsplash more useful by hanging a glass or wooden towel bar from the underside of the white pine shelf. Simply screw a ready-made bar to the pine or make your own by screwing two blocks of wood to the pine, drilled to accept a ½-inch diameter dowel.

This simple design can be used behind nearly any free-standing fixture in the bathroom or kitchen. Simply select or cut down a door to fit the size of the space. Doors can be cut and installed around corners to take advantage of odd shapes and spaces. You can also use wood doors for a continuous backsplash behind kitchen counter units. The bottom edge of the doors should sit on the counter. You can use the shelf on top for spices and supplies, and you can screw hooks into the underside and edges of the shelf to hang equipment and utensils.

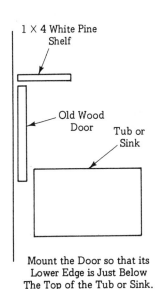

1 X 4 White Pine Shelf

Old Wood Door

Tub or Sink

Mount the Door so that its
Lower Edge is Just Below
The Top of the Tub or Sink.

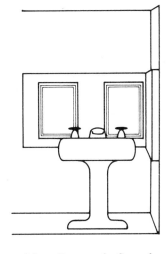

A Long Door can be Cut and
Mounted to Serve as a
Backsplash Around a Corner.

FIGURE 9-7. How to use a door as a backsplash.

In brief

1. Find or buy an old door of the right size.
2. Carefully strip the paint from one side of the door and all the edges.
3. Locate the position of the studs beneath the plaster and mark their position high on the wall.
4. Position the door with the bottom edge nearly flush with the fixture rim.
5. Nail the door to the wall with long finishing nails. Avoid nailing through the door panels.
6. Cut a piece of white pine into a 1 × 4-inch strip, sand the edges, and mount it with finishing nails to the top edge of the door.
7. Finish the door and shelf with three coats of urethane.

STRIP UTENSIL HANGERS

Tools and supplies needed

Circular saw
Tape measure
Hammer
Drill and bits
Level
1 × 12-, 2 × 6-, or 1 × 3-inch lumber
2½-inch finishing nails
2-inch screw hooks or L hooks
¼-inch diameter wood doweling
Wood screws

Procedure

If you follow the open plan for your kitchen you should get most of your tools, utensils, and pans up on the wall where they will take up less space than in cabinets. Simple wood strips mounted on the wall with nails, hooks, or dowels in them are a good way to hang kitchen tools. The strips can be as short as 1 foot and as long as 10 feet (or longer, whatever your needs and wall space dictate). One 2-foot-long strip of 1 × 12-inch white pine with 12 finishing nails driven into it at 2-inch intervals can hold up to 30 small kitchen tools—more than the contents of a typical cabinet drawer.

To make a strip hanger, simply cut board lumber to fit the wall space. You can use the broad width of 1 × 12-inch white pine to keep tools and pots from marring the wall, or you can mount 2 × 6-inch board and count on the extra depth of the wood to keep tools and pots from banging against the wall. You can even use thin, 1 × 3-inch furring strips to hang small utensils that won't cause much damage to the plaster even if they are banged about. Nearly any lumber will do. Select good-looking pieces because they will be in plain sight on your walls.

Once you have cut the length you need you should finish the lumber by sanding any rough edges and selecting the lumber's best side to turn outward. Mark the points where you plan to drive nails, screw hooks, or mount dowels. A spacing of one hanger every 2 inches across the strip's length is about right for most uses. Drive nails, drill and mount screw hooks, or drill ¼-inch holes for the dowels. If you use dowels, cut 2½-inch lengths with a hack saw. Coat the ends of

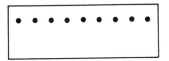

A Single Strip of Scrap Wood
with Finishing Nail Hangers
Can Hold a Drawer Full
of Kitchen Utensils.

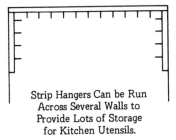

Strip Hangers Can be Run
Across Several Walls to
Provide Lots of Storage
for Kitchen Utensils.

FIGURE 9-8. Uses for strip hangers.

the dowels with white glue or epoxy glue and drive the dowel pieces into the holes with a hammer.

Find the studs and mark their position on the wall. Place the completed strip on the wall (6 feet above the floor is about right for most people) and mark where the studs are with a pencil on the strip. Use a level on the strip to make sure that it's straight. Drill holes through the strip and into the studs. Then mount the strip to the wall with screws. Finish the strip by applying urethane varnish or a penetrating wood stain, or leave the wood unfinished.

In brief

1. Cut board lumber to fit the wall space. Finish the lumber by sanding the rough edges.

2. Mark the spacing for the hangers on the lumber. One hanger every 2 inches is recommended. Drive nails, drill and mount screw hooks, or drill ¼-inch holes for dowels.

3. If you use dowels, cut 2½-inch lengths with a hack saw. Coat the ends of the dowels with glue and drive the pieces into the holes in the lumber.

4. Mark the position of the studs on the wall. Place the strip on the wall and mark the position of the studs on the strip. Drill holes through the strip and into the wall. Mount the strip with screws.

TOWEL AND PAPER HOLDERS ————————————

Tools and supplies needed

Drill and bits
Adjustable hole drill
Tape measure
Circular saw
Hack saw
Scrap pieces of pine
½-inch diameter wood dowel
Sandpaper

Procedure

You can use scraps and waste ends of 1 × 12 white pine to make towel and paper holders for the bathroom and kitchen. These simply designed holders can be left unfinished or they can be urethaned to provide a glossy woodgrain finish.

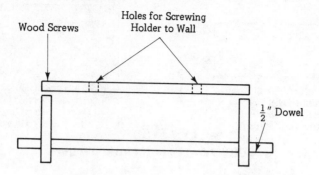

FIGURE 9-9. Basic design for a holder.

To make a toilet paper holder, cut a piece of scrap into an 8 × 4-inch oblong. Cut two more pieces into 4 × 4-inch squares. Sand all of the edges smooth. Drill a hole slightly larger than the ½-inch dowel in each of the squares. Center these holes 1 inch from the edge and 2 inches from the sides of the squares.

Assemble the holder by drilling holes from the back of the oblong into the edges of the two squares. Use two holes for each square and secure them with wood screws. Drill two holes in the oblong for securing the holder to the wall. Insert a dowel cut to a length of 10 inches into the two holes of the holder.

To make a towel holder, cut a piece of scrap into a 22 × 4-inch oblong. Cut two more pieces into 4 × 4-inch squares. Sand all of the edges smooth. Drill a hole slightly larger than the ½-inch dowel in each of the squares. Center the hole 1 inch from the edge and 2 inches from the sides of the square.

Assemble the holder by drilling holes from the back of the oblong into the edges of the squares. Use two holes for each square and secure them with wood screws. Drill two holes in the oblong for securing the holder to the wall. Insert a

dowel cut to a length of 24 inches through the holder's two holes.

In brief

1. Cut scrap pine into one oblong and two squares.

2. Sand all the edges smooth.

3. Drill a hole slightly larger than the ½-inch dowel in the two squares.

4. Assemble the holder by drilling and screwing from the back of the oblong into the edges of the two squares.

5. Drill two holes in the oblong for securing the holder into the wall.

6. Insert a dowel cut to the proper length into the holder's two holes.

RECYCLING OLD BATHROOM FIXTURES ——

Tools and supplies needed

Hack saw
Pipe wrench and extension handle
Adjustable wrench
Valve seat grinder

Valve seat wrench

Screwdriver

Washers

Packing material

Valve seats

Brass waste water kit

Pipe joint compound

Cloth tape

Penetrating oil

Procedure

The key to recycling old porcelain and cast iron tubs and sinks is to renew their faucets and waste water pipes. Old porcelain fixtures will generally romain serviceable if you adapt or replace their metal parts. The porcelain will clean up with a bleaching cleanser and scrub brush; it's the faucets and drains that usually cause problems.

If you have a nice old faucet that is faulty you can often save it by grinding the valve seats, installing new washers, and repacking the valve stems. Begin by removing the handles of the faucet from the valve stems. Use a screwdriver to loosen a set screw (which might be hidden under a decorative cap). Pull the handles off the valves, using a drop of penetrating oil to loosen reluctant handles.

Wrap a piece of cloth adhesive tape around the packing nuts on the faucet to avoid damage when you apply an adjustable wrench. Turn the nuts counterclockwise to remove them. Remove the valve stems by twisting them counterclockwise out of the faucet. (You can slip the handles on the stems temporarily to do this.) Once the stems are free, remove the old washers from them and install new ones of the same type and size.

Feel the condition of the valve seats in the faucet by inserting your index finger. If the seats against which the washers rest feel rough to your touch they will probably have to be smoothed. Use a seat grinder tool, which you can buy at a plumbing store. It is a simple tool that fits into the faucet with the same threads as a valve stem. Follow the package instructions for the particular grinder you buy. In general, you will have to set an adjustment nut to align the grinder so that it is square with the valve seat. Give the grinder a few turns with light pressure to dress the valve seat smooth.

Reassemble the valves, using petroleum jelly on the threads of the stem and packing nut to make the reassembly easier. Examine the packing material or washer under the packing nut. If it looks worn or shrunken, replace it with new material. Form the plastic, rubber, or lead packing into a circle and place it in the body of the nut.

Test the faucet by connecting the sink or tub to the water supply pipes. If the faucet still leaks after the renewal procedures you have taken, you will have to replace the valve seats. Disassemble the faucet and remove the valve seats with a screwdriver or valve seat wrench (a special tool for removing hex-head seats). Turn the screwdriver or wrench counterclockwise to remove the seats. Take the seats to a plumbing shop and obtain exact replacements. Install the new seats with pipe joint compound on their threads, and reassemble the faucet, using new washers on the valve stems if the previous ones were damaged by contact with the old, rough seats.

Drains and their related pipes are often rotted or deteriorated on old sinks and tubs. Happily, new waste water kits

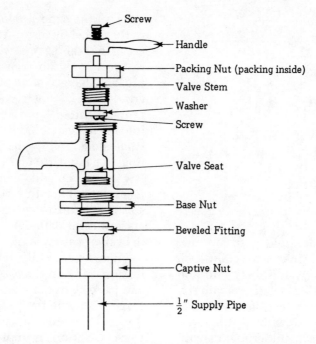

Screw
Handle
Packing Nut (packing inside)
Valve Stem
Washer
Screw
Valve Seat
Base Nut
Beveled Fitting
Captive Nut
$\frac{1}{2}$" Supply Pipe

FIGURE 9-10.   The anatomy of a typical old faucet.

of brass and chrome-plated brass are available that will tie the old fixture into the house drainage system. Remove the old drain tubes and fittings from the fixture. Use large-jaw multi-pliers and pipe wrenches to get a grip on the fittings. Use penetrating oil on tough joints and, if necessary, use a 3-foot-long steel pipe that will fit over the handle of your pipe wrench to get extra leverage.

When the pipes are free, draw a diagram of your fixture showing where the drain outlets are, the distance between them, and the distance from the fixture to the house's drain line in the floor. Take this information to the plumbing store to guide you in the selection of materials. For a free-standing bath tub, you will want a brass waste water kit composed of overflow tube, drain tube, tee fitting, and tail piece. For a free-standing or pedestal sink you will want a chrome-plated S trap kit and a 4-inch-long chrome-plated tail piece with drain fittings. These kits can be cut down with a hack saw to fit nearly any fixture and installation.

Install the waste water kits as shown in the illustrations. Use all of the washers provided with the kits. The drain pieces that secure to the fixture usually have two soft rubber washers, one on the finished side of the fixture and one on the unfinished side. The tubes and fittings of the kits are sealed with rubber ring washers (also called O rings) that slip on the tubes between the securing nuts and the tee or trap piece. Cut the tubes to the proper length with a hack saw. File or use sandpaper to remove rough edges from your cuts.

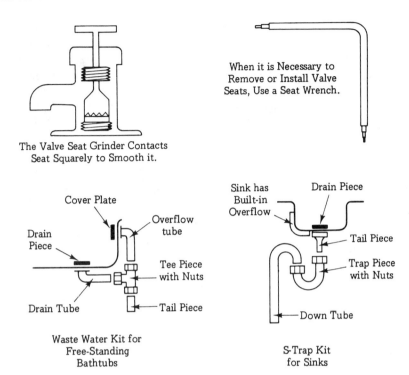

The Valve Seat Grinder Contacts
Seat Squarely to Smooth it.

When it is Necessary to
Remove or Install Valve
Seats, Use a Seat Wrench.

Cover Plate

Drain
Piece

Overflow
tube

Tee Piece
with Nuts

Drain Tube

Tail Piece

Waste Water Kit for
Free-Standing
Bathtubs

Sink has
Built-in
Overflow

Drain Piece

Tail Piece

Trap Piece
with Nuts

Down Tube

S-Trap Kit
for Sinks

FIGURE 9-11. Details of bathroom fixture restoration.

In brief

1. Deal with an old faucet by disassembling it and renewing its critical parts. Remove the faucet handles, packing nuts, and stems. Remove the washers from the base of the stems and replace them.

2. Feel the valve seats with your finger; if they are rough, use a grinder to smooth them. Square the cutter with the seat and apply light pressure and a few turns to smooth the seat.

3. Reassemble the faucet with petroleum jelly on the threads. Inspect the packing nut material and replace

it if it is deformed, dried out, or damaged. Connect the faucet to the water supply and test it.

4. If the valve still leaks, the seats need to be replaced. Disassemble the faucet and remove the old seats with a screwdriver or hex-head wrench. Take the old seats to a plumbing store and buy exact replacements. Install them with pipe joint compound and reassemble the faucet.

5. Remove old drain tubes and fittings from tubs and sinks with a pipe wrench, multi-pliers, penetrating oil, and an extension handle. Draw a diagram of the fixture complete with dis-

tances between outlets and fixture-to-branch drain line.

6. Buy a brass kit for a tub or a chrome-plated kit for a sink. Install the fittings with the washers and nuts provided in the kits. Cut the tubes to size with a hack saw and use a file to smooth rough edges.

Tips

If a fixture that you want to recycle is worn to the point that the porcelain finish won't clean up, you can have the fixture recoated by a porcelain refinishing service. These services (check the Yellow Pages) can apply a new bonded coating to the old porcelain. The service is relatively expensive, but it can be a way for you to save an especially fancy or treasured fixture that you've acquired.

If you don't care to renew the existing faucets of a fixture you can remove them and replace them with a single modern faucet. Replacement and reproduction faucets are available that will allow you the convenience and reliability of modern hardware and still be in tune with the old lines of the fixture. When you go shopping for a replacement faucet take the "center" measurement of your fixture with you. A center measurement is the distance between the centers of the two faucet mounting holes in the fixture, typically 4, 6, or 8 inches.

MISCELLANEOUS PROJECTS

SOLDERING TECHNIQUE

Tools and supplies needed

Propane torch
Soldering iron or gun
Steel wool
Paste-style acid flux
Flux brush
Plumber's 50/50 solder wire
Electronic rosin-core solder wire
Cellulose sponge

Procedure

Soldering of metal is such a useful repair and recycling technique that it is worth covering in detail. There are two basic kinds of soldering—mechanical and electrical. Mechanical soldering is for repairs and assembly of parts that are made of copper, brass, tin, and galvanized steel. For the projects in this book most mechanical soldering will be for securing copper and brass plumbing products.

Mechanical Soldering. A joint to be soldered must be clean. This is best accomplished by buffing it with medium steel wool. Rub until both mating surfaces are bright. Flux is then applied to both surfaces to prepare the metal to receive solder and to keep the surfaces clean while they are being heated. Common plumber's paste flux is a good choice. It is applied to the surfaces with a small brush so that oils and dirt from your hands don't contaminate the surface. Most plumber's fluxes are corrosive if left on the metal after soldering, so you should clean the finished joint with detergent and clean rags after it has cooled.

The important thing to remember about soldering is to apply the heat *to the material being soldered,* not to the solder itself. You want to heat the metal so that it will melt the solder wire as it is touched to the joint. If the metal is hot enough it will suck solder into the joint by capillary action.

The best heat source for mechanical soldering is a hand propane torch. Use a medium (pencil flame) fitting for general plumbing fittings and most small-scale metal joints. You can purchase a large diameter (1 inch or larger) fitting for the torch to solder large pipes (over 1-inch diameter) and big projects.

Point the flame at the metal, not the joint. Play the flame along the material to thoroughly heat the general area, especially if the joint is a long one. Keep the heat on the area and touch the solder wire to the joint. If the solder wire doesn't immediately melt, remove it and continue heating the area. The area has been heated properly when the solder wire melts immediately upon contact with the joint. As the solder melts, feed it along the joint. If you are working with plumbing fittings, the joint will take only enough solder to fill it—any excess will drip off the fitting. If you are soldering a flat joint you will have to watch for excess solder running out from under the joint. Keep the flame on the area until you are finished feeding solder to the joint.

Remove the flame and leave the joint undisturbed for several minutes while the solder hardens. On small plumbing fittings you can hasten the process by applying a wet rag to the joint to cool it, but first let the joint sit undisturbed for a full minute.

When the joint is cool, clean it of flux by wiping it with strong detergent and rags. You can polish the joint by rubbing with medium and then fine steel wool.

The finished soldered joint should have a bright and smooth appearance. Solder that looks dull or rough signals a poor joint (perhaps not enough heat or flux for a good bond).

A bad joint can be cleaned and resoldered. Heat the area with the torch and pull the joint apart by hand. (Use gloves or pliers to handle heated surfaces.) While the solder is still molten, wipe it from the joint with a piece of steel wool. You won't get all of it off, but you will take off any solder that is not firmly adhered to metal. After the joint has cooled, clean the area by buffing it with steel wool, apply flux, and solder as described above.

Electrical Soldering. Electrical soldering differs from mechanical soldering in that not only is a strong mechanical bond important but a good electrical one is too. Electrical soldering is employed for wire connections, splices, and electrical and electronic components. Since mechanical soldering flux is corrosive, it is never employed in electrical soldering. Instead, a thin solder wire (typically .062 gauge) with a rosin core is used. As the solder wire melts into the connection, the rosin flux flows and performs its function of cleaning and preparing the metal for a good bond. Since the rosin flux is noncorrosive, the joint doesn't need to be cleaned after it is soldered.

The heat source for electrical soldering is an electric iron or gun. For most work a 45-watt pencil style soldering iron is fine. If you do a great deal of electrical and electronic work, a 150-watt soldering gun (featuring near-instant heating) is worth the investment. Since flame never touches the electrical joint and the iron or gun tip is kept clean during soldering, electrical soldering is a very clean and surgical technique compared to mechanical soldering.

Prepare the connection by first making a strong mechanical connection with the wire or component. Wrap or crimp wires and leads by hand or with needlenose pliers. The solder should be responsible for a good electrical connection; let the wrapping or crimping take care of the mechanical connection.

Prepare the soldering iron tip for good work by heating it and applying some rosin-core solder to its surface. Rub the wire on the tip until it is coated with molten solder and flux. Then wipe the tip on a wet cellulose sponge to remove any excess solder. This procedure is called tinning. The tip should appear bright when it is properly tinned. Keep that bright look on the tip continuously while soldering. Use the sponge frequently while you work to wipe excess solder and flux from the tip. If the tip tarnishes (usually from too much heating), clean it with steel wool or a file and retin it before soldering.

Apply the heated and tinned tip to the electrical connection. Allow the area to heat up before touching the rosin-core solder to the connection, not the tip. When the connection is properly heated it will melt the solder wire. Remove the tip from the connection as soon as the solder melts. You usually need to melt only a small amount of solder to make the joint. Cover the connection, but don't overflow it. Excess blobs of solder can cause short circuits or damage to components.

Allow the connection to cool without disturbing it. If you move a wire or component before the solder hardens, it will cause a poor bond. Check the appearance

Solder Here

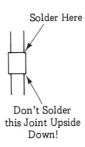

Solder Here

Don't Solder
this Joint Upside
Down!

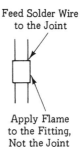

Feed Solder Wire
to the Joint

Apply Flame
to the Fitting,
Not the Joint

First Make Strong Mechanical
Connections by Crimping or Wrapping,
Then Apply Solder to Make a
Superior Electrical Connection.

FIGURE 10-1. Soldering techniques.

of the solder when it is hard—it should be smooth and bright. A bad joint can be unsoldered by heating and wiping or suctioning the solder away. (Electronics stores sell bulb-type desoldering tools.) Often simply reheating the joint and then allowing the solder to recool will produce a proper joint.

In brief

1. Clean metal parts with steel wool. Apply plumber's flux with a brush. Apply heat to the material, not to the joint or the solder wire. When the area is properly heated the joint will draw solder into itself by capillary action.

2. Clean the finished joint with detergent, rags, and steel wool. If the soldered joint doesn't appear smooth and bright, melt the solder again, pull the joint apart, clean, and resolder.

3. Use an electrical soldering iron or gun and rosin-core solder for electrical soldering. First make a strong mechanical connection by crimping or wrapping.

4. Tin the heated soldering tip by applying rosin-core solder and wiping off the excess on a wet sponge. Apply the tip to the connection. Allow the area to heat up; then apply the solder. Remove the tip from the connection and allow the connection to melt the solder.

5. Watch that you don't apply too much solder, and when the joint is cool check to make sure that the solder appears bright and smooth. A bad joint can be reheated with the tip and allowed to reharden. Molten solder can also be carefully wiped or suctioned away from the connection.

Tips

Prepare a good working surface by putting down bricks or concrete blocks for safe mechanical soldering. Since electrical soldering is precision work, you can often work right in the appliance or device or over a simple heat-resistant mat laid on a table.

In electrical soldering it is usually not necessary to clean wires or parts before connecting them. Usually the parts are new, the wire has been newly stripped, or the part has a bright plated finish. If you are working with older, tarnished or corroded components you should clean them before making the joint. Use fine sandpaper, a penknife, steel wool, and emery boards to scrape and buff joint surfaces to a bright appearance. Because electrical soldering employs a mild rosin flux it is important for used parts to be extra clean before soldering to ensure a good electrical joint.

When soldering plumbing fittings it is often difficult to avoid soldering an upside down joint. You are putting the item together and suddenly you find that a tee or a sleeve needs to be soldered, but its joint is facing the floor. Avoid this situation by advance planning or by turning the whole object over if possible. You don't want the force of gravity to fight the capillary action of the joint taking solder into itself. Solder joints on the horizontal or from above only.

RECYCLING OLD ELECTRICAL EQUIPMENT

Tools and supplies needed

AC test lamp or battery continuity tester
Screwdriver
Knife
Electrical supply cords
Miscellaneous electrical supplies

Procedure

One of the most rewarding recycling activities involves working with older electrical equipment. This country has produced some truly original popular culture in the form of electrical household appliances. The profusion of irons, radios, toasters, hot plates, fans, coffee-makers, waffle irons, record players, TV sets, heat and sun lamps, and other items that you find at an average flea market or garage sale is testament to our national obsession with labor-saving and enter-tainment appliances. Most people are caught up in the newest appliances and devices being advertised, so a steady stream of used but serviceable appliances goes to market.

You may not want many of these appliances. After all, who really needs an electrical countertop roaster or oven that does the same thing your stove can do? But you might want to buy and use an odd or old appliance that catches your fancy. Appliances from the 1950s and before are becoming collectible for their styling (streamlined irons and toasters that look as if they are ready for a trip to the moon)

and their innocent expression of faith in technology.

You might have a need for a used major appliance—a refrigerator or a vacuum cleaner, perhaps. These appliances are readily available and are worth tuning up with a few minor repairs to keep them in service for many more years. Such appliances show up at flea markets, thrift shops and auctions, and in classified ads, used furniture warehouses, and apartment building liquidations. Refrigerators, vacuum cleaners, fans, and other big appliances from the 1930s that still function are common. It can be fun to own a vintage appliance that not only looks interesting but functions efficiently too.

Replacing Line Cords. Most appliances are in workable condition but have worn line cords. Of the nonworking appliances, approximately 50 percent will function if their line cords are replaced. For safety and for the majority of broken appliances, replacement of the line cord should be the first step you take in recycling.

Replace the cord with one of the same type. Appliances have different current requirements, and a cord that serves for an old tube radio or television set will be inadequate for an iron or sun lamp. In general, the following types of cord will serve these appliances:

Plastic or rubber parallel cord—TVs, radios, small fans, record players.

Cotton- or plastic-covered reinforced cord— hanging lamps and fixtures, portable appliances (light current draw).

Vacuum cleaner cord—light-duty cleaners, sweepers, polishers.

Junior hard service cord—hand tools and portable appliances subject to dampness and some abuse.

Hard service cord—large electrical tools and portable appliances subject to dampness and very hard usage.

Cotton-covered heater cord—heating element appliances in dry places.

Rubber- or plastic-covered heater cord—heating element appliances in damp places.

If you bring the old cord into an electrical supply house and mention the kind of appliance you have, the counter person can supply you with a replacement or can advise on a substitute cord that will perform well. It is best to let the counter person suggest a suitable plug for the cord, since each kind of cord has its own plug requirement.

Electrical stores also stock a large number of replacement cord sets (cords with suitable plugs and terminals already attached). These cord sets are great for a quick, professional-looking replacement on irons, countertop heating appliances, some radios and TVs (that use a safety interlock cord device), power tools, and most other portable appliances. Some cords come with strain relief devices such as flexible sleeves, wire springs, and plastic bushings already mounted, which greatly simplifies professional quality repairs.

Testing. If an appliance doesn't respond to replacement of its line cord, you can try a few simple measures to see whether or not it can be recycled. The first check is to use a continuity tester. These devices (either an AC type that plugs into a wall socket or a self-powered battery model) are available for a few dollars and will allow you to check for broken components and grounded appliances.

To check for broken components, first isolate the component from the appliance. You may have to remove it entirely from the appliance to do this. Then make the suspected component part of the tester circuit. If you clip the two test leads to a switch and the lamp lights when you turn the switch on, the switch is good. If the tester doesn't light the switch is broken, and when it is replaced the appliance will probably return to normal operation. This testing for broken components is called *continuity testing*—you are checking to make sure that a component offers a continuous circuit for electricity to pass. Here is a partial list of components that should be tested for continuity:

Line cords
Hook-up wires
Switches
Heating elements
Contact points
Coils
Fuses
Indicator lamps
Solenoids
Relays
Timers

To check for grounding, clip one tester lead to a point in the appliance's circuit and touch the other lead to the metal frame of the appliance. If the lamp lights, you have a grounded appliance (a loose wire or component is touching the frame of the appliance), and you should correct that condition before doing any more work on the appliance.

Another inexpensive tester is a neon hot circuit tester. This will tell you if an outlet, plug, or circuit is carrying current. Simply touch the tester leads to the two poles of the circuit. If the lamp lights, you have current present. The neon tester is a good check to make sure that current to the circuit you are working with is off.

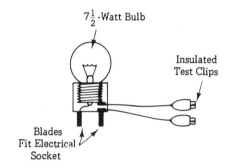

FIGURE 10-2. A test lamp.

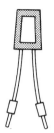

FIGURE 10-3. A neon hot-circuit tester.

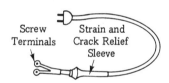

FIGURE 10-4. A heavy-duty appliance cord.

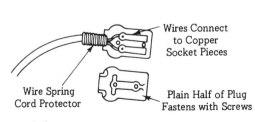

FIGURE 10-5. An appliance plug cord for heaters, toasters, irons, etc.

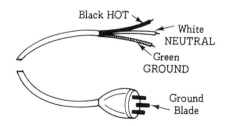

FIGURE 10-6. A heavy-duty, three-wire, grounded plug and cord for major appliances, refrigerators, air-conditioners, power tools, etc.

The Bulb in the Tester
will Glow if the Circuit is Good.

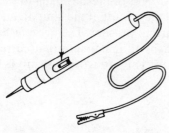

FIGURE 10-7. A penlight-battery-powered continuity tester.

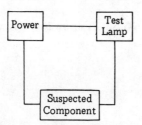

FIGURE 10-8. Continuity testing makes the suspected item part of the circuit.

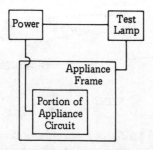

FIGURE 10-9. A grounding check establishes whether the appliance frame has become connected to the appliance circuit.

In brief

1. Replace worn and broken line cords. Select a cord and plug recommended by an electrical supply store for your particular appliance and use. Buy complete appliance cord sets for professional repairs on small appliances.

2. Use an AC or battery continuity tester to check for broken components or wires. Isolate the suspected component from the circuit and connect it to the test leads. If the tester lights up, the component is good.

3. Clip one lead to a portion of the circuit and the other lead to the metal frame of the appliance to check for grounding. If the tester lights, some component or wire is touching the frame of the appliance, and it must be repaired before any more work proceeds.

4. A good safety measure is to use a neon hot circuit tester. If the tester glows when inserted into the circuit you are going to work on, there is current present and you are warned.

Tips

The AC tester is good for appliance testing because it puts real house current through the circuit. Be sure to handle the clips carefully—don't make yourself part of the circuit. Get an AC tester with well insulated probes or clips.

A battery tester is safer to use and works fine on cords and small components. It generally won't have enough power to check components with a lot of resistance (heating elements, coils, etc.), so you need an AC tester as well.

Old electrical equipment that contains tubes (nearly every radio, TV, record player, or other entertainment device before 1960) can often be recycled. Tubes are the most vulnerable components since they are fragile and are subject to heat and vibration. A large electronics store will have a tube tester available for you to test suspected components. Simply remove the tubes from their sockets (using pieces of masking tape to mark tubes and their sockets for accurate reassembly) and take them to be tested.

If you have outsized tubes from the 1940s or earlier that can't be tested and replaced by use of a modern tube tester, you can often substitute modern style tubes that will perform the same functions as the old tubes. Go to a radio and TV repair store and ask them to wire new tube sockets into the equipment. Modern tubes can then be plugged in. The work is straightforward (there are standard substitution tables for all tubes), and most shops should be able to handle it for you. Your equipment won't be all original, but it will function and its appearance won't be affected.

RESTORING AND PRESERVING NEON SIGNS*

Tools and supplies needed

Drill and bits
Pliers
Needlenose pliers
Penknife
Screwdrivers
Wood screws

*This project was prepared under the guidance and supervision of Leonard Davidson of Davidson Design Studio, Philadelphia, Pennsylvania.

Screw hooks and eyes
Electrical tape (plastic or friction)
High tension cable (15,000 volts rating)
Artist's paint brush
2-inch-wide paint brush
Neon tube supports
Copper tie wire
Fishing line
Galvanized picture wire
Black enamel paint

Procedure

Neon signs from store windows, roadside displays, and old commercial buildings are intriguing bits of American popular culture. From its introduction in the 1920s to its decline in popularity in the late 1950s the art and craft of bending glass tubes, fitting them with electrodes, and filling them with neon or argon gas was practiced all over America. Multicolored neon signs and designs became part of the modern landscape. From the simple blue or green neon-outlined clock in a country gas station to the giant animated neon sign spectaculars of Times Square in the 1930s, neon was the way we celebrated and advertised our way of life. If you have fond memories of going to the movies and passing through a magical neon-festooned lobby, or if you like the beauty of gracefully bent glass and appreciate the skill and ingenuity behind these cleverly designed objects, you will probably want to restore and display some neon in your home.

Old neon signs are often sold at auctions and flea markets. They might range from complete two- and three-color beer signs to individual letters that have been salvaged from a larger sign. You might see a sign hanging, unused, in a window. Often you can buy old neon signs from shop owners who no longer want them. Or it might be that a building is slated for demolition or renovation and the owner is willing to sell you the old neon signs that would be thrown out anyway.

If you find an old neon sign and negotiate for its sale, you are faced with the problems of dismantling, transporting, testing, repairing, and installing it in your home. The following procedures should provide you with the information you need to do these things successfully.

Dismantling and Transporting. When dismantling a neon window sign, first check to make sure that the sign is unplugged. Then disengage the transformer (a copper coil in a rectangular metal casing) from the neon tubes (which are lightweight and very breakable). Find the transformer. (It will be hanging from hooks or chains or screwed to a wall or window frame.) Disconnect the two high tension leads that run from the transformer to the electrodes on the neon tubes. If possible, disconnect the leads at the transformer (or cut the leads with wire cutters) to avoid putting stress on the delicate and breakable glass-enclosed electrodes of the neon sign.

After the leads are detached, unhook or unscrew the transformer. Then remove the neon tube itself by cutting the wires that hold it to the window frame. If the tube is small you can hold it with one hand while you cut the hanging wires with your other hand. If the piece is large or awkward to hold, use a helper to cut the wires while you hold the neon tube with both hands.

Handle the tube by the frame (the transparent glass tubes or rods that hold the whole assembly together) if it has one. If the sign is frameless, handle it by hold-

ing the straight sections of tube. You should avoid putting stress on the delicate bends, connections, and electrodes of the tube. Carefully lay the sign on a flat surface—flat side (viewing side) down— for transporting it. A rug, blanket, or foam pad will serve to keep it from contacting hard metal surfaces.

Testing and Repairing. When you get the neon sign home, test it. Reattach the wiring as you found it and plug the transformer into your house current. Switch on the transformer pull cord (if it has one). If the sign lights up brightly, you are in great shape and you can proceed to cleaning and installing.

If the neon lights up dimly with flickering, it could mean several things. First, the gas could be slowly leaking from the tube through a hairline crack. The only solution to this would be to have a sign shop inspect and repair the tube and refill it with gas. Second, the transformer might not be powerful enough because it is deteriorating from old age. Last, the electrode wires might be imperfect. (These are the wires that come out of the neon tubes and connect to the high tension leads.) Unwrap the electrode connections, supporting the electrodes with your fingers as you work, and inspect them. If the wires are corroded, broken, or loosely attached, correct the situation. This may require taking the unit to a sign shop to have the electrodes replaced.

If the sign lights up but buzzes loudly, your high tension leads or the glass tubes may be touching a surface that conducts electricity. If this is not the case, you have a weak transformer that will eventually have to be replaced. If the sign doesn't light up at all, the transformer is dead or the neon has leaked completely out of the tube. If inspection reveals a crack or break, get the tube repaired at a sign shop.

Since the transformer is important to the whole set-up, you should test yours if the neon is not functioning correctly. If you can establish that the transformer is good, then you know that your problem is with the neon itself and its associated electrodes and connections. To test a transformer, disconnect the high tension leads from the electrodes on the neon. Position the leads so that they are away from each other, the transformer, and any conductors. Plug the transformer in, switch it on, and test each lead separately. Hold the lead by the insulation and bend it so that the bare wire approaches the metal case of the transformer. If the unit is good there should be a ½-inch arc of electricity from the lead to the case. Test the other lead in the same way. If both leads have a healthy ½-inch arc, the unit is good. Be careful not to touch the bare wires of the high tension cables as you test them.

If you buy a new transformer be sure to take the information from the old transformer rating plate with you to get a new one of the right capacity. Look at the rating for the "secondary voltage." (It will be somewhere between 3,000 and 15,000 volts and 20 to 30 milliamps.) If the transformer is missing or there is no rating plate, a sign shop or neon supply house will be able to provide you with a proper transformer if you can give them the total footage of the sign (include all the bends and turns) and the diameter of the tubing. It is also important to tell the store personnel whether the sign is filled with neon or argon gas. The only way to know this is to describe the color of the lit sign

(if you or the previous owner have seen it lit) or to bring the sign in for inspection and testing by the store.

Getting the proper size transformer is very important. If the transformer is too weak for the sign the installation will buzz, the light will flicker, and the transformer will burn out quickly. If the transformer is too powerful for the sign, the neon will run hot and the electrodes will burn out prematurely.

If the high tension leads have deteriorated or are too short for the new installation, buy a length of 15,000-volt high tension cable from the sign shop to cut into two new leads for the sign. You can substitute automobile ignition cable for high tension cable, but be sure that it has stranded metal conductors and is rated at 15,000 volts or better.

If you plan to mount the sign on a wall or other surface instead of hanging it, be sure to buy glass and metal tube supports at the sign shop. You should use one tube support for about every 1 to 2 feet of neon tubing you plan to mount. The sign shop or neon supply house can sell you porcelain or glass tube insulators for running high tension cable through walls and other solid surfaces. You can also buy glass tubes and rods for making or replacing frame units on your sign.

Cleaning. Once you have the neon sign functioning, you can proceed to clean and mount it. If the neon tube is small enough to fit inside a bathtub or shallow pan, place it there; otherwise, place it on a flat surface outside where you can apply liquids. Make a solution of dishwashing detergent and warm water. Place the neon tube in it or apply it with a soft bristle paint brush. Use the brush to work the detergent into tight places and

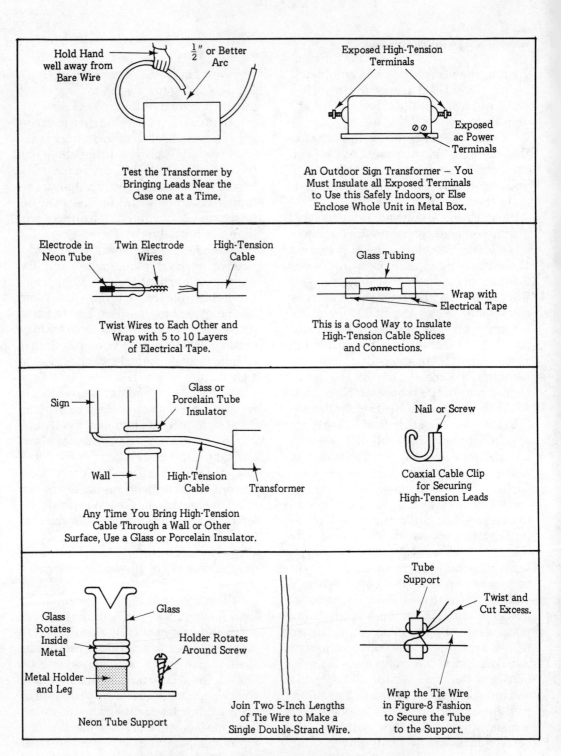

FIGURE 10-10. Hints for restoring neon signs.

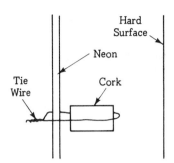

FIGURE 10-11.   Protect hanging neon by installing cork bumpers on the tubes.

to remove any caked and dried dirt. Be very gentle as you clean, and allow the detergent time to work on the dirt. Rinse the tube with fresh water and allow it to air dry.

If the neon has grease or paint spots that won't come off with detergent and brushing, use a single-edge razor blade to gently remove them. Support the tube as you go over it with the razor. Don't scrape off the black paint that has been applied to block out unwanted portions of neon light.

After the neon is dry, use a small artist's paint brush to restore the blocked out portions of the sign. Apply a special neon block-out paint (available at sign shops) or use a thick flat or gloss black enamel. If you use an enamel, let it sit in a shallow dish for a few hours to thicken before applying it—you want a thick, opaque paint to prevent light from showing through. After the paint is dry, hook up the sign and turn it on. Carefully inspect your blocking out work—you will probably find places that need to be retouched.

Mounting.   The final step is the mounting and permanent hook-up of the neon. It is important to mount the sign in a place where there are no conducting or flammable materials. A window is an excellent place to mount neon. The glass panes are nonconducting and nonflammable. Other possible mountings would be a plaster wall, a piece of plexiglass, or a sheet of plastic laminate.

If you choose to hang the neon, you must drill and screw two or more screw eyes into a solid surface and run picture hanging wire, copper tie wire, or monofilament fishing line from them to two or more points on the neon. In general for simple, small pieces a two-line hanging is adequate.

If you want to mount the neon on a wall or nonconducting surface you can use glass tube supports and soft copper tie wire (20 to 30 gauge). Have a helper hold the neon against the wall while you mark points on the wall where supports should be positioned. The supports should be close to the electrodes at the beginning and end of the run of tubing and every 1 to 2 feet in between. Place the supports so that they will contact the frame (preferable) or the neon tubing. Alternate supports high and low on the wall so that the neon is balanced. Drill holes and install the supports to the wall with wood screws (and plastic anchors if necessary). The glass supports rotate within their metal holders and on the screw mounting so you can cup them exactly under the glass.

Have your helper hold the sign next to the wall while you position and secure the supports to the tubing. Take two 5-inch lengths of tie wire and place them together to act as one wire. Loop the wire under the tube support wings and over the glass in a figure-8 fashion, and then twist the wire tight with a pair of pliers. Cut the excess wire with a pair of wire cutters.

The transformer should be mounted to a window frame or on a wall near the neon tube. You want a direct route to the neon for the high tension leads. The transformer shouldn't be more than 5 feet away from the neon electrodes if possible. Cut the old high tension leads (or the new cable) to fit, strip the ends, and attach them to the electrodes and transformer leads. It is important to keep the high tension leads from crossing each other or any other wire (stereo, extension cords, etc.) or conducting material. You can secure the high tension leads to walls, woodwork, or the ceiling if you wish by using plastic cord clips sold at electric and electronic supply houses. Ask for heavy-duty cord clips or coaxial cable clips. First the clips are secured to the support surface, and then the high tension cable is placed in the flexible plastic holder. This way, there is no chance of damaging the high tension leads during installation.

It doesn't matter which high tension lead goes to which electrode. Twist the wires around each other and tightly insulate each connection with five to ten wraps of electrical tape. If you are running high tension wire through a wall or other surface from a remote transformer, use a glass or porcelain tube insulator in the surface to insulate the high tension lead. A very good way to insulate bare wire high tension connections is to use a small length of glass tube over the splice and then wrap the whole unit with electrical tape. When insulating the electrode connections, be very careful not to break them off by wrapping too violently.

In brief

1. Dismantle the neon sign after it's been unplugged. Disconnect the high tension leads at the transformer end. Remove the transformer. Holding the sign, cut the hanging wires to remove it.

2. Transport the neon sign on a soft, flat surface, flat side down. Handle the sign by the frame pieces or straight sections of tubing.

3. Reattach the sign at home and turn it on. If it works, clean and install it. If the neon lights dimly or flickers, check for a hairline crack or a weak transformer. Also check high tension leads and electrode wires for poor connections.

4. If the sign buzzes loudly, the sign or wires are in contact with a conducting material or you have a weak transformer. Replace it. If the sign doesn't light up at all, test the transformer. If it's good, you probably have a bad neon tube.

5. Test the transformer by bringing the high tension leads near the transformer case, one at a time. If you get

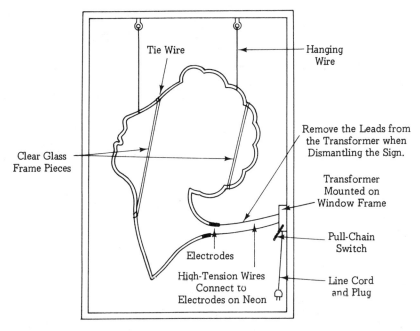

FIGURE 10-12. **A typical window-frame mounting for a neon sign.**

a healthy ½-inch arc from both leads, the transformer is good.

6. Buy a new transformer, high tension cable, insulators, and tubing supports at a sign shop or neon supply house. Give the shop the rating for the old transformer (or the length, diameter, and color of your tube) to get a new one of the proper size. If your tube needs repairs, the sign shop can do them for you.

7. Clean the neon tube by soaking and brushing it with a detergent solution. Use a soft paint brush to clean hardened dirt. Rinse gently with fresh water and allow to air dry. Clean grease or paint spots with a razor blade.

8. Use a small artist's brush to restore the blocked out portions of the sign.

Use a thick black paint and follow the old blocking or use your common sense to separate letters and designs. Turn on the sign to check your work.

9. Hang the neon sign from screw eyes and picture wire or monofilament. A two-point hanging is usually enough for a small piece.

10. Mount the sign on a wall or other nonconducting and noncombustible surface by holding it to the wall, marking points for tube supports, drilling and screwing on tube supports, and securing the sign to the supports with tie wire.

11. Mount the transformer near the sign with a clear path for the high tension cables. Don't cross the cables with each other or any other wire.

Secure the high tension cables with cord or coaxial clips if you wish.

12. Connect the cables to the transformer and to the neon electrodes by twisting the wires. Insulate the connections by wrapping tightly with electrical tape. An alternate method is to use a small tube of glass over the bare wires and then wrap the whole unit with tape.

Basic rules for safe installation and operation of neon

1. Neon glass tubing (especially old recycled signs) is fragile and can break very easily. If the glass breaks while the neon is in operation, shut the power off immediately. High voltage electricity will eventually find a way to break or burn through most materials in its search for a ground.

2. Shut down the neon immediately if the installation malfunctions (breaks, overheating, flickering, loud buzzing), and correct the cause before turning it on again.

3. Transformers need ventilation—don't install them in tight airless areas. They shouldn't be run for more than 8 hours continuously. Business installations have timers to ensure an overnight cool-down period.

4. Never run neon when no one is present in the room. It is not advisable to run neon when children or animals are present. Neon is best mounted where it won't be touched or bumped. Unplug the unit when it's not in use.

5. Always hang or mount neon on or near nonconducting and noncombustible surfaces. At a minimum, the neon should be 3 inches away from any possible conducting surface. Electrodes and high tension cables must be insulated by glass, porcelain, or heavy tape wrapping to minimize shock and fire hazard.

6. Never substitute any other kind of cable for high tension wire. Use only neon high tension cable or automobile ignition cable (either must be rated at a minimum of 15,000 volts).

Tips

Look in the Yellow Pages under "Signs" and "Sign Supplies" to locate sign shops and supply houses that handle neon. If you live in a remote location, some of the larger supply houses in big cities will mail order parts and equipment to you.

A sign shop can handle repairs to the neon tube itself. Following are some of the services:

Repair of breaks and cracks in the tubing and repumping of gas into the tubing.

Installation of new electrodes and electrode wires.

Repositioning of electrodes (for, example you might want to have electrodes changed from perpendicular to parallel with the sign to make installation easier in your space).

Changing the color of certain signs. (This is done by putting argon gas and mercury into former neon gas tubes.)

Repair parts and service prices vary tremendously in this business, so it will pay you to do research by phone before you bring your tube into a shop. Price variations of from $15 to $75 for the same repair are typical.

Sometimes the twin metal leads coming out of the glass-encased electrode on the neon tube will be broken off from metal fatigue. If the leads are broken flush with the glass it will be impossible to make a standard twisted connection to the high tension lead. In this case the tube can sometimes be salvaged with a special fitting available from sign shops. It is a cap that contains a number of fine metal whiskers that conduct electricity. The cap is placed over the broken electrode wires and crimped into place. The high tension lead is then attached to the cap and the whole unit is insulated with tape or glass tube and tape.

MAKING A HOOD ORNAMENT LIGHT ——————————

Tools and supplies needed

Drill and bits

Circular saw

Screwdriver

Tape measure

Knife

Hot glue gun

12-volt illuminated hood ornament

Doorbell transformer

Long-neck canopy toggle switch

Lamp cord

Self-tapping plug

Scrap white pine

Wire nuts

Sandpaper

Wood screws

Procedure

This is a fanciful project for people who have a sense of humor about our national love affair with automobiles. Large custom auto supply stores and mail order catalogs offer many different styles of hood ornaments. Some of these ornaments feature idealized women, mythological figures, animals, and popular culture figures, and some are electrically lit. Generally the figure will have colored plastic wings or a transparent base through which the illumination passes. Some of these ornaments are cast from classic molds that have been around since the 1920s, 30s, and 40s. Such inexpensive chrome and plastic ornaments are ideal for creating a novelty light that will brighten a dark corner of your living space. This design uses a common doorbell transformer to break down house current into a low voltage to run the automobile lamp in the ornament.

Begin by constructing a simple box to mount the ornament and house the electrical parts. Cut four pieces of pine 8 × 6 inches and two pieces 6 × 4½ inches. Sand all the edges of the pieces smooth with medium and fine sandpaper.

Assemble the box using wood screws driven into pilot holes. If you have a hot glue gun you can quickly assemble all but the bottom of the box by squeezing a bead of glue on the edges of the lumber. Leave the bottom of the box unassembled for the moment.

Position the ornament on the top of the box and mark where holes will have to be drilled to accept the mounting bolts that come with the ornament. Also mark the position and size of the hole necessary to admit the 12-volt light bulb and socket that come with the ornament. Drill holes for the bolts and the light. Secure the ornament with the bolts supplied. If the bolts aren't long enough to clear the underside of the pine, use stove bolts of the proper length and with the same diameter as the stock bolts.

On the back of the box drill a hole for

the canopy toggle switch and a ⅜-inch hole to admit lamp cord to the box. Install the toggle switch in the box and thread an 8-inch length of lamp cord into the box. Tie a knot in the lamp cord so it can't be pulled out of the box. Strip ½ inch of insulation from each end of the lamp cord with a knife. Cut an 8-inch length of lamp cord and split the conductors apart to come up with two 8-inch lengths of hook-up wire. Strip ½ inch of insulation from the ends of the hook-up wires.

Attach one end of the power supply cord to a terminal on the transformer. (Make sure the terminals say "primary side" or "110 VAC".) Attach the other end of the power cord to one of the wires coming from the toggle switch. Attach a length of hook-up wire with one end on the other primary terminal of the transformer and the other end on the remaining wire of the toggle switch. Secure all the bare wire connections with wire nuts.

From one terminal on the secondary side of the transformer, run a length of hook-up wire to one of the bolts on the hood ornament. Secure the wire under the bolt head or nut. Attach the wire from the light bulb and socket to the remaining secondary terminal on the transformer.

Attach the transformer to the bottom piece of the box with wood screws. Slip the light bulb and socket up into the hood ornament. Secure the bottom piece to the box by drilling and driving four screws. Install a self-tapping plug on the free end of the line cord.

In brief

1. Construct a box to mount the ornament and electrical components. Cut four pieces 8 × 6 inches and two pieces 6 × 4½ inches. Sand the edges smooth.

2. Assemble all but the bottom piece of the box with screws or hot glue from a gun. Position the ornament and drill

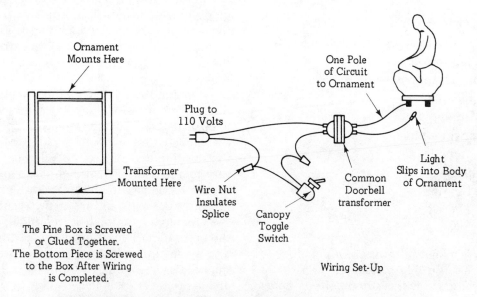

Ornament Mounts Here

Transformer Mounted Here

The Pine Box is Screwed or Glued Together. The Bottom Piece is Screwed to the Box After Wiring is Completed.

Plug to 110 Volts

Wire Nut Insulates Splice

Canopy Toggle Switch

One Pole of Circuit to Ornament

Light Slips into Body of Ornament

Common Doorbell transformer

Wiring Set-Up

FIGURE 10-13. Procedures for making a hood ornament light.

the necessary holes for bolts and the light bulb. Install the ornament.

3. Drill holes for the canopy toggle and the line cord. Install the toggle and feed the cord into the box. Tie a knot for strain relief in the cord. Cut 8 inches of line cord and split the conductors. Strip ½ inch of insulation from all the conductors.

4. Attach one power supply wire to a terminal on the transformer's primary side. Attach the other supply wire to one of the switch wires. Attach a hook-up wire to the other primary terminal and connect the other end of the wire to the remaining wire of the switch. Use wire nuts to secure bare connections.

5. Attach hook-up wire from a secondary terminal on the transformer to a bolt on the hood ornament. Attach the light bulb wire to the remaining secondary terminal.

6. Screw the transformer to the bottom of the box. Slip the bulb and socket up into the ornament. Drill and screw the bottom to the rest of the box. Install a self-tapping plug on the line cord.

CUTTING BOTTLES AND JUGS

Tools and supplies needed

Bottle cutting kit
Glass cutter
Goggles
Gloves
Kerosene
Emery cloth
Silicon carbide wet/dry paper
Electrical supplies

Procedure

By using one of the available bottle cutting kits from a variety store or hobby shop, you can recycle glass bottles and jugs into a number of interesting projects. Industrial designers are paid large amounts of money to design interesting and attactive-looking glass containers. It is very simple to take advantage of these good-looking objects and use them as lampshades, bowls, ash trays, vases, and food containers.

You can find bottles in the trash, at recycling centers, and at flea markets and junk shops. Some of the more interesting bottles can be obtained from restaurants and bars that serve wines and bottled water. Inexpensive bottles that you might purchase for a dollar or less include thick 1950s and earlier soda, beer, and milk bottles with etched and painted designs and lettering.

For efficient cutting, a bottle must be clean. Soak the labels off in a sink of hot, soapy water. Scrape off any tough labels with a single-edge razor blade or sharp knife. To get bottles squeaky clean on the outside, spray them with ammonia-based window cleaner and wipe them dry with a clean cloth or paper towels.

Types of Cutters. There are three basic kinds of bottle cutters available. One is the *scribe and tap* model, which allows you to use the bottle's neck and mouth as a guide and support for running a glass cutter around the bottle and then fracturing the scored line from within the bottle. Another model is a *cradle cutter*, which has a base on which you place the bottle. The base is adjusted to place the cutter where you want it, and then the bottle is rotated against the cutter to score a cut line. The break is then accomplished by heating and cooling the cut line in quick succession. A third type of cutter is the *hot wire* model. This device permits you to place a loop of resistance heating wire around a bottle and then apply electrical current to the wire, which causes the bottle to break. A combination cradle and hot wire cutter is also available that uses a hot wire to finish a break started by scoring the bottle with a cutter wheel.

Which cutter you choose is up to you. The wheeled cutters are generally cheaper and more available than the hot wire models. Regardless of the model you choose, be sure to follow the manufacturer's instructions for use. The important thing with wheeled cutters is to keep the cutter wheel at a perfect right angle to the glass surface and to scribe only a light hairline around the bottle. Too deep and wide a line will cause the bottle to break unevenly.

Freehand Cutting. You can't use a cutter kit to work on square or oddly shaped bottles. With these you can try freehand scribing with a common glass cutter. Use a block of wood, a sturdy can, or some other support to hold the cutter at an even height. Lubricate the cutter by dipping the wheel into kerosene. Hold the cutter in place on the support and rotate the bottle against it to produce a fine score line. If the cutter skips when making corners, complete the line around the bottle and then go over the missed areas to connect the line. Don't draw the cutter back across the score line—you will dull the cutter wheel and make a frothy, wide score line that will break unevenly. The sound the cutter should make is like that of tearing tissue paper. If you hear a grinding sound from the cutter, it means

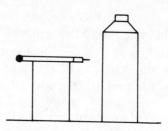

FIGURE 10-14. **Use a support block to freehand square a squarish bottle.**

that you are pressing too hard or are going over a previously scored line.

The break of a squarish bottle is accomplished by heating and cooling the score line. Light a candle and rotate the score line in the flame. Make two passes of the flame over the score line and then move the bottle out of the flame and make two more passes about ½ inch above the flame. Cool the score line with a cube of ice. Rub the ice quickly around the line. The combination of heat and cold will cause a break along the line. If the bottle doesn't come apart on your first attempt, repeat the heating and cooling procedure until it does.

Making Your Own Cutter. You can make a hot wire device for breaking bottles that have been scored by a pivot point or cradle cutter. Simply buy a length of nickel/chrome heating element wire (often called *nichrome wire*) from an appliance store or electrical supply house. Connect it to the screw terminals on a porcelain cleat-type lamp socket. Screw a plug base into the socket, which will allow you to plug in a power cord. Make up a length of power cord with heavy-duty plugs on both ends. One end of the cord will plug into a wall socket and the other end will plug into the porcelain socket.

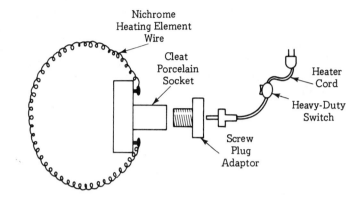

FIGURE 10-15.   A homemade, heating-type bottle breaker.

Use heater cord and install a heavy-duty line switch in the cord for power control to the heater wire.

Take a round bottle that you have scored with a cutter. Place the heater wire on the score line and adjust one of the screw terminals on the porcelain socket to take up any slack in the wire. Put eye goggles on and plug the power cord into the porcelain socket and then into a wall outlet. With the line switch, turn the power on for about 2 seconds and then turn it off. The wire should heat rapidly and cause the bottle to break on the score

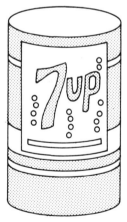

Thick, Old, Deposit-Style
Soda Bottles with Tops
Cut off Become Pencil
Holders, Flowerpots,
Match Cups, etc.

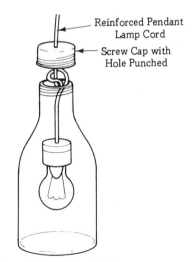

Reinforced Pendant
Lamp Cord

Screw Cap with
Hole Punched

Quart Beer or Soda Bottles
with Bottoms Removed
Make Nice Lamps.

FIGURE 10-16.   Two household items made from bottles.

line. You should be able to hear the fracture being made in the glass. Complete the break by moving the wire around the diameter of the bottle until it covers the portion not fractured. Cycle the power on and off as before to complete the break.

In brief

1. Select a score and tap, cradle style, hot wire, or combination bottle cutter. Follow the manufacturer's directions for use. Soak the labels off and clean the bottle with window cleaner before cutting.

2. Cut an oddly shaped bottle freehand by laying a glass cutter across a support piece and rotating the bottle against it. Lubricate the cutter with kerosene. Finish the break by heating the line in a flame and cooling it with an ice cube. Repeat the heat/cool cycle until the bottle fractures.

3. Make a hot wire bottle breaker with a length of heater wire, porcelain socket, electrical plugs, cord, and a plug base. Place the wire on the score line and quickly cycle the heat on and off until the bottle fractures. Complete the break by moving the wire to the unbroken section of the bottle and cycling the heat on and off.

Tips

You must use eye and hand protection when cutting bottles. Glass can break unexpectedly, and you must be prepared. Lay sheets of newspaper over your work surface to catch glass dust, splinters, and shards. Deposit waste glass in a sturdy cardboard box.

Check the uniformity of thickness of your bottle before attempting a cut. If the bottle is poorly formed, with thick and thin sections, it won't cut very easily. Place the bottle on a flat surface and roll it to check for this—the thickest section will always come to rest on the underside of the bottle. You can mark the thick and thin parts of the bottle with a felt pen and at least be aware of the situation when you tap or heat.

The cut end of the bottle should be sanded to smooth the edges. Most bottle cutting kits will give you a supply of emery cloth or silicon carbide sandpaper to start with. Hold the paper flat on a table and rub the glass on it in circular strokes. You can use an electric drill fitted with a sanding disk to speed up this work. Simply mount the drill in a vise and press the bottle to the spinning disk. For a really fine finish on the glass use a #220 wet/dry emery cloth. Wet the cloth with a bit of water before starting to smooth the glass.

MAKING DISPLAY BASES FOR ART WORK

Tools and supplies needed

Circular saw
Tape measure
Hot glue gun
Drill and bits
White pine lumber
Plate glass
Spray paint
Old heating grilles
Wood screws

Procedure

If you have a treasured piece of art such as a sculpture, casting, or rare collectible, you can show it off to good advantage with a museum-style pedestal base. White pine 1 × 12-inch lumber is perfect for the job. It's smooth and uniform and will glue or screw together to make a base that you can paint, urethane, cover with sheet goods, or leave natural.

You can cut white pine to make a base of any height. The recommended heights for normal use are 8, 24, and 48 inches. Cut four pieces of 1 × 12-inch lumber to the height required. Cut one more piece for a top 9¾ × 11¼ inches. Cut four cleat pieces to hold the top in place. Make the cleats 9¾ × 1 inches.

Assemble the four height pieces as shown in the illustration. The quickest way to assemble the lumber is to use a hot glue gun. Simply squeeze a bead of glue along the edge of one board, press it to another, and hold it for 60 seconds. A glue gun will let you put the base together in 15 minutes or less, and there won't be any screw heads showing on the surface

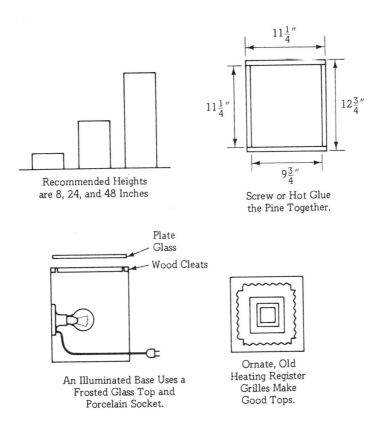

Recommended Heights
are 8, 24, and 48 Inches

Screw or Hot Glue
the Pine Together.

Plate
Glass
Wood Cleats

An Illuminated Base Uses a
Frosted Glass Top and
Porcelain Socket.

Ornate, Old
Heating Register
Grilles Make
Good Tops.

FIGURE 10-17. How to construct display pedestals.

of the project. If you don't have a glue gun you can drill and screw the base together with 1½-inch wood screws.

After the four height pieces are secured, fasten the four cleat pieces inside the top of the base to support the top piece. Place the cleats ¾ inch below the top edge of the base so that the top piece will sit flush with the top edge. Use hot glue or 1-inch screws to fasten the cleats. Lay the top piece in place on the cleats and secure it with screws or hot glue.

In brief

1. Cut four pieces of 1 × 12 lumber to the height required. Cut a top piece 9¾ × 11¼ inches. Cut four cleats 9¾ × 1 inches.

2. Assemble the height pieces with hot glue or wood screws. Using screws or hot glue, fasten the cleats inside the top end of the base. Indent the cleats so that the top piece will sit flush with the project.

3. Lay the top piece in place on the cleats and fasten it with screws or hot glue.

Tips

The base can be illuminated by substituting a ⅛-inch-thick piece of glass for the top piece. Indent the cleats ⅛ inch from the top of the base so that the glass will sit flush with the unit. Paint the underside of the glass with white spray paint to diffuse the light. Screw a porcelain flush-mount socket with a 25- to 60-watt bulb inside the base about 4 inches below the glass plate. Wire the socket with lamp cord and install a line switch and plug on the cord. You might want to drill a few vent holes

in the base to prevent heat build-up (especially important if the base is a short one and you are using a bright bulb).

You can also use salvaged iron or steel fancy heating grilles that you find in the trash or at a flea market or auction. These decorative grilles only need to be wire brushed and spray painted to bring their details back. You could simply lay a grill on top of the base instead of a lumber top piece or you could build the base to the dimensions of a grille, recessing the piece on cleats so that it is flush with the top of the project.

ADAPTING SALVAGED WOODWORK

Tools and supplies needed

Paint stripping supplies and tools
Drill and bits
Adjustable hole drill
Hack saw
Screwdriver
Epoxy glue
Sandpaper
Scrap pine or other wood
1½-inch wood screws
½-inch wood dowel

Procedure

Occasionally you will come across some beautiful examples of late 19th and early 20th century woodwork. These hand- and machine-carved pieces were the building blocks of domestic architecture. Builders ordered this fancy work from catalogs listing hundreds of different styles. Many fine old houses have staircases and porches embellished with carved, turned, and molded brackets, balusters, and ornamental pieces.

When houses are remodeled or torn down, some of these pieces become available for purchase. Often you will come across cardboard boxes of porch gingerbread and stair balusters at flea markets and auctions. These fine pieces of wood sometimes go begging because no one knows what to do with them. Unless you are restoring an old house and you can find enough woodwork to do over an entire porch or staircase, there doesn't seem to be much use for these architectural delights. Here are some ideas for recycling these pieces so that they survive to be appreciated and loved again.

The first step in working with these items is to clean and strip them thoroughly. Many times their finish is rough and battered. Use chemical stripper, a wire brush, a putty knife, small pointed scrapers, and steel wool to get all the paint and finish off them.

Candlesticks. To make a pair of candle holders from a single turned baluster piece, cut equal lengths off the ends of the piece. (Often the piece will be chewed up on both ends.) When you have two square ends, measure the piece and cut it in half. You should have two identically detailed halves. If the two baluster pieces don't match, you will have to use more than one whole baluster to cut into two candle holders.

Cut two 5-inch diameter discs from scrap lumber. Use an adjustable hole drill to cut plugs from the scrap and then sand any rough edges on the discs with medium sandpaper. Set your hole drill to a 1-inch diameter and drill two holes 1½ inches deep in the top of the baluster piece to hold the candles. Remove the wood plugs from the holes by breaking them out with a screwdriver and then cleaning the hole further with a penknife. Drill a ½-inch hole in the center of each disc. Drill ½-inch holes in the bottom of

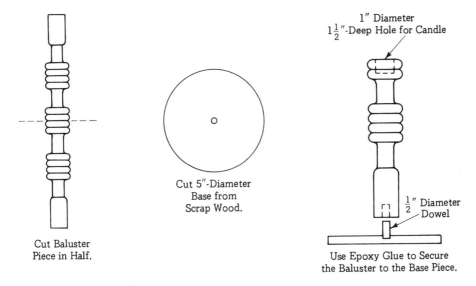

Cut Baluster
Piece in Half.

Cut 5″-Diameter
Base from
Scrap Wood.

1″ Diameter
1½″-Deep Hole for Candle

½″ Diameter
Dowel

Use Epoxy Glue to Secure
the Baluster to the Base Piece.

FIGURE 10-18. How to make a candle holder from salvaged wood.

the two baluster pieces 2½ inches deep.

Cut two 3-inch lengths of ½-inch dowel with a hack saw. Coat the dowels with epoxy glue. Fasten the dowels to the wood discs and drive the units into the holes of the baluster pieces. Allow the glue to cure before finishing the candlesticks.

Shelf Brackets. To make porch brackets into shelf brackets, simply drill ½-inch diameter holes in the brackets to receive glued ½-inch dowels. Drill matching holes in the wall through to the underlying studs to receive the rest of the dowels. The procedure is much like that described for constructing a floating shelf/sideboard. Be sure to use a magnetic stud finder to establish the position of the studs beneath the wall before planning the shelf. Finish the project by cutting and mounting a length of lumber (pine or stair tread) to bridge the two wall-mounted brackets.

Bookends. Porch brackets can also make nice bookends. You will need to cut four pieces of lumber (about 6 inches wide) the length and height of the brackets to serve as backing and support pieces for the brackets. Use screws and epoxy glue to fasten the lumber pieces to the brackets.

In brief

1. Clean and strip the old wood pieces with chemical stripper, a wire brush, scrapers, and steel wool.

2. Cut off the bad ends of a baluster and cut the baluster into matching halves. Cut two 5-inch discs from scrap wood. Drill two 1-inch-diameter holes in the tops of the balusters and break the wood out with a screwdriver and penknife.

3. Drill ½-inch-diameter holes in the discs and in the bottom of the balusters. Cut two 3-inch lengths of ½-inch wood dowel.

4. Coat the dowels with glue and drive them into the discs. Drive the remaining part of the dowels into the bottoms of the balusters.

5. Hang brackets on the wall by drilling holes in the brackets and the wall to

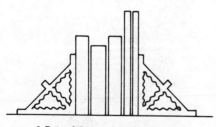
A Pair of Stripped and Restored Porch Brackets Make Nice Bookends.

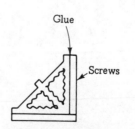
Attach Scrap Pine Pieces to the Bracket for Extra Support.

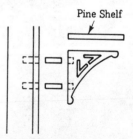
Porch Brackets can Become Shelf Brackets Using Invisible Dowel Supports.

FIGURE 10-19. How to make bookends and shelf brackets from salvaged wood.

receive lengths of ½-inch dowel. Use a stud finder to establish the position of the studs as you did for the floating shelf/sideboard.

6. Cut and mount a length of lumber to bridge the two brackets and form a shelf.

7. Make bookends out of two brackets by cutting four pieces of lumber to act as backing and support pieces for the brackets. Use screws and epoxy glue to secure the lumber to the brackets.

8. Finish these projects by painting, varnishing, or staining.

MAKING AN AUDIO CASSETTE RACK ——————

Tools and supplies needed ——————

Circular saw
Tape measure
Drill and bits
Hammer
Screwdriver
Sandpaper
1 × 12-inch white pine
1½-inch wood screws
1½-inch finishing nails

Procedure ——————————

Here is a design for a rack to hold audio tape cassettes. The rack holds thirty cassettes in ten rows of three each. The rack supports and displays the cassettes so that it's easy to read the labels on their edges. The spacing of ¾ inch between rows of cassettes makes it easy to pull out and replace individual units without disturbing the others.

Take a 5-foot piece of 1 × 12-inch white pine and cut it as shown in the illustration on page 228. Use a piece of pine that is free of large knots, and cut two pieces 30¾ × 2 inches and twelve pieces 13½ × 2 inches. When all of the pieces are cut, smooth their edges with medium and then fine sandpaper.

Drill a series of pilot holes in the two long pieces of pine. Space them as shown in the illustration—½ inch in from the sides of the wood and ¾ inch from each other with the exception of the starting holes, which are placed ⅜ inch in from the edge of the wood. Use a small-diameter bit (a 1/16-inch will do nicely).

Change the bit in your drill to one suitable for drilling pilot holes for the 1½-inch wood screws. Assemble the two long pieces and two of the short pieces on a smooth surface to form a box. Place the two short pieces within the two long pieces. Drill eight pilot holes for screws in the appropriate starter holes and through to the edges of the short wood pieces. Drive screws through the holes to secure the box.

Assemble the rest of the project by placing one short rack piece after another in the box and securing it with 1½-inch finishing nails driven through the pilot holes and into the edges of the rack pieces. Use a spare piece of white pine to space the rack pieces accurately: Put the spacer piece in place, butt a rack piece to it, drive nails to secure the rack piece, draw the spacer piece out, and repeat the process.

When you are finished you will have a rack that sits on a table or shelf or can be mounted to a wall. The rack will hold a good-sized collection of cassettes, and the three cassettes per row design will allow you to organize the rack horizontally by artist or type of music. If you want to give the rack a shiny finish you can spray urethane varnish from an aerosol can. The rack is too full of tight corners for the finish to be applied by brush.

In brief

1. Cut a 5-foot piece of white pine into two 30¾ × 2-inch pieces and twelve 13½ × 2-inch pieces. Smooth all the edges with medium and fine sandpaper.
2. Drill 1/16-inch pilot holes in the two long pieces. Change to a larger bit for screw pilot holes. Assemble the project into a box and drill and fasten 1½-inch screws to secure the frame.

3. Assemble the rest of the rack pieces by using a spare piece of pine. Put the spacer in place, butt a rack piece against it, drive finishing nails to secure, withdraw the spacer piece, and repeat.
4. Finish the rack by applying spray urethane varnish.

Tips

This rack can be condensed or expanded to accommodate your individual needs. To facilitate accurate construction, however, it might be better to build more than one 30-cassette unit and then gang the units together to provide for mass storage.

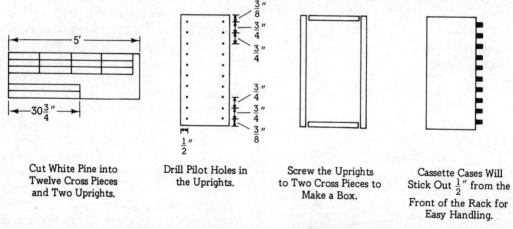

Cut White Pine into Twelve Cross Pieces and Two Uprights.

Drill Pilot Holes in the Uprights.

Screw the Uprights to Two Cross Pieces to Make a Box.

Cassette Cases Will Stick Out ½″ from the Front of the Rack for Easy Handling.

FIGURE 10-20. How to make a cassette rack.

Index

HOW TO (index to step-by-step procedures)